Diversity and the Transition to Adulthood in America

SOCIOLOGY IN THE TWENTY-FIRST CENTURY

Edited by John Iceland, Pennsylvania State University

This series introduces students to a range of sociological issues of broad interest in the United States today and addresses topics such as race, immigration, gender, the family, education, and social inequality. Each work has a similar structure and approach as follows:

- introduction to the topic's importance in contemporary society
- overview of conceptual issues
- review of empirical research including demographic data
- cross-national comparisons
- discussion of policy debates

These course books highlight findings from current, rigorous research and include personal narratives to illustrate major themes in an accessible manner. The similarity in approach across the series allows instructors to assign them as a featured or supplementary book in various courses.

1. *A Portrait of America: The Demographic Perspective,* by John Iceland

2. *Race and Ethnicity in America,* by John Iceland

3. *Education in America,* by Kimberly A. Goyette

4. *Families in America,* by Susan L. Brown

5. *Population Health in America,* by Robert A. Hummer and Erin R. Hamilton

6. *Religion in America,* by Lisa D. Pearce and Claire Chipman Gilliland

7. *Diversity and the Transition to Adulthood in America,* by Phoebe Ho, Hyunjoon Park, and Grace Kao

Diversity and the Transition to Adulthood in America

Phoebe Ho, Hyunjoon Park, and Grace Kao

UNIVERSITY OF CALIFORNIA PRESS

University of California Press
Oakland, California

© 2022 by Phoebe Ho, Hyunjoon Park, and Grace Kao

Library of Congress Cataloging-in-Publication Data

Names: Ho, Phoebe, 1984- author. | Park, Hyunjoon, author. | Kao,
    Grace, author.
Title: Diversity and the transition to adulthood in America / Phoebe Ho,
    Hyunjoon Park, and Grace Kao.
Other titles: Sociology in the 21st century (University of California
    Press) ; 7.
Description: Oakland, California : University of California Press, [2022] |
    Series: Sociology in the twenty-first century ; 7 | Includes
    bibliographical references and index.
Identifiers: LCCN 2021060185 (print) | LCCN 2021060186 (ebook) |
    ISBN 9780520302655 (cloth) | ISBN 9780520302662 (paperback) |
    ISBN 9780520972544 (ebook)
Subjects: LCSH: Adulthood—United States. | Young adults—United
    States. | Minorities—United States. | Immigrants—United States. |
    Cultural pluralism—United States. | United States—Economic
    conditions.
Classification: LCC HQ799.97.U5 H6 2022 (print) | LCC HQ799.97.U5
    (ebook) | DDC 305.240973—dc23/eng/20211223
LC record available at https://lccn.loc.gov/2021060185
LC ebook record available at https://lccn.loc.gov/2021060186

31 30 29 28 27 26 25 24 23 22
10 9 8 7 6 5 4 3 2 1

We dedicate this book to all the immigrant and minority young people in the United States today, but especially to June and Jean Park and Collin Tse, who have begun to embark on their own journeys to adulthood.

Contents

Illustrations

TABLES

Acknowledgments

We are grateful for support from the Laboratory Program for Korean Studies through the Ministry of Education of the Republic of Korea and the Korean Studies Promotion Service of the Academy of Korean Studies (AKS-2016-LAB-2250002). Phoebe Ho acknowledges support from the Department of Sociology at the University of North Texas. Phoebe Ho and Hyunjoon Park are thankful for the University of Pennsylvania's Sociology Department, Population Studies Center, and the James Joo-Jin Program in Korean Studies. Grace Kao gratefully acknowledges support from the Department of Sociology, Faculty of Arts and Sciences, MacMillan Center, and Council on East Asia at Yale University.

This project benefited from support and comments from the members of the Korean Millennials Lab, directed by Hyunjoon Park. In addition to Grace Kao, its other faculty fellows, Seung-kyung Kim, Joongbaeck Kim, and Jaesung Choi, all offered valuable feedback through various stages of this project. Previous postdoctoral fellows Gowoon Jung and Soo-Yeon Yoon offered helpful comments. Student research assistants Kennan Cepa, Yun Cha, Sangsoo Lee, Daesung Choi, and Hyejeong Jo all made valuable contributions.

Drafts of several sections of the book were presented at the 2018 International Workshop on Young Adults in East Asia in Taipei, the 2019 conference Diverse Stories of Coming of Age among East Asians and Asian Americans in Seoul, the 2020 Korean Millennials Conference in New Haven, CT, and the 2021 Virtual International Conference on Youth in Transition. We are grateful to all the participants of these conferences, especially Hiroshi Ishida, Kuo-Hsien Su, Paul Chang, Youngshin Lim, Yi-Lin Chiang, Rourke O'Brien, Emma Zang, Hwansoo Kim, Meera Choi, Hannah Tessler, Keitaro Okura, and Esther Chan.

We thank John Iceland for editing this series and for including us in it. We also appreciate the time and helpful comments of our anonymous reviewers, as well as those who were willing to be identified (Robert Crosnoe and Jennifer Glick). Of course, the book would not be here without the sage advice and support of our editor, Naomi Schneider.

Finally, we are indebted to our families and friends, especially Keith and Shu Ho, Roxana Ho, Candice Ho, Alvin Ho, Andrea Ho, Andreana Ho, Hyunsuk Kim, June Park, Jean Park, Jeff Rubidge, Suzanne Nichols, Vivian Louie, Wonseok Lee, Vivi Michael, Virginia Chang, Jane Kao, Mary Kao and family, and Christine Kao and family, all of whom offered various types of moral support that are always crucial, but were especially needed during the COVID-19 pandemic.

Introduction

DEFINING AND GIVING CONTEXT TO
THE TRANSITION TO ADULTHOOD

Most of us have a sense of what it means to become an adult. Children and adolescents imagine what their lives will be like when they "grow up." Parents envision the types of adults their children will become and hold expectations of their children's schooling, careers, and future families. There are many examples of coming-of-age films and novels focusing on young people on the cusp of adulthood. Often these characters are still living with their parents but are in conflict with them. They may be working part-time, earning enough for spending money but not enough to live on their own. They are perhaps imagining life after they finish school or if they are continuing their education, they picture life at college away from their parents. These characters are often interested in romance and they usually do not yet have children.

Take, for example, *Real Women Have Curves* (2002), *Dope* (2015), and *The Half of It* (2020), three contemporary coming-of-age movies. The protagonists of these movies—Ana, Malcolm, and Ellie—are all navigating their final year in high school. All of them are preoccupied with finishing school and decisions about whether and where to attend college. Romantic pursuits play a central role in their stories, as do family relationships. The protagonists also grapple with societal expectations of who they should become. Yet we also see how their personal identities and the social contexts in which they are embedded profoundly shape their experiences. Ana is the daughter of working-class Mexican immigrant parents who are supportive of her going to college, but not at the expense of leaving the family home or in lieu of working to help support the family. Malcolm, the high-achieving son of a Nigerian father and African American mother living in a disadvantaged neighborhood, has his eyes set on Harvard, but his skeptical high school counselor suggests that a student with his background is unlikely to gain admission. Ellie immigrated from China to rural Washington with her family when she was a child, where her ethnicity and sexual identity made her a social outcast. She struggles between her desire to escape her small hometown and her sense of obligation to her widowed father. Most audience members watching these movies will probably find some aspects of Ana, Malcolm, and Ellie's stories that resonate with them. As audience members, we expect that these protagonists will learn some lessons about "growing up" by the end of the movie. However, it may be harder for us to determine exactly what becoming an adult entails. When do individuals reach adulthood? How do we know when someone has become an adult? Do all Americans have the same ideas about what constitutes adulthood? Is adulthood an inevitable outcome that results when one reaches a certain age, or do individuals have to complete certain goals in their lives in order to be considered adults?

We argue that definitions of adulthood result from interactions between personal experiences, which are often shaped by social forces beyond the individual, and societal expectations of adulthood. The contrast between what today's young people experience and societal expectations of them can make the transition to adulthood a fraught process. In 2016, "adulting" (defined as "the practice of behaving in a way characteristic of a responsible adult, especially the accomplishment of mundane but necessary tasks") made the shortlist for the *Oxford English Dictionary*'s "Word of the Year"—meaning it was one of the few words that "reflect the ethos, mood, or preoccupations" of the year and would have "lasting potential as a word of cultural significance."[1] A 2019 *Parade* magazine article described the proliferation of "adulting" classes, designed to teach young people the life skills needed to be successful adults. As the principal of one such "adulting" school remarked, "Young adulthood is a frustrating place to be—everybody's asking, 'Who am I?' and 'How do I?'"[2] Clearly, becoming an adult is not a seamless process for young people today, and many might wonder what it takes to be an adult.

Moreover, the American narrative of adulthood is largely based on a White middle-class ideal, but is it the case that these norms and behaviors apply to all young people? In an impressive overview of trends in the markers of adulthood over the twentieth century, Elizabeth Fussell and Frank Furstenberg examined the experiences of young people across race, nativity, and gender. They write:

> Remarkably little research has focused on the experience of "average" black youth, instead, focusing on those at risk of delinquency . . . Likewise, few have looked at the experience of the foreign born, who experience the additional transition of international migration in their life course. In addition, the life-course experiences of women, especially black women and foreign-born women, [have] been neglected except for issues relating to marriage and childbearing.[3]

The authors highlight the lack of research that provides a "big picture" of the transition experiences that are shared by and that are distinct across diverse populations of young people in the United States. While the authors acknowledge the importance of considering racial and immigrant diversity, they were only able to focus on native-born Black men and women, native-born White men and women, and foreign-born men and women. Their reliance on a century's worth of census data limited the breadth of racial and ethnic categories available to them.

Racial and ethnic diversity in the United States is increasing more quickly among young people than the general population, with nearly five in ten young people (ages six to twenty-one) belonging to racial and ethnic minority groups in 2018, compared to fewer than two in ten in 1968.[4] The arrival of new immigrant groups since the easing of immigration restrictions in the mid-1960s has also contributed to the racial and ethnic diversity of the United States. In 2018, the foreign-born population in the United States exceeded forty-four million people, making up almost 14 percent of the total population. This is a remarkable increase from 1970, when the foreign-born comprised only 5 percent of the total population.[5] Moreover, about three-quarters of today's immigrants are from Asia or Latin America (with growing numbers from Africa). In contrast, the vast majority of the foreign-born in 1970 were from Europe or Canada.[6] The growth of the immigrant-origin population, as well as its racial and ethnic diversity, means that a single story of the transition to adulthood based on native-born White young people likely misrepresents and over-simplifies contemporary experiences of the transition to adulthood. Youth from immigrant families and their parents may bring different ideals of adulthood from their countries of origin.

In a rare example of research focusing on the transition to adulthood among immigrant-origin young people, Rubén Rumbaut and Golnaz Komaie provide comparisons of Hispanic and Asian first-generation (those who are foreign-born and entered the United States at age thirteen or older), 1.5-generation (those who are foreign-born and entered the United States before age thirteen), and second-generation (those who are native-born but have at least one foreign-born parent) young people, as well as third-plus generation (those who are native-born with native-born parents) White and Black young people, on various markers of adulthood.[7] In showing how the completion of markers of adulthood varies across immigrant generations within the same ethnic group, the authors illus-trate the relevance of nativity in the transition to adulthood. The study also highlights ethnic heterogeneity, challenging the conventional use of pan-ethnic categories, such as Hispanic and Asian, that tend to mask differ-ences in experiences among groups presumed to share similar cultural attributes. Through interview data, Rumbaut and Komaie also point out the unique and serious challenges faced by undocumented immigrant young people in the transition to adulthood. Many of these young people experience frustration over their inability to get a driver's license, to finish schooling, to obtain a full-time job, or to attain many other goals.

Given that the population of current and future young adults is increas-ingly racially and ethnically diverse, with many coming from immigrant families, it is vital that we examine the diversity of experiences in the tran-sition to adulthood. Prior research finds that broad social trends—such as the growth in college attendance and delays to marriage and parenthood—have affected all young people. However, these shifts are more visible for some groups than others. For example, Black young people (ages twenty to thirty-four) are more likely than their White peers to be single and to have never married.[8] Immigrant young people—even those who arrive in the United States at relatively younger ages—also differ from their native-born peers in terms of their experiences. At ages eighteen to thirty-four, they are, on average, more likely than their native-born peers to be full-time students, to have experienced marriage, and to have children of their own.[9] Even though researchers and the general public are increasingly aware of how the transition to adulthood has changed for young people today, surprisingly little research has taken a systematic approach to understanding how race, ethnicity, and nativity intersect with other social categories, such as gender and social class, to affect the outcomes of young people. As such, this book examines the experiences of White, Black, Hispanic, and Asian native-born and immigrant young men and women (a fuller description of the groups examined is provided in chapter 1). Only by examining how such intersectional identities affect these young people's experiences can we determine the multitude of patterns that constitute transitions to adulthood today. These are the issues we attend to throughout this book.

DEFINING ADULTHOOD

Definitions of the stages of the life course are not fixed, but rather change according to societal context. For example, in the United States, childhood as we picture it today looks vastly different from childhood in earlier periods of American history, when children were expected to work and contribute to the family economy from an early age.[10] The same is true for how we understand young adulthood in the United States. When researchers speak about the transition to adulthood, we typically mean the period of time during which young people begin to acquire new rights, responsibilities, and roles associated with adulthood. One of the reasons that the transition to adulthood sparks interest among researchers and the general public, however, is that these rights, responsibilities, and roles are no longer as sharply defined for today's young people as they were for past generations. Both research on and public perception of what constitutes adulthood tend to focus on particular accomplishments, including finishing school, working full-time, establishing residential independence (away from the parental home), getting married, and becoming a parent.[11] Research that emphasizes the acquisition of new roles as markers of adulthood finds that for many young people, acquiring such roles is more difficult and takes longer now than in the past.[12] For example, in 2012, Frank Furstenberg and Sheela Kennedy found that "only about one-fifth of men and one-third of women had completed [all] transitions [by age 30], a striking decline even from the beginning of the decade . . . . Adulthood, *as traditionally defined,* is now achieved only by a minority of men and women."[13]

Some researchers have argued that because the traditional markers of adulthood no longer seem to closely match the experiences of many young people today, we should revisit these conceptions. Psychologist Jeffrey Arnett has proposed *emerging adulthood* as a distinct life stage that occurs whenever young people experience a large gap in time between the end of their adolescence and entering "adult roles" in work and relationships.[14] The period of emerging adulthood is characterized primarily by its subjective and cultural aspects. The literature on emerging adulthood emphasizes how young people think and feel about their accomplishments and positions in society relative to the idea of adulthood, especially in the context of prolonged role transitions in contemporary societies.[15] Arnett argues that young people in the United States today think of the transition to adulthood in "intangible, gradual, psychological, and individualistic terms."[16] Rather than placing importance on the accomplishment of specific roles, young people today instead focus on psychological and individual characteristics such as responsibility, independent decision-making, an equal relationship with parents, and financial independence as key criteria for defining adulthood.

Of course, how young people think and feel about adulthood is difficult to measure using survey data. Moreover, there is little systematic research that compares how diverse groups of young people conceptualize adulthood. In one study, Arnett investigated how Black, Hispanic, and Asian young people (ages eighteen to twenty-nine) differed from their White peers in their beliefs about criteria for adulthood. Arnett found that young adults across groups agreed that independence in deciding personal beliefs and accepting responsibilities for one's actions were characteristics of adulthood. However, there was less consensus on other dimensions of adulthood. Compared to their White peers, Black, Hispanic, and Asian young people were more likely to support notions of adulthood that involve role transitions—including traditional adulthood milestones such as the completion of education, full-time employment, marriage, and parenthood. Black, Hispanic, and Asian young people were also more likely than their White counterparts to emphasize "family capacities"—such as being able to support a family, care for children, and run a household.[17] These differences point to the importance of understanding patterns of attainment of traditional adulthood milestones across race, ethnicity, and nativity.

It is also challenging to separate young people's thoughts and feelings about adulthood from the structural conditions that have placed traditional adulthood milestones out of reach for many. That is, have young people always taken an individualistic and subjective approach to defining adulthood, or has this arisen out of necessity as young people increasingly find themselves struggling to meet traditional markers of adulthood? Young people's feelings about whether they are adults are also highly age-dependent. Even during the period of emerging adulthood (typically covering ages eighteen to twenty-nine, as in Arnett's studies), there is much variation in whether young people consider themselves adults. In one of Arnett's studies, fewer than 10 percent of eighteen-to-twenty-nine year-olds responded "no" when asked whether they feel they have reached adulthood. Younger people were more likely to respond "yes and no" to the question and among those ages twenty-four to twenty-nine, the majority gave an emphatic "yes" response.[18] The early twenties seem to be a particularly unsettled age. Looking beyond these tumultuous years allows us to consider how young people who are more likely than not to *feel* they are adults are faring on milestones strongly associated with adulthood.

In this book, we emphasize five traditional adulthood milestones: (1) finishing school, (2) working full-time, (3) establishing residential independence from parents, (4) getting married, and (5) becoming a parent. We examine these milestones separately and also in relation to each other. We focus on these milestones for a number of reasons. First, even though these milestones may have lost some of their importance in practice, they still signify adulthood to most Americans. A recent study by Kennan Cepa and Frank Furstenberg examined American attitudes toward traditional markers of adulthood and found that individuals "define adulthood similarly and hold relatively similar views about the timing and importance of adult milestones."[19] Other research has also revisited how the accomplishment of traditional markers impacts young people's perceptions of adulthood. Young people who have moved out of their parents' homes, who have married, or who have become parents are all more likely than their peers who have not reached these adulthood milestones to report that they feel like adults.[20] In other words, the experience of role transitions remains meaningful in determining feelings of adulthood. However, we want to emphasize that it is not our view that every person aspires to these milestones. In fact, two of the three authors of this book have not completed all of the adult milestones we measure, but most people (ourselves included!) would still consider us adults. We argue, however, that the five milestones are meaningful and common in widely understood narratives of adulthood.

Second, focusing on traditional adulthood milestones allows us to systematically compare the experiences of today's young people to those of previous generations. Research on how young people think and feel about adulthood is quite recent, so we know less about how young people have historically defined adulthood for themselves. However, there is a large literature on young people's attainment of markers of adulthood across different generations. Hence, we can compare the patterns seen in this book with past research. As we describe in later chapters, the most dramatic changes include the increasing length of time spent in school and in the parental home, in addition to delayed marriage and parenthood.

Finally, and perhaps most importantly, we argue that it is essential to look beyond individualistic explanations and toward patterns formed by intersectional group identities. Although we acknowledge young people's agency in defining adulthood for themselves, taking a purely individualistic view of the transition to adulthood tends to obscure the social contexts that shape their opportunities. Recent and ongoing economic and social changes have significantly altered how young people experience the transition to adulthood. Comparative research examining different countries and societies also reveals the relevance of social institutions and culture for young people's opportunities.[21] Yet young people undergoing the transition to adulthood may blame themselves for failing to meet societal norms.[22] Rather than castigating young people for a perceived inability or unwillingness to accept adult roles (as, for instance, when older generations complain about Millennials), we instead seek to place the shifts in how young people complete traditional markers of adulthood (i.e., finishing school, working full time, establishing residential independence, getting married, and becoming a parent) within the broader context of contemporary economic and social changes.

CONTEMPORARY CONTEXT AND CHALLENGES FOR YOUNG PEOPLE

The experiences involved in the transition to adulthood can change over time, as shifting educational, economic, family, and welfare institutions collide with existing cultural norms and attitudes. Jeffrey Arnett points to four "revolutions" from the 1960s and 1970s that have changed how young people enter adulthood today. First, the "Technology Revolution" transformed the American labor market from a manufacturing-based economy to a skills-based service economy that requires young people to attain more education than in the past. Second, the "Sexual Revolution" brought about by the introduction of the birth control pill allowed young people to enter into sexual relationships outside of marriage, leading to delays in marriage and parenthood. Third, the "Women's Movement" opened up many more educational and occupational opportunities for women, and also contributed to delays in marriage and parenthood. Fourth, the "Youth Movement" cast traditional markers of adulthood (such as marriage and parenthood) less as accomplishments and more as perils to be delayed for as long as possible.[23] The wide reach of such social changes on young people's lives is difficult to fully encapsulate, but suffice it to say that most research agrees the landscape of social norms and opportunities for young people today is vastly different from that of the past.

Young people today also experience the transition to adulthood in the context of widescale economic challenges (e.g., the Great Recession and the COVID-19 pandemic), growing economic inequality, and significant labor market changes. A cohort that enters the labor market during a recession and one that does so during a period of economic growth experience very different life opportunities, not just at the beginning of their work lives, but throughout their careers. For example, Frank Furstenberg and Sheela Kennedy argue that one reason why "growing up is harder to do" is because the Great Recession and its subsequent slow economic recovery have had "profound and potentially permanent consequences for the adult transitions of young men and women today."[24] At the time of writing, we are in the middle of the COVID-19 pandemic, which will also likely have a lasting impact on the socioeconomic attainment of young people whose educational and work careers have been disrupted.

Since the late 1970s, income inequality in the United States has risen sharply. It is now at the highest level seen in the past one hundred years. The top 10 percent of American families collectively earned half of all total pre-tax income in 2015, a level of income inequality that outpaces that of other highly developed countries.[25] The United States also ranks high among developed countries in the ratio of wage returns to skills— that is, Americans with greater skills (usually as a result of their education) earn considerably more in the labor market than Americans with fewer skills.[26] This means that educational attainment is a key determinant of young people's eventual economic success. Research shows declines in job quality among young workers since the 1970s, including lower rates of employment, lower median wages, and fewer "decent" jobs. This is especially the case for those who lack college credentials.[27] Even as higher education has taken on increasing importance for young people's life chances, it has become more unaffordable.[28] Disinvestment in public higher education systems has increased the amount of time and money it takes to complete a college degree. Even middle-class college students can find themselves at risk of downward mobility as they are saddled with educational debt and face limited career options.[29] The need to be competitive in the labor market also means that more young people are pursuing advanced degrees, which further lengthens the time spent in school and possibly delays marriage and parenthood.[30]

The economic precariousness of young people's situations has implications for other dimensions of the transition to adulthood. A Gallup report found that Millennials (which they defined as those born between 1980 and 1996) have a hard time finding jobs they want and that their higher levels of education than previous generations might even make them overqualified for the jobs they can obtain. Millennials also express lower levels of engagement with their work and are more prone to switch jobs, an indicator of job dissatisfaction.[31] Moreover, both their lower levels of work experience relative to older workers and the service industries in which they are concentrated make them more susceptible to economic downturns. According to an analysis by the Economic Policy Institute, unemployment rates among young workers (ages sixteen to twenty-four) in the United States rose from 8 percent to 24 percent between spring 2019 and spring 2020 as COVID-19 spread; the corresponding increase in unemployment rates among older workers was from 3 percent to 11 percent.[32] Even highly educated young people experience employment challenges. Interviewed in a *Vox* article on recent college graduates struggling to find employment during the COVID-19 pandemic, twenty-four-year-old Kyle says, "I've probably applied to around 1,400 positions . . . . That number sounds crazy, but that's pretty much all I've been doing."[33]

Young people in the United States now remain in their parents' homes for a longer period of time compared to previous generations.[34] Moreover, the age at first marriage in the United States has steadily increased since the mid-1950s, reaching thirty for men and twenty-eight for women in 2019, and the marriage rate has fallen substantially over the last few decades.[35] It is easy to see why young people, faced with declining labor market prospects, might stay in or return to the parental home and delay or even forego marriage and parenthood. Researchers have also noted more complicated patterns in the transition to adulthood among young people today.[36] An adulthood milestone is not always permanent—once attained, some milestones can be revisited. For example, young people might move out of and back into the parental home multiple times or they might return to school after working for some time. Moreover, the links between markers of adulthood are increasingly tenuous. One notable change in family formation is the weakening association between marriage and parenthood, with increasing shares of births occurring before marriage.[37] The COVID-19 pandemic has brought into sharper focus the vulnerability of young people on the edge of adulthood, with many having lost their jobs and a majority now residing with their parents.[38] Kyle, the recent college graduate mentioned above who is struggling to find a job, voices many of the anxieties young people are experiencing today: "Will I ever own a house because right now, the positions I do qualify for barely pay enough to live . . . . My girlfriend and I have cried about it. Are we going to have a shot at a life the older generation has?"[39]

HOW RACE, ETHNICITY, AND NATIVITY MATTER
FOR THE TRANSITION TO ADULTHOOD

The theoretical perspectives and broader social contexts we summarize should apply to all young people. One of the major themes of this book, however, is that existing theoretical perspectives are not always well suited to describing the experiences of young men and women from a range of racial, ethnic, and immigrant backgrounds. Research has shown that vast racial, ethnic, and gender differences in socioeconomic status persist. We also know that different groups of young people vary in their attainment of traditional adulthood milestones.[40] As the United States becomes increasingly diverse, our conceptualizations of the transition to adulthood must also be continually revisited and updated.

Moreover, while the economic and social changes in the United States over the past several decades have touched the lives of virtually all Americans, they have arguably had a greater impact on racial and ethnic minorities. For example, during the Great Recession (between 2007 and 2009), the wealth of Hispanic families declined by 66 percent and the wealth of Black families by 53 percent, compared to a decline in wealth of 16 percent among White families.[41] The COVID-19 pandemic, which began in 2020 and is still ongoing at the time of this writing, has hit racial and ethnic minority young workers much harder than White young workers, with Black, Hispanic, and Asian/Pacific Islander young workers experiencing higher rates of unemployment (ranging from 28 to 30 percent), compared to their White peers (about 21 percent).[42] Longstanding systemic racial and ethnic inequalities in housing, employment, and education also continue to constrain racial and ethnic minority young people's opportunities.[43] Thus, another recurring theme throughout this book is the continued salience of race and ethnicity for young people's transitions to adulthood, especially in relation to their educational attainment.

The distinct experiences of immigrant-origin young people are also a particular focus of this book. Variations in the social and economic resources of immigrant families and communities mean that immigrant young people often experience the transition to adulthood differently from their native-born peers. Although there is a robust literature on how immigrants and the children of immigrants adapt to life in the United

States, there is limited research on immigrant young people that encompasses multiple markers of adulthood and that also attends to their racial and ethnic diversity.[44] For example, there is an abundance of research on the educational outcomes of immigrant-origin youth, but such studies are rarely accompanied by research on when they leave the parental home, marry, or have children.[45] Moreover, major studies of immigrant youth tend to focus on specific geographic locations such as New York City or Southern California.[46] These locations are important because of their concentrations of immigrant groups, but an obvious drawback is that their localized contexts produce particular patterns that are not necessarily generalizable to the broader population of immigrant young people. For example, the high cost of living in New York City might lead to longer delays in leaving the parental home than is the case elsewhere in the United States.[47] Thus, this book offers a rare holistic look at how immigrant young people in the United States compare to their native-born peers across racial and ethnic groups in the transition to adulthood.

A final recurrent theme of this book is the importance of educational attainment for understanding other adulthood milestones. The completion of schooling is typically the first marker on the road to adulthood for young people. The educational paths young people take—attaining an undergraduate or advanced degree or stopping after or even before high school graduation—set them on particular trajectories in the transition to adulthood. For example, research shows that the marriage gap by educational attainment has increased over time, with the more-educated more likely to marry.[48] Previous studies also find that the increase in single motherhood is more apparent among women without college degrees than among women with college degrees.[49] As we will see in subsequent chapters, the attainment of an array of adulthood milestones diverges significantly by educational attainment. However, we also pay close attention to instances in which racial, ethnic, immigrant, and gender differences persist even among similarly educated young people. For example, research indicates that during the Great Recession, White and Asian individuals who did not graduate college lost more of their wealth compared to White and Asian college graduates. In contrast, Black and Hispanic college graduates lost more wealth than Black and Hispanic individuals who did not graduate college. Among some of the potential explanations for these inequalities include the fact that college-educated Black and Hispanic families saw greater decreases in their home values during the Great Recession and have not experienced increases in "real income" compared to college-educated White and Asian families.[50] Thus, this book also focuses on racial, ethnic, immigrant, and gender variations at both the upper and lower range of educational attainment.

OVERVIEW OF CHAPTERS

Our book is organized as follows, and each chapter can be read separately. Chapter 1, Understanding the New Face of America: Racial and Ethnic Diversity and Immigration, provides a brief overview of historically important immigration regulations that have affected the makeup of the US population. We document the changing racial and ethnic demographics of the United States, and pay special attention to the youth population. We discuss structural and cultural explanations that are commonly applied to explain differences in outcomes among racial and ethnic minority and immigrant youth. We also describe the primary source of data for this book (the American Community Survey) and the sample of young people whose experiences form the backbone of our analyses in subsequent chapters.

Chapter 2, Getting Ahead, Falling Behind: Education and Employment, focuses on two traditional markers of adulthood: completion of education and labor force participation. The educational attainment and labor force participation of young adults are important and interrelated indicators of socioeconomic status, so we focus on research on the school-to-work transition. We find that Asian and White young adults have higher rates of bachelor's degree completion than their Black and Hispanic counterparts. This advantage is visible for both immigrant and native-born youth as well as for both men and women. Educational attainment is crucial because while the completion of one's education is itself often seen as a marker of adulthood, the level of education attained is of consequence for other markers of adulthood, including full-time work, residential independence, marriage, and parenthood. Thus, the remaining milestones are examined in light of the educational attainment of young people.

Earning a college degree is highly related to having a full-time job—young adults with more education are consistently more likely to be employed full-time than their peers with less education, while young adults with no college experience are significantly more likely to be unemployed or out of the labor force. However, there are also consistent patterns that demonstrate the role of race, ethnicity, and nativity in labor force participation. Among college-educated men, White men maintain an advantage in full-time employment but among college-educated women, minority women are typically more likely than White women to be employed full-time. At the lower end of the educational attainment spectrum, immigrant minority men are more likely to be working full-time than their native-born counterparts, but the opposite is true for immigrant minority women.

In chapter 3, Settling In, Settling Down: Household and Family Formation, we turn to residential independence and family formation (marriage and parenthood) as markers of adulthood. Independent living away from the parental home is an important symbol of adulthood in the American imagination, but being able to do so is usually dependent on having adequate financial resources. Traditionally, living independently was tied to marriage, but today, this is less often the case. The Pew Research Center finds that more than half of Millennials are unmarried and close to half of those aged eighteen to twenty-nine were living with a parent in 2020.[51] As we describe in this chapter, young people who have attained bachelor's or higher degrees are more likely than their less-educated peers to have established their own households and to be married. White young people tend to be more likely than their minority peers to be residentially independent and married at all levels of education. Young women with college degrees are typically less likely to be mothers and much less likely to be unwed mothers compared to their peers with lower levels of educational attainment. We also find greater differentiation in family formation outcomes by race, ethnicity, and nativity among young people who do not have a bachelor's degree. Put differently, we see fewer racial and ethnic differences among those with at least a bachelor's degree. This suggests that having a college degree may have a larger impact on the family formation outcomes of minority young people compared to their White peers.

Next, in chapter 4, Connecting Milestones: Profiles of Adulthood, we bring all the milestones together. In other words, we move away from looking at education, employment, residential independence, marriage, and parenthood separately and instead focus on the interrelatedness of these milestones. To do this, we start with young people's educational attainment and then evaluate the patterns of attaining the four remaining milestones. We argue that the educational routes taken significantly shape the attainment of other adulthood milestones. We focus primarily on the patterns that are substantively meaningful (for example, having attained all of the milestones or none of the milestones) and that are common among young people. We review how race, ethnicity, nativity, and gender shape the typical profiles of adulthood seen among young people with varying levels of educational attainment, and discuss the implications for their future socioeconomic standing. College-educated young people are more likely to be working full-time, with some living as independent singles and others having already established families; as such, we argue that they are more likely to be on their way to a middle-class life with less economic hardship. In contrast, young people who have less than a bachelor's degree have much more varied profiles of adulthood. Many native-born minority young people who lack a college education have yet to attain any of the traditional milestones associated with adulthood, making their futures look uncertain. Compared to native-born young people, immigrant young people without college degrees are more likely to have accomplished many of the family formation milestones, giving them a clearer pathway to working-class adulthood.

Chapter 5, Exploring a Mosaic of Experiences: Ethnicity, Immigrant Status, and Sexual Orientation, addresses additional forms of diversity among young people—including ethnic variation among Hispanic and Asian Americans, undocumented immigrant status, and sexual orientation—and makes the point that the meaning of adulthood evolves alongside the identities of young people. We highlight ethnic differences within Hispanic and Asian pan-ethnic groups by comparing the completion of adulthood milestones across five Hispanic groups (Mexican, Puerto Rican, Cuban, Salvadoran, and Dominican) and across five Asian groups (Chinese, Filipino, Asian Indian, Vietnamese, and Korean). Once again, we emphasize the importance of educational attainment. Among Hispanic young people, Mexican Americans are the least educationally advantaged while Cuban

Americans are the most educationally advantaged. These differences translate into outcomes that show a slower path to marriage and parenthood for the latter compared to the former. Among Asian Americans, Chinese Americans tend to have higher levels of educational attainment and exhibit a slower path towards family formation compared to most other Asian American groups. We also summarize previous work on undocumented immigrant young people, whose transitions to adulthood are profoundly impacted by their lack of legal status—often, their educational, employment, and even romantic aspirations are blocked. Lastly, we show how sexual minority young people are mostly excluded from the conversation around the transition to adulthood, particularly when discussing traditional adulthood milestones like marriage and parenthood. We also find that sexual minority young people often define adulthood in relation to their sexual identities. We stress how a heteronormative approach to marriage and parenthood has functioned as a dominant narrative of the transition to adulthood, further marginalizing the diverse experiences of young people who are sexual minorities.

Finally, chapter 6, Envisioning the Transition to Adulthood Today and in the Future, presents an overview of our main findings and considers the future of adulthood. We summarize the book's findings on the relevance of educational attainment for labor force participation, residential independence, marriage, and parenthood. In particular, we emphasize how a college degree can help offset differences by race, ethnicity, nativity, and gender. However, we also point out instances where race, ethnicity, and nativity continue to be significant stratifying forces that lead to different experiences in the transition to adulthood. We point out that race, ethnicity, and nativity tend to matter more for young people without college degrees than for their peers with college degrees. We also note that the well-being of young people depends on social policies that are relevant to most American families. Policies that increase the affordability and equity of educational and occupational training opportunities as well as policies that improve the living and working conditions of working-class and poor families will help put young people on firmer ground as they begin their journeys into adulthood. We conclude with some predictions about the transition to adulthood. We believe that precarity and resiliency alike will characterize the experiences of most young people in the near future.

The chapters ahead will present data for a nationally representative, cross-sectional sample of young adults, collected between 2013 and 2017. This means that our findings can be generalized to the larger populations of the subgroups we examine. While we can be confident in our measurement of milestones traditionally associated with adulthood, these data do not allow for a comparison of the actual attitudes and beliefs young people today have about what it means to be an adult, nor can we follow how young people's transitions evolve as they age. These limitations aside, we are able to provide a broad overview of the experiences of a large and diverse cohort of young people in the midst of their transitions to adulthood. In the next chapter, we begin with a look at the growing racial and ethnic diversity in the US population, and how this increased diversity has contributed to differences in the transition to adulthood.

1 Understanding the New Face of America

RACIAL AND ETHNIC DIVERSITY AND IMMIGRATION

Give me your tired, your poor,
Your huddled masses yearning to breathe free,
The wretched refuse of your teeming shore.
Send these, the homeless, tempest-tost to me,
I lift my lamp beside the golden door!

These famous lines from the oft-quoted poem by Emma Lazarus are engraved on the pedestal of the Statue of Liberty. The poem portrays America as a "golden door" open to all who seek a better life. The United States owes much of its racial and ethnic diversity to immigrants, but also to Native Americans, enslaved Africans and their descendants, and to its empire-building and territorial expansion (such as the annexation of Texas and Hawai'i and the colonization of the Philippines and Puerto Rico). From its origins, the United States has granted the rights of citizenship to only a segment of its population, based largely on gender, race, and national origin. The unequal treatment of racial and ethnic minority populations in the United States lives on in contemporary racial and ethnic inequalities that pervade all aspects of life, from day-to-day interactions to socioeconomic well-being and health across the life course.[1]

In this chapter, we briefly review how immigrant exclusion laws from the 1880s to 1920s and the loosening of restrictive immigration policies after World War II have contributed to racial and ethnic diversity in the United States. We then turn to describing the racial and ethnic composition of the US population today, with an eye towards the young adult population that is the focus of our book. In describing this population, we pay special attention to the intersections of race, ethnicity, nativity, and socio-economic status. We describe how research has advanced both structural and cultural explanations for why experiences in the transition to adulthood might differ by race, ethnicity, and nativity before describing the data used in this book.

MAJOR IMMIGRATION LEGISLATION IN US HISTORY

While the United States prides itself on being welcoming of all individuals, in reality our first laws limited citizenship, and the rights that come with it, to certain individuals. The 1790 Naturalization Act allowed only a "free White person" to naturalize (i.e., become a citizen). Though the 1875 Page Act began to restrict the entry of Asian labor migrants, it was really the 1882 Chinese Exclusion Act that first targeted a group for exclusion on the basis of national origins. Specifically, it banned Chinese laborers from entry into the United States and barred those who were already in the United States from naturalization for ten years. The Geary Act of 1892 extended this law for an additional ten years. In 1907–8, the Gentlemen's Agreement (named because it emerged from an agreement between the US and Japanese governments) effectively barred Japanese immigration to the United States. The 1917 Immigrant Act (Asiatic Barred Zone Act) ended immigration from other Asian countries (with the exception of the Philippines, then a US colony). From there, the United States moved to further limit immigration by targeting countries in Southern and Eastern Europe with the 1921 Emergency Quota Act and the 1924 Immigration Act (Johnson-Reed Act). The goals of the latter act were not only to limit immigration, but also to preserve the composition of the US population as it was in 1890, before the arrival of the vast majority of immigrants from Eastern and Southern Europe, who were viewed as undesirable and less assimilable.

After World War II, the United States enacted the Immigration and Nationality Act of 1952 (McCarran-Walter Act), which first created preferential categories for skilled workers and family members.[2] It was not until the Immigration and Nationality Act of 1965 (Hart-Celler Act) that the United States removed strict immigration quotas based on national origins. At the signing of the act, President Lyndon B. Johnson remarked:

This bill that we will sign today is not a revolutionary bill. It does not affect the lives of millions. It will not reshape the structure of our daily lives, or really add importantly to either our wealth or our power. Yet it is still one of the most important acts of this Congress and of this administration. For it does repair a very deep and painful flaw in the fabric of American justice. It corrects a cruel and enduring wrong in the conduct of the American nation.[3]

As is clear from President Johnson's remarks, neither politicians nor policymakers at the time anticipated how much the Hart-Celler Act would affect the composition of the US population. In fact, the Hart-Celler Act has fundamentally changed the racial and ethnic makeup of America. It ended restrictions on immigration from many regions around the world and as a result, immigration to the United States shifted from largely European countries to Asian and Latin American countries. Moreover, the act included family-oriented preferences for immigrants (for example, a relative of a US citizen or permanent resident) as well as preferences for highly skilled immigrants.[4] All these changes have left an indelible mark on the contemporary immigrant-origin population in the United States.

CONTEMPORARY RACIAL AND ETHNIC DIVERSITY

Today, the United States is more diverse than ever in terms of race and ethnicity. Data from the 2020 decennial census show that about 58 percent of the US population identified as White non-Hispanic, 19 percent as Hispanic, 12 percent as Black non-Hispanic, and 6 percent as Asian non-Hispanic.[5] Between 2010 and 2020, the share of the US population that was non-White grew and the share that was White declined, meaning that racial and ethnic minorities drove population growth in the United States.[6] The US Census projects that by 2060, non-Hispanic Whites will make up less than half of the US population while all other racial and ethnic groups will increase in size.[7] More than a quarter of the one hundred largest metropolitan areas in the United States—including New York, Los Angeles, Dallas, and Atlanta—are already majority-minority, meaning that non-Whites as a whole make up more than half of the population.[8] Immigration also drives US population growth and racial and ethnic diversity. The US Census Bureau estimates that under a hypothetical scenario of zero immigration (in which the population changes only through births and deaths), the US would experience a population decline, as well as less growth or even declines in the size of racial and ethnic minority groups.[9]

One reason racial and ethnic diversity in the US population is expected to increase is because the minority population is younger than the White population. For example, consider the most common age of the population—the age of the largest share of the population. For White Americans, the most common age is fifty-eight, followed by twenty-nine for Asian Americans, twenty-seven for Black Americans, and eleven for Hispanic Americans. Another way to understand the relative youth of the non-White population is by using the median age of the population—the age at which half the population is older and half the population is younger. The median age for White Americans is forty-four compared to thirty-one for racial and ethnic minorities. More than half of racial and ethnic minorities are part of the Millennial and younger generations (generally those born 1981 and later) while more than half of White Americans belong to older generations.[10] In fact, the school-age population in the United States is already majority-minority. The National Center for Education Statistics reports that of the 50.7 million US students enrolled in public elementary and secondary schools in 2017, 48 percent were White, 27 percent were Hispanic, 15 percent were Black, and 5 percent were Asian.[11]

In the 1970 Census, just after the passage of the Hart-Celler Act, less than 5 percent of the US population was foreign-born (about 9.2 million people). By 2018, close to 14 percent of the US population was foreign-born (about 44.8 million people).[12] When we talk about the immigrant-origin population, we usually refer to those who are first-generation immigrants (who are foreign-born) and those who are second-generation immigrants (who are born in the United States and have at least one foreign-born parent). Together, first- and second-generation immigrants make up about a quarter of both the youth and adult population in the United States.[13] As we alluded to earlier, the US foreign-born population is also racially and ethnically diverse. In 1960, 84 percent of the foreign-born population was born in Europe or North America. By 2018, the composition had shifted such that more than three-quarters of the foreign-born population came from Asia or Latin America.[14] With respect to national origins, the most common birthplace of immigrants in the United States is Mexico (about 25 percent of immigrants). Other top countries where US immigrants were born include China, India, the Philippines, and El Salvador.[15]

The implications of the growing racial and ethnic diversity in the US population for the transition to adulthood are unclear because most theories about the transition to adulthood are based on earlier, less diverse generations. However, what is apparent is that we can no longer think of the typical young American as someone who is White and middle-class. How the "average" American young person transitions to adulthood today must also include the life experiences of racial and ethnic minorities and immigrants from a range of socioeconomic backgrounds.

RACIAL, ETHNIC, AND IMMIGRANT VARIATION IN SOCIOECONOMIC STATUS

In order to examine the transition to adulthood that contemporary young adults experience, we also have to understand the relative differences in their family resources. The legacy of racially discriminatory policies, such as residential and school segregation, is reflected in the socioeconomic disparities found across racial and ethnic groups in the United States today. Moreover, US immigration policies—such as those that give priority to family members of citizens or to skilled immigrants with high levels of education—have also shaped the socioeconomic profiles of racial and ethnic groups with greater shares of foreign-born individuals.

A large body of sociological research has focused on understanding the extent of and potential explanations for racial and ethnic inequalities across a range of socioeconomic measures (including educational attainment and earnings) and demographic measures (such as rates of marriage and parenthood). In *Race and Ethnicity in America* (another book in this series), John Iceland provides an overview of such differences. Broadly, Black Americans experience higher rates of poverty and lower rates of college completion compared to White Americans, and they experience higher rates of residential segregation. Although Hispanic Americans with recent immigrant origins tend to show social mobility across generations, they are still socioeconomically disadvantaged, with lower average educational attainment and higher rates of poverty compared to White Americans. Asian Americans tend to outpace other groups in college completion and have rates of poverty on par with that of White Americans (and lower than those for Black and Hispanic Americans).[16] These socioeconomic differences shape the resources and opportunities available to different racial and ethnic groups of young people as they make the transition to adulthood. We do not mean to imply that upward social mobility is not possible for young people from disadvantaged racial and ethnic minority groups; rather, the average Black or Hispanic young person coming of age often does so from a less advantaged starting point compared to the average White or Asian young person.

Today's immigrants not only vary by national origins, shaping racial and ethnic diversity in the United States, but also bring with them a wide range of socioeconomic backgrounds. For example, more than half of immigrants born in Mexico have less than a high school degree, while more than 70 percent of immigrants born in South Asia have at least a bachelor's degree. Overall, Asian and African immigrants are among the most educationally advantaged, while Hispanic immigrants (especially those hailing from Mexico and the rest of Central America) are among the least educationally advantaged.[17] The wide variation in the educational levels of immigrant adults means that some children of immigrants grow up with two parents with advanced or professional degrees, while others may have parents who have little formal education. These differences vary systematically by race and ethnicity even though on the whole, immigrant parents have lower levels of education than native-born parents. About one in five children of immigrants have parents with less than a high school education compared to fewer than one in ten children with native-born parents. Likewise, about 36 percent of children with immigrant parents have at least one college-educated parent compared to 42 percent of children of native-born parents.[18] Since parental resources influence the transition to adulthood for young people, these differences in family resources are important to keep in mind as we document divergent pathways in the transition to adulthood.

STRUCTURAL AND CULTURAL EXPLANATIONS FOR SOCIOECONOMIC DIFFERENCES

The variation in family socioeconomic background across racial, ethnic, and immigrant groups means that young people are not on equal footing at the starting line to adulthood. Still, family socioeconomic background alone does not fully explain racial, ethnic, and immigrant differences in the attainment of important adulthood milestones. To understand such persistent differences, researchers often turn to *structural* and *cultural* explanations. Both structural and cultural perspectives recognize the role of family socioeconomic status, but they diverge in their emphasis on which additional factors are most important in accounting for the remaining racial and ethnic differences across a variety of outcomes.

Structural explanations emphasize broader social forces that shape the opportunities and experiences of racial and ethnic minority and immigrant youth. Some of the explanations that researchers consider structural include the unequal treatment of minorities and immigrants, which affects patterns of residential and school segregation. For example, research shows that compared to middle-class White neighborhoods, middle-class Black neighborhoods are much more likely to be spatially connected to poor neighborhoods.[19] This means that the resources and networks of even middle-class Black families are more likely to be limited compared to those of middle-class White families. As described by Kimberly Goyette in *Education in America* (another book in this series), racial and ethnic minority children are also more likely to attend high-poverty schools. Fewer than one in ten White students attend schools where more than 75 percent of the student body is eligible for free or reduced-price lunch (a measure of school poverty), compared to more than one in ten Asian students, more than three in ten Hispanic students, and more than four in ten Black students. In other words, the average White or Asian student is less likely to be in school with disadvantaged peers compared to the average Black or Hispanic student. Schools that have majority-minority student populations also tend to have less experienced teachers.[20] These structural conditions shape the educational opportunities available to individuals from an early age and continue to impact educational outcomes and the transition to adulthood at later ages.

Cultural explanations tend to focus on specific beliefs and behaviors attributed to particular racial and ethnic groups and how they shape young people's transitions to adulthood. In a study by one of the authors of this book, high schoolers from different racial and ethnic groups were asked about labels associated with their own racial and ethnic groups and also about their thoughts on members of other racial and ethnic groups. In their responses, adolescents tended to invoke common stereotypes—for example, associating White and Asian students with studiousness and academic achievement and Black and Hispanic students with poorer academic achievement.[21] These stereotypes might lead people to believe that there are innate cultural differences that result in some groups valuing education more highly than do other groups.

However, commonplace beliefs about group cultures tend to differ from how social scientists think of culture. Sociological research is not just concerned with describing group-level patterns of differences in beliefs and behaviors, but also seeks to understand why these differences exist. For example, early work by John Ogbu suggested an "oppositional" culture among Black and other disadvantaged racial and ethnic minority students, one that associated school achievement with "acting White," as one reason for education achievement gaps.[22] Ogbu's work generated significant debate because some took these findings to mean that certain minority groups did not value education and were, in essence, responsible for their own lower academic achievement. However, even in Ogbu's original work, student attitudes are only one part of a broader "cultural-ecological" theory that emphasizes societal context. How some groups become "involuntary minorities" and how they are subsequently treated by society are also part of the social context that shapes the attitudes, values, and behaviors of minority groups.[23] Sociological studies tend to challenge purely cultural perspectives and instead emphasize the connections between culture and social processes. For example, research has found that racial and ethnic minority students have engagement in school that is as high or higher than White students, but also that Black and Hispanic students' educational expectations decline over time, while Asian and White students' expectations remain steady, suggesting that it is how minority students are treated in and out of schools that shapes their educational goals rather than innate cultural differences.[24]

Defining culture and trying to measure its independent impact on individuals is difficult. An alternative is to consider how culture and structure interact to shape behaviors and beliefs. Sociologist David Harding, for example, has proposed the concept of "cultural heterogeneity" to explain how neighborhoods contribute to educational inequalities. Harding argues that disadvantaged neighborhoods have "competing and conflicting" cultural models that make it difficult for young people to construct effective paths to educational goals.[25] One potential result is that a young person in a disadvantaged neighborhood may aspire to college but receive mixed signals about the importance of or steps to get to college from others in their neighborhood. Conflicting messages and poor information make it difficult for them to reach their aspirations. Thus, while we could consider the educational aspirations held by individuals or groups of individuals as part of their cultural understandings of the world, the particular mix of educational aspirations across neighborhoods is strongly influenced by societal features such as the existence of pronounced residential segregation by income and race.

Other research has expanded the concept of cultural heterogeneity to explain differences in educational and occupational attainment across racial and ethnic groups. In their Los Angeles-based study of young adult children of immigrants, Jennifer Lee and Min Zhou argue that Asian Americans tend to share one dominant "success frame" that emphasizes high educational attainment and specific professional occupations while other groups have more varied success frames.[26] These success frames can be viewed as cultural attributes of specific groups, but are shaped by broader social structures, such as the makeup of different immigrant streams. Some immigrant groups are positively selected, meaning they tend to be made up of individuals with greater socioeconomic resources (such as more education), compared to nonmigrants from their countries of origin, while other immigrant groups might be negatively selected, meaning members of these groups tend to have lower than average socioeconomic resources compared to nonmigrants from their countries of origin. Lee and Zhou argue that some Asian immigrant groups, like the Chinese, are actually hyper-selected because they have rates of bachelor's degree attainment that are higher than both the average adult in China and the average adult in the United States. Using this comparison of bachelor's degree attainment, they define Vietnamese immigrants as positively selected and Mexican immigrants as negatively selected. The hyper- and positive selectivity of Chinese and Vietnamese immigrants on educational attainment—itself a product of US immigration laws—can help explain why some Asian Americans seem to focus on educational attainment. Asian Americans might also anticipate discrimination in the labor market and view greater educational attainment as a means for countering such discrimination.[27] Again, while we might consider the educational aspirations of different racial and ethnic groups as a part of their culture, we should also recognize that these aspirations are formed within specific societal contexts.

Another example of combining cultural and structural perspectives to explain group differences in beliefs and behaviors related to the transition to adulthood is apparent in research by Kathryn Edin and Maria Kefalas that examines why low-income young women choose to have children outside of marriage. At first glance, this might seem to indicate cultural differences between poor and middle-class women in how they view marriage and motherhood. However, Edin and Kefalas point to broader structural issues—such as the lack of employment options for young men in their neighborhoods—that make marriage more elusive for poorer women. Edin and Kefalas find that such women have very high standards for marriage that are difficult to realize given their circumstances, but that they are confident in their abilities to be good mothers. Rather than delay motherhood until after marriage, poor young women instead opt to have children before marriage.[28] Thus, Edin and Kefalas argue that low-income mothers have not turned away from marriage but rather that structural conditions constrain their marriage opportunities.

STRUCTURE AND CULTURE IN IMMIGRANT ASSIMILATION THEORIES

As we stated earlier, some immigrant-origin young people have parents with limited formal schooling who work in the informal economy as domestic workers or laborers while others have parents with PhDs who work at research universities or in the high-tech sector. However, despite their very different socioeconomic resources, their race, ethnicity, and immigrant background bind them together and their experiences are often not the same as those of their White and native-born peers.[29] Theories of how young people of recent immigrant origins will fare in the United States tend to emphasize assimilation—meaning that over time, minority groups are expected to become more like the American "main-stream" (often understood as White and middle-class) both in terms of their cultural beliefs and their average socioeconomic status. Early immigrant assimilation theories, based largely on the experiences of European-origin immigrants, tended to treat the process as relatively smooth. However, more recent assimilation frameworks often consider how the racial and ethnic diversity of contemporary immigrant groups might lead to differing processes and levels of integration.[30] Other scholars reject the assimilation framework for describing the outcomes of immigrant groups.

A recent report from the National Academies of Sciences, Engineering, and Medicine found that second-generation immigrants (i.e., the US-born children of immigrants) show educational progress over first-generation immigrants across most racial and ethnic groups. This pattern serves as evidence of "rapid educational integration."[31] However, the average level of education varies significantly for immigrants by region of origin. This means that while most children of immigrants will surpass their parents' level of educational attainment, there is still considerable racial and ethnic variation. For example, on average, first-generation immigrant women ages fifty to fifty-nine from Mexico have about eight years of formal education, while those from India have close to fifteen years of formal education. Among second-generation immigrant women ages twenty-five to thirty-four, Mexican Americans average about twelve years of education while Indian Americans average about sixteen years of education.[32] For both groups, there is an improvement in educational outcomes across generations and in fact, the change in levels of education between first- and second-generation Mexican Americans is even more dramatic than the corresponding change between first- and second-generation Indian Americans, given the lower starting point of the former. However, in terms of absolute levels of education, second-generation Indian Americans still fare better than second-generation Mexican Americans.

Even though there is general improvement in socioeconomic attainment across immigrant generations, the existence of racial and ethnic variations among immigrant-origin groups has spurred sociologists to revise classic assimilation theories. One prominent example is *segmented assimilation theory*. As the name suggests, segmented assimilation theory argues that there are multiple segments of society into which immigrants and their children can assimilate. The level of parental resources as well as structural factors such as the strength of co-ethnic communities and receptivity of society all shape the likelihood of whether immigrant-origin young people will experience upward mobility into the American "mainstream," working-class "stagnation," or downward mobility into "deviant" lifestyles.[33] According to segmented assimilation theory, immigrant groups that are more positively selected and that face neutral or positive receptions in the United States are more likely to experience upward mobility across generations, while immigrant groups that are negatively selected, especially those that experience strong societal discrimination, are more likely to experience downward mobility and to share outcomes more like those of disadvantaged native-born minority groups.

While some challenges might be widely shared among immigrant families—for example, lower levels of English fluency that prevent immigrant parents from helping their children with schoolwork or applying to college—information shared among co-ethnics can supplement the modest resources of individual families.[34] Immigrants often rely on their ethnic community as they adapt to life in their new country. Their ethnic communities not only provide useful information, such as where to find a job or how to access social services, but also serve to reinforce social norms.[35] The resources that stem from such social networks are sometimes referred to as *social capital*. The availability of beneficial social capital is often dependent on the social class composition of immigrant groups. For example, because Chinese immigrants tend to be positively selected, working-class Chinese immigrant families can benefit from the resources of robust ethnic communities with larger shares of middle-class families. Through their middle-class co-ethnics and the ethnic businesses that cater to them, working-class Chinese families can get information about the best schools in their neighborhoods, college-prep courses, and services such as after-school tutoring and cram schools.[36] For racial and ethnic minority and immigrant groups with smaller shares of middle-class families, these resources are not as widely available via their co-ethnic communities, so their stock of social capital may be lower.

Researchers have also proposed a variety of cultural explanations for why the children of immigrants seem to experience more positive educational and behavioral outcomes compared to their third-generation peers (those born in the United States to US-born parents).[37] The cultural beliefs and practices of immigrant families may be a factor. For example, some immigrant parents might be more likely to promote the importance of the family over the individual. This general sense that an individual's desires are superseded by obligations to one's family—sometimes termed familism—is thought to be especially applicable to Asian and Hispanic families because it is akin to cultural notions of filial piety in parts of Asia and to the idea of *familismo* in parts of Latin America.[38] Placing the family over the individual can lead to better educational outcomes since children may feel more obligated to their parents and thereby study harder and avoid "risky" behaviors.[39] Research by Vivian Louie and Robert Smith describes the "immigrant bargain" between children and their immigrant parents, in which children feel obligated to repay their parents' sacrifices by following rules and focusing on their schoolwork.[40] Such research suggests that if there is a difference in the parent-child relationships of immigrant and nonimmigrant households, it will be that children of immigrants feel more obligated or tied to their parents than children of native-born parents.

However, an emphasis on familism might also mean that parents want to keep their children in closer physical proximity and thus prevent their children from moving away from home to attend a more prestigious university or to pursue additional work opportunities.[41] Some immigrant families may even have a preference for parent-child coresidence, although it is unclear whether these behaviors stem from cultural preferences or economic constraints.[42] The conflict between family obligations and personal development is on full display in the movie *Real Women Have Curves* (2002), in which high-achieving Ana confronts a roadblock to her college dreams because her working-class Mexican immigrant parents prefer that she find a job and live at home before marrying and starting her own family. Similarly, developmental psychologist Andrew Fuligni writes that the academically successful young adult children of East Asian immigrant families may be "torn" between the sense of obligation they feel to provide assistance to their families and the broader opportunities available to them after completing college.[43]

Other cultural explanations focus broadly on the outlook of immigrant families. John Ogbu contrasted the experiences of "voluntary" immigrant minorities with those of "involuntary" and nonimmigrant minorities, arguing that because the former choose to come to the United States, they maintain and pass on beliefs about the importance of education for socioeconomic mobility to their children, while the latter doubt educational institutions work for them.[44] Other research discusses the possibility that because immigrants are more naïve than non-immigrants about the effects of discrimination against minorities, they remain more optimistic about their children's outcomes, a phenomenon termed "immigrant optimism."[45] Note, however, that immigrant optimism (and its positive benefits on the educational aspirations of the children of immigrants) is widely found across immigrant groups. If we consider immigrant optimism to be a cultural attribute, it is one that stems from the process of immigrating and not one that is inherent to particular racial or ethnic groups.

Extending these cultural explanations, we might expect that immigrant young adults would be more likely than non-immigrants to complete a college degree, less likely to establish an independent household separate from their parents, and more likely to marry and have children. We might even anticipate native-born Hispanic and Asian young people, who are perceived as coming from cultures that emphasize familism, to behave differently from their native-born White peers. However, our analyses in the coming chapters do not support a simple story in which minorities and immigrants place greater value on family formation compared to their White and native-born peers. Rather, our findings demonstrate complex differences by race, nativity, and gender.

YOUNG ADULT DIVERSITY

Now that we have a sense of the diversity of the US population by race and ethnicity and of the contribution of historical and contemporary immigration to such diversity, we can better understand the demographics of the young adults that we focus on in this book. Our data on young people originates from the American Community Survey (ACS), a yearly survey conducted by the US Census Bureau, compiled by IPUMS USA.[46] The ACS includes about 3.5 million households every year and has a high response rate.[47] The ACS stems from the "long form" version of the survey that until 2000 was administered to a subsample of individuals in the decennial census. Today, the only survey used for the decennial census is a "short form" that asks fewer questions. Since our research questions go beyond those asked in the short form, we turn to the ACS. Importantly, the ACS includes measures of nativity as well as information on the adulthood milestones we outlined in the introduction. Another advantage of the ACS is that it is compiled into "period" estimates that cover population characteristics over a time span of five years. Using five-year estimates provides larger samples of subpopulations of young people for which we would otherwise lack reliable data.

In this book, we focus on young men and women who were ages twenty-five to thirty-four between 2013 and 2017. The oldest among this cohort of young people were born in 1979 and the youngest were born in 1992. Almost all of these young people are part of the "Millennial" generation, the largest living adult generation in the United States.[48] Since educational attainment is a stratifying feature of the transition to adulthood—meaning that the amount of education young people attain is a clear dividing line in experiences with other adulthood milestones—we also primarily focus on young people who are not currently enrolled in school, since we do not yet know what level of education those still enrolled will attain. Throughout the book, we emphasize racial, ethnic, and immigrant diversity among this group of young people, showing how native-born and immigrant White, Black, Hispanic, and Asian young men and women are faring in the transition to adulthood.

In our sample, the native-born population consists of young people who were born in the United States (including Puerto Rico and US territories). The immigrant population in our sample is a subset of the first generation. While the immigrant young people in our sample are foreign-born, they migrated to the United States at age 13 or younger and have likely spent almost all of their adolescence in the United States. Often, the term *immigrant-origin youth* encompasses both first-generation immigrants and second-generation children of immigrants. One reason for our decision to include only immigrant young people who migrated by age thirteen is that the ACS does not include information on parental place of birth. Without this information, we cannot determine second-generation immigrant status. We can, however, determine first-generation immigrant status, since we know whether an individual is foreign-born or not, and we also have information that allows us to calculate age of arrival in the United States.

More importantly, the group of first-generation immigrant young people we focus on are "decimal generations."[49] We analyze this group of "1.5-generation" (who arrived ages 6–12) and "1.75-generation" (who arrived ages 0–5) immigrant young people because we are interested in the transition to adulthood that occurs in the United States and not elsewhere. The immigrant young people we describe in this book have experiences that make them not quite first or second generation. Compared to their first-generation peers who immigrated as teenagers or older, 1.5- and 1.75-generation young people are more likely to have been exposed to the norms and expectations of adulthood in the United States. However, they are also likely to stand apart from their second-generation peers, who were born in the United States to immigrant parents, in terms of language acquisition and the composition of their peer groups.[50] We examine the experiences of these 1.5- and 1.75-generation immigrant young people in relation to the larger body of research on immigrant-origin youth, paying attention to outcomes where generational differences are notable.

How do our restrictions influence the makeup of our sample? Figure 1 gives a simple demographic breakdown of the more than 1.4 million young people in our sample, compared to the full sample of twenty-five-to-thirty-four-year-olds in the ACS 2017 five-year file. These estimates are statistically weighted to adjust for population representativeness. Since we include only White, Black, Hispanic, and Asian native-born young people as well as their counterparts who immigrated as children in this book, our sample has fewer racial and ethnic minorities than the general population of twenty-five-to-thirty-four-year-olds in the United States. In our sample of young people, about 66 percent are White,

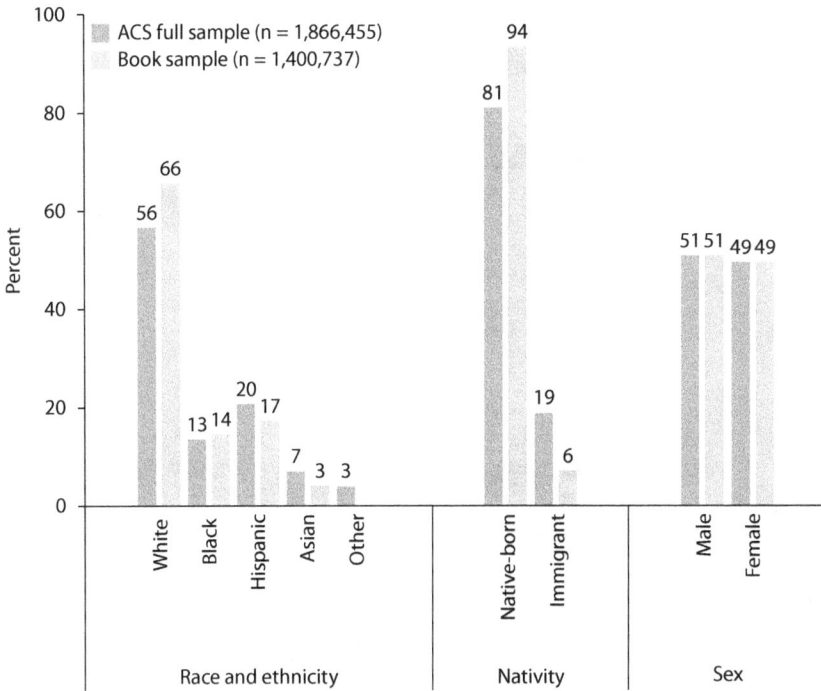

Figure 1. Characteristics of ACS full sample and book sample, by race and ethnicity, nativity, and gender.

SOURCE: US Census 2017, Five-Year Estimates; Ruggles et al. 2021.

17 percent are Hispanic, 14 percent are Black, and 3 percent are Asian. In total, about one in three young adults in our sample are racial and ethnic minorities. Because we are interested in the transition to adulthood in the United States and restrict our sample of immigrant young people to those who spent their childhoods in the United States, 94 percent are native-born young people and 6 percent are immigrants. As figure 1 shows, if we were to include all immigrant twenty-five-to-thirty-four-year-olds regardless of the age at which they immigrated, almost 20 percent of the sample would be immigrants. Like the ACS full sample, our sample is about evenly split between men and women.

Figure 2 provides a more detailed look at the composition of our sample in terms of nativity and immigrant generation across racial and ethnic groups in comparison to the larger ACS sample. This gives a better sense

Percent

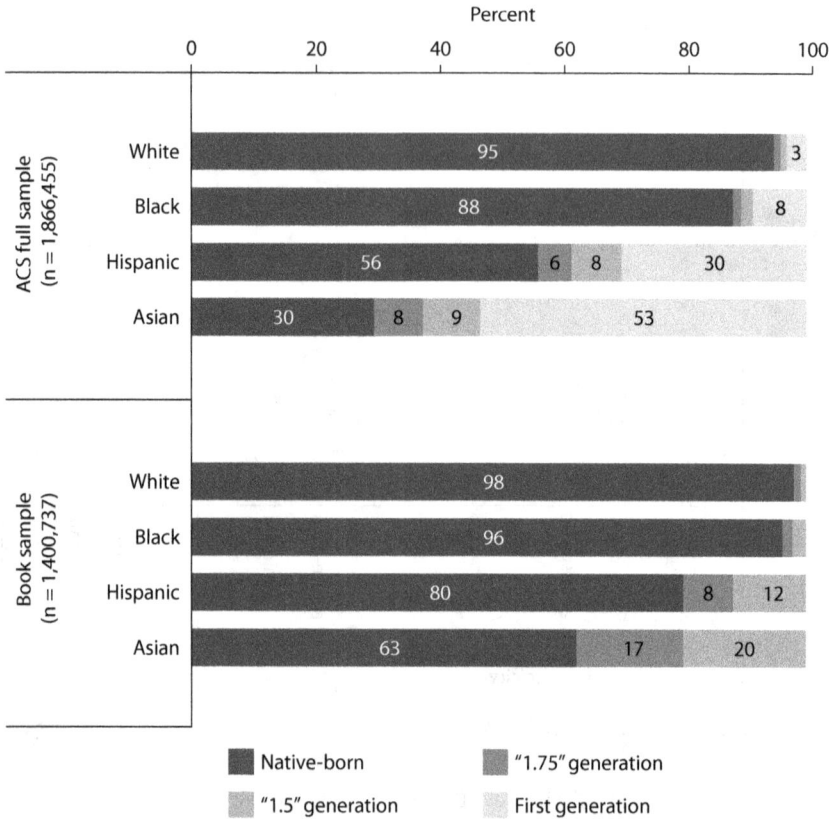

Figure 2. Nativity and immigrant generation of ACS full sample and book sample, by race and ethnicity.

SOURCE: US Census 2017, Five-Year Estimates; Ruggles et al. 2021.

of why nativity is relevant for describing the experiences of many young people, especially Hispanic Americans and Asian Americans. Among the twenty-five-to-thirty-four-year-olds in the ACS full sample, the foreign-born (including first, 1.5, and 1.75 generations) make up 70 percent of the Asian population, 44 percent of the Hispanic population, 12 percent of the Black population, and 5 percent of the White population. However, since our focus is on the 1.5 and 1.75 generations, who come of age in the United States, our sample excludes first-generation immigrants (who, in this case, immigrated at age fourteen or older). Since first-generation young people make up a larger share of the Hispanic and Asian population, this decision affects these groups more. As seen in figure 2, excluding first generation young people who migrated at age fourteen or older means that in our sample, the majority of young people across racial and ethnic groups are native-born. Nevertheless, about one-fifth of Hispanic young people and close to two-fifths of Asian young people in our sample are 1.5- or 1.75-generation immigrants.

Whether their experiences in the transition to adulthood differ meaningfully from their native-born peers is a question we examine. On the one hand, any differences we find between the native-born and immigrant young people in our data might understate the extent to which immigrant origins play a role in the transition to adulthood, since some of the second-generation immigrant young people included among the native-born might be like their 1.5- and 1.75-generation peers in comparable ways (for example, on measures of adulthood that might be related to having immigrant parents, such as leaving the parental home). On the other hand, identifying and providing context for any differences between 1.5- and 1.75-generation immigrant young people and their native-born peers gives us a fuller picture of how the transition to adulthood is experienced today by a much more diverse group of young people than considered by most previous research. Our next chapters examine how race, ethnicity, nativity, and gender together affect the transition to adulthood, beginning with educational attainment and labor force participation in chapter 3.

2 Getting Ahead, Falling Behind

EDUCATION AND EMPLOYMENT

In the foreword to a 1973 report entitled *Youth: The Transition to Adulthood,* produced by the Panel on Youth of the President's Science Advisory Committee, sociologist James Coleman wrote, "With every decade, the length of schooling has increased, until a thoughtful person must ask whether society can conceive of no other way for youth to come into adulthood." At the time, Coleman and other members of the panel argued that the United States had already gone through a "work phase" in its treatment of youth, one in which young people were expected to become economic contributors to their families as early as possible, and was now in a "schooling phase," with young people expected to stay in school as long as possible to improve their economic opportunities. Although the authors of the report hoped that the United States would move into a third phase in its treatment of young people, one that included but was "neither defined by nor limited to" schooling, one could argue that the life chances of youth in the United States today are more than ever inextricably linked to their educational credentials.[1]

The completion of education is viewed by a majority of Americans as one of the most important milestones in the transition to adulthood.[2] But exactly how much education is needed for a smooth school-to-work transition? Though opinions vary, a casual survey of mainstream American television shows and movies, particularly those depicting contemporary family life, reveals the normative expectation of going to (and presumably graduating from) college. Many coming-of-age movies concern moving away to attend college and experiencing college life. Getting into college, paying for college, and finishing college are major storylines of family sit-coms like *Black-ish* (and its spin-off *Grown-ish*), *The Middle*, and *Modern Family*, for example. The critically acclaimed *Ladybird* (2017) revolves around the self-named titular character's decision whether to attend college close to home or across the country. And in the comedy *Booksmart* (2019), studious high school protagonists Amy and Molly decide to let loose for one night to celebrate their admission into college.

The importance of attending college is further reinforced by numerous media outlets. *U.S. News and World Report* provides a multitude of college rankings, including best liberal arts college in the Midwest, best college in a small town, and top party school, among others. Popular websites like College Confidential, which boasts many discussion forums on college admissions (including one for parents), also give readers information about the college experience. Further cementing the centrality of college-going for today's young people, in 2018 the *New York Times* began a newsletter for and written by college students and recent graduates.[3] These media outlets and many others depict going to college as a major rite of passage for today's young people. For many parents, having their children attend college is crucial because it can increase social mobility and preserve existing socioeconomic advantages.[4] The importance of a college education and the anxieties it can produce among families is evident in the 2019 college admissions scandal, the result of a federal investigation dubbed "Operation Varsity Blues" that involved wealthy and celebrity parents convicted of cheating and bribing college officials at prestigious institutions in order to gain admission for their children.[5]

The levels of education young people attain are of obvious importance for understanding their school-to-work transition experiences. Young adults who do not go on to college can join the workforce earlier, but their experiences in the labor market and the types of jobs available to them are also more limited.[6] Take, for example, the following accounts of unemployed and marginally employed young high school graduates featured in the *Philadelphia Inquirer*. Twenty-one-year-old Betsy, employed at a short-term job paying ten dollars an hour, describes with obvious frustration applying to a receptionist position only to learn the employer wanted a college graduate. Brian, an unemployed thirty-one-year-old, morosely predicts, "There'll be one low-wage job after another ahead of me. It's just a nightmare."[7] A large body of research confirms that having a college education is critical for one's chances of securing a stable, well-paying job and that the earnings advantage associated with a college education has become even more substantial over time in the United States.[8]

In this chapter, we examine young people's educational attainment and labor market experiences, as well as the interrelatedness of these two markers of adulthood. First, we document the shares of young adults still pursuing education. We then move to young adults who are not currently enrolled in school, showing the shares who fit into three categories of educational attainment: high school or less, some college, and bachelor's or higher degree. We compare these educational distributions by race, ethnicity, nativity, and gender. Next, we turn to the school-to-work transition, showing full-time employment and labor force participation rates of young adults in relation to their level of educational attainment. Lastly, we compare educational attainment and the labor force participation of young adults in the United States to their peers from more than a dozen countries. As we covered in chapter 1, young people in the United States today come from more diverse backgrounds than in past generations. Hence, we emphasize the significant racial, ethnic, immigrant, and gender differences apparent in educational attainment and labor market outcomes, and how these disparities begin to define particular pathways to adulthood. The differences we refer to throughout the text are statistically significant ($p < 0.05$) unless otherwise noted, meaning we are reasonably certain that the comparisons reflect actual differences between groups rather than chance occurrences.

TRENDS IN EDUCATION: COLLEGE-FOR-ALL AND THE TRANSITION TO ADULTHOOD

Pursuing higher education is now a significant part of the transition to adulthood for most adolescents in the United States. Kimberly Goyette finds that in 1980, less than half of high school sophomores expected to complete a bachelor's degree compared to more than three-fourths of students in 2002. Goyette also finds that over this period, parental education declined in importance in explaining students' educational expectations. In 1980, about 38 percent of high school sophomores whose parents lacked college degrees expected to complete a bachelor's degree compared to more than 72 percent of their peers with college-educated parents, a more than 30-percentage point difference. By 2002, the gap had narrowed to a 13-percentage point difference (79 percent versus 92 percent).[9] The changes in high school students' expectations are also borne out in college enrollment trends: in 1980, only about half of high school graduates were enrolled in college in the fall following their graduation compared to nearly 70 percent of high school graduates in 2018.[10] Moreover, families increasingly invest in activities to boost students' academic credentials in preparation for college. Studies show that families with the resources to do so often seek to enroll their children in a variety of extracurricular activities, from sports to chess, in a bid to increase their children's educational competitiveness.[11] Likewise, there has been a significant increase in the share of high school students who participate in educational activities outside of school, including test preparation courses, tutoring, and private college counseling.[12]

However, college completion rates do not match the "college-for-all" ethos that is increasingly the norm in the United States. In 2019, about 39 percent of twenty-five-to-twenty-nine-year-olds had completed four years of college. Though this is an increase over the 26 percent of young people who had done so in 1980, it is still far below the vast majority of today's high schoolers who expect to complete college.[13] While some young adults may never enroll in any kind of higher education, others may enroll for a short period of time and leave before obtaining a bachelor's degree. Some may leave after having earned certificates or associate's degrees while still others take longer than the traditional four years to graduate. Indeed, among students who entered four-year colleges in 2010, less than half graduated within four years and less than two-thirds graduated within six years.[14]

One reason for the increasing length of time to bachelor's degree completion today is the growing share of students who begin their higher education at two-year institutions, such as community colleges. In 1980, fewer than one in five recent high school graduates (19 percent) enrolled in two-year colleges in the following fall compared to about one in four high school graduates (26 percent) in 2019.[15] Research suggests a "community college penalty" in the completion of bachelor's degrees, even after accounting for student demographics and academic achievement.[16] Some of the delay in bachelor's degree completion can also be attributed to a decrease in institutional resources available to and spent on students as well as to the increase in the number of students who work while attending college, usually out of financial necessity.[17] For example, in public colleges and universities—the types of institutions that are meant to provide broad access to higher education—the cost of tuition, fees, room, and board increased 31 percent between 2006–7 and 2016–17 (adjusting for inflation).[18] To cover the growing cost of higher education, many more students now turn to education loans. Just over half of students who began college in 1995–96 took out federal loans compared to nearly two-thirds of students who began college in 2003–4.[19]

Young people are also now more likely to pursue graduate and professional credentials, prolonging their time spent in school. Between 1994 and 2009, the share of recent four-year college graduates enrolled in graduate education (including master's, doctoral, and professional degrees) increased from less than 16 percent to nearly 25 percent (although recent estimates show a subsequent decline).[20] As with trends in the financing of undergraduate education, education loans are increasingly a part of young people's pursuit of graduate education. In the 1999–2000 academic year, about 45 percent of graduate degree completers had student loans associated with their graduate education, compared to 54 percent in the 2015–16 academic year. Moreover, the average amount owed for graduate school increased from about $33,300 to nearly $71,000 (in current dollars) during the same time frame.[21] Though many young people pursue graduate education in a bid to increase their knowledge and skills for the labor market, it often takes considerable time and financial resources to do so.

Educational inequalities have long been stratified by race, ethnicity, and nativity in the United States. Black and Hispanic students tend to experience worse educational outcomes compared to their White peers, while Asian students often fare better. While the Black-White and

Hispanic-White gaps in educational attainment have narrowed over time, the persistence of such disparities is an area of ongoing research and policy debates.[22] Differences in educational attainment are largely attributable to racial and ethnic differences in family socioeconomic status (such as parental education, parental occupation, and family income and wealth), as well as to school, neighborhood, and community characteristics.[23] Many of these differences can be traced to discriminatory policies and practices (such as unfair housing and labor markets) that have persisted across generations.[24] Thus, while almost all adolescents expect to graduate from college, they begin their journeys to higher education from very different starting points.

The post-1965 wave of mass immigration also spurred research on the educational outcomes of young immigrants and the children of immigrants. One consistent finding is the significant intergenerational progress made in educational attainment: most second-generation immigrants (whom researchers typically define as the native-born children of immigrant parents and sometimes immigrants who arrived as young children) do as well or better than their third-generation peers (who are native-born with native-born parents) within racial and ethnic groups.[25] For example White, Black, Asian, and to some extent Hispanic students from immigrant families generally outperform their co-ethnic peers who are not from immigrant families.[26] However, immigrant groups migrate under different circumstances (e.g., as refugees, high-skill workers, low-skill workers) and come with varying levels of resources (e.g., education, English fluency, family and ethnic community ties). Variations in resources and experiences play a pivotal role in shaping the educational attainment of immigrant-origin youth relative to their native-born peers.[27]

Finally, while gender is not the primary focus of this book, recent trends in educational attainment are important for understanding how gender profoundly shapes young people's transitions to adulthood. As documented by Thomas DiPrete and Claudia Buchmann, women began outpacing men in college degree completion in the 1980s. This gender gap has widened in subsequent decades. Male students are more likely than female students to drop out of high school, to earn a GED certificate over a high school diploma, and to delay college entry after completing high school. All of these are risk factors for college readiness and completion.

However, women's labor market outcomes (such as their occupational fields and earnings) do not always reflect this educational advantage.[28] While some gender gaps in education have changed over time, gender gaps in the labor market persist, pointing to the complex role of gender in understanding how young people reach adulthood milestones.

The sociological literature on racial, ethnic, immigrant, and gender differences in educational outcomes suggests that observed patterns are less a question of individual ability and more an issue of persistent inequality in the structure of educational and labor market opportunities. We delve more deeply into this research after first showing patterns of continued enrollment and educational attainment.

Continued Enrollment in Higher Education

Most Americans believe education should be completed by about age twenty-two, though in reality a nontrivial proportion of young people are still in school well into their mid-twenties and beyond.[29] On the one hand, continued enrollment in undergraduate education in young adulthood might pay off in the future in terms of improved job opportunities. On the other hand, extended delays in completing a bachelor's degree might lead to dropping out and no improvement in labor market outcomes. Researchers sometimes consider older undergraduate students to be "at risk" because of individual factors (such as greater chances of attending part-time, having dependents, and having fewer financial resources) and institutional factors (such as enrollment in less-than-four-year institutions).[30] Young adults pursuing graduate education may be better positioned in the labor market. Research shows that an increasing portion of the economic benefits of higher education lies in advanced degrees and that individuals with master's, doctoral, or professional degrees enjoy significantly greater earnings.[31] To gain a clearer picture of which groups of young adults tend to stay in school across an extended period of time and which are especially likely to pursue advanced degrees, figure 3 shows the share of twenty-five-to-thirty-four-year-olds who are still enrolled in school, focusing on those enrolled in undergraduate (at any level) and graduate education. The very small share of young people who are enrolled in education below the college level are not shown. Throughout the

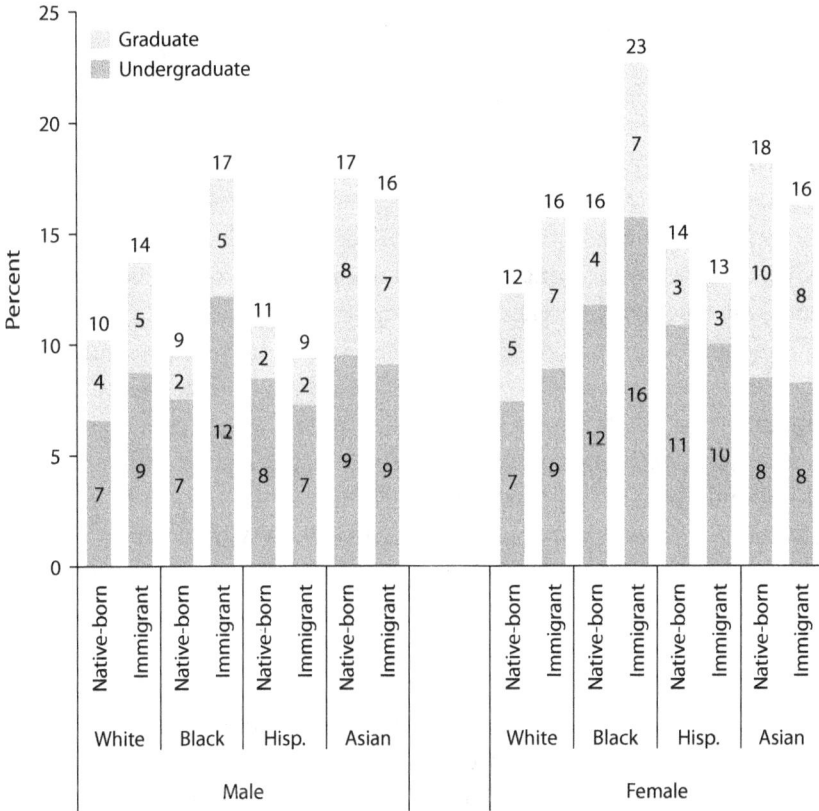

Figure 3. Percentage of young adults (ages twenty-five to thirty-four) enrolled in undergraduate and graduate education, by gender, race and ethnicity, and nativity. Undergraduate and graduate enrolled may not sum to total enrolled due to rounding.

SOURCE: US Census 2017, Five-Year Estimates; Ruggles et al. 2021.

chapter, including in the figures, "native-born" includes anyone born in the United States (including Puerto Rico and US territories) while "immigrant" includes foreign-born young people who immigrated to the United States by age thirteen or younger; foreign-born young people who immigrated after age thirteen are excluded from our analysis.

Most twenty-five-to-thirty-four-year-olds who are still enrolled in school are enrolled at the undergraduate level. Among native-born young men, rates of undergraduate enrollment do not vary much by race or ethnicity, ranging from 7 to 9 percent. Among immigrants, however, Black men have higher rates of undergraduate enrollment (12 percent) and Hispanic men lower rates (7 percent) compared to White men (9 percent). Furthermore, Black and Hispanic young women are generally more likely than their male peers to still be enrolled as undergraduates though this is not the case for White and Asian young people.

However, the consequences of continued enrollment in undergraduate education well into young adulthood are not clear, and it is difficult to conclude whether differences in undergraduate enrollment at these ages represent an advantage or disadvantage. We can, however, be more confident that young people who pursue and complete graduate education will eventually fare better in the labor market. Figure 3 shows that among the native-born, Asian men outpace White men in graduate enrollment, while Black and Hispanic men are less likely than White men to be pursuing advanced degrees. About 4 percent of native-born White men are enrolled in graduate education, which is half the share of native-born Asian men (8 percent) but twice the share of native-born Black and Hispanic men (2 percent for both). Similar racial and ethnic patterns are apparent among immigrants, with Asian men having the highest rates of graduate enrollment, followed by White, Black, and Hispanic men. Both native-born and immigrant Asian women have higher rates of enrollment in graduate education compared to their White peers while native-born and immigrant Hispanic women have lower rates.

Turning to differences between the native-born and immigrants within each racial and ethnic group reveals an immigrant *advantage* for White and Black young adults: compared to their native-born peers, White and Black immigrant men and women are more likely to be enrolled in graduate-level education. For instance, the share of immigrant Black men pursuing graduate degrees (5 percent) is more than double the share of native-born Black men (2 percent). The share of immigrant White women enrolled in graduate education (7 percent) is greater than that of native-born White women (5 percent). Among Hispanic and Asian young adults, however, there is no clear immigrant advantage: native-born and immigrant young people are enrolled in graduate education at comparable rates. Finally, while young women generally outpace young men in graduate enrollment, these differences are not especially large.

KEY FINDINGS

- The majority of young adults who are still enrolled in education at ages twenty-five to thirty-four are enrolled at the undergraduate level.
- Asian young adults tend to have higher rates and Black and Hispanic young adults lower rates of continued enrollment in graduate education relative to White young adults, a pattern that generally holds across gender and nativity.
- There is an immigrant advantage in graduate enrollment among White and Black young adults but not among Hispanic and Asian young adults.
- Young women are generally more likely than their male peers to still be pursuing undergraduate or graduate education at ages twenty-five to thirty-four.

Understanding Continued Enrollment

As we noted earlier, it is difficult to draw conclusions about the racial, ethnic, immigrant, and gender patterns we have shown without knowing whether currently enrolled young adults ultimately complete their degrees. Research suggests that young people who delay entry into college tend to come from socioeconomically disadvantaged families and to have experienced academic difficulties, which may make college completion more challenging.[32] Moreover, changes to the financial landscape of higher education make any delay in college completion a costly burden. Research by the College Board found that in 2015–16, the vast majority of students at four-year colleges and universities had unmet financial need beyond the grant aid they received.[33] Many students and their families must rely on loans in order to finance their higher education.[34] Thus, young adults today are not only spending more time pursuing education, but they and their families are also incurring significant debt in the process.[35] This puts many young people in an especially precarious position as they make the school-to-work transition, particularly for those who take on educational debt without completing a degree.

Research also finds that first-generation college students (students who are the first in their family to attend college), lower-income students, and disadvantaged racial and ethnic minority students are less likely to complete postsecondary education.[36] Marginalized young people may end up drifting in and out of colleges without a terminal degree and with few job prospects.[37] Tanya, one of the young people profiled in *Not Quite Adults*, a trade press book based on research by Richard Settersten and Barbara Ray, exemplifies the challenge of pursuing a college credential over an extended period of time, especially for nontraditional students. Tanya is a twenty-nine-year-old community college student with three children of her own who juggles both a full-time and a part-time job. Reflecting on the long road ahead to a college credential (at this point she is aiming for an associate's degree), Tanya remarks, "It makes you not want to go at the rate I'm going."[38] Even young people who pursue graduate education in a bid to increase their future earnings potential can expect significant variations in the payoff to their degrees by field of study.[39]

A more optimistic perspective of continued enrollment is that these young people are making an investment in their future. Settersten and Ray argue that young people who opt out of college because they want to avoid debt might find some temporary success in the labor market, but this is a much less secure path than strategically taking on educational debt to finance a college education that may lead to a more stable and lucrative career. Settersten and Ray suggest that a more practical strategy for students is to attend lower-cost public universities rather than elite universities. In their view, it is the degree, not the institution that matters.[40] Higher education is also positively correlated with a number of outcomes beyond an individual's economic well-being. These outcomes include improved health, family stability, and social connections. Studies have even shown broader community benefits of having a more educated populace, including lower crime rates and less reliance on public assistance.[41] Particularly for women with children, having a college or advanced degree is positively related to a range of children's health, behavioral, and socioeconomic outcomes.[42] This means that the education young adults pursue has immediate and longer-term consequences not only for themselves but also for their offspring. Thus, continued enrollment into adulthood, while not necessarily the "ideal" many young adults hold, probably yields benefits to them and any children they may have.

Educational Attainment by Race and Ethnicity

Patterns of educational attainment for young adults not currently enrolled in school are shown in figure 4. We present patterns by race, ethnicity, and nativity for males and females ages twenty-five to thirty-four. Though people return to school at all ages, it is reasonable to assume that the majority of these young adults have completed their education. Young adults are grouped into three categories based on the highest level of education they have attained: (1) "high school or less" refers to those with a high school diploma (or equivalent, such as a GED) or less education, (2) "some college" refers to those with at most some college experience (including sub-baccalaureate degrees such as associate's degrees) but no bachelor's degree, and (3) "bachelor's degree or higher" refers to those who have completed a bachelor's or higher degree (including those with master's, professional, or doctoral degrees).

Figure 4 shows significant racial and ethnic differences in educational attainment. For native-born White men, educational attainment is split fairly evenly across the three categories. Educational attainment is more skewed for men in other racial and ethnic groups. More than 50 percent of native-born Asian young men are college graduates (i.e., "bachelor's degree or higher"). In contrast, more than 50 percent of native-born Black and Hispanic young men have no college experience (i.e., "high school or less"). Among immigrant young men, we see similar patterns of racial and ethnic differences, with 52 percent of Asian men having earned at least a bachelor's degree compared to 43 percent of White men, 26 percent of Black men, and 11 percent of Hispanic men.

For native-born and immigrant women, racial and ethnic patterns largely mirror those found among men. About 44 percent of native-born White young women and 51 percent of immigrant White young women have bachelor's degrees compared to 69 percent and 63 percent of their respective Asian counterparts. Native-born and immigrant Black and Hispanic women are less likely than their White peers to have completed a bachelor's degree, with less than 40 percent of immigrant Black women, less than 25 percent of native-born Black and Hispanic women, and less than 20 percent of immigrant Hispanic women having done so.

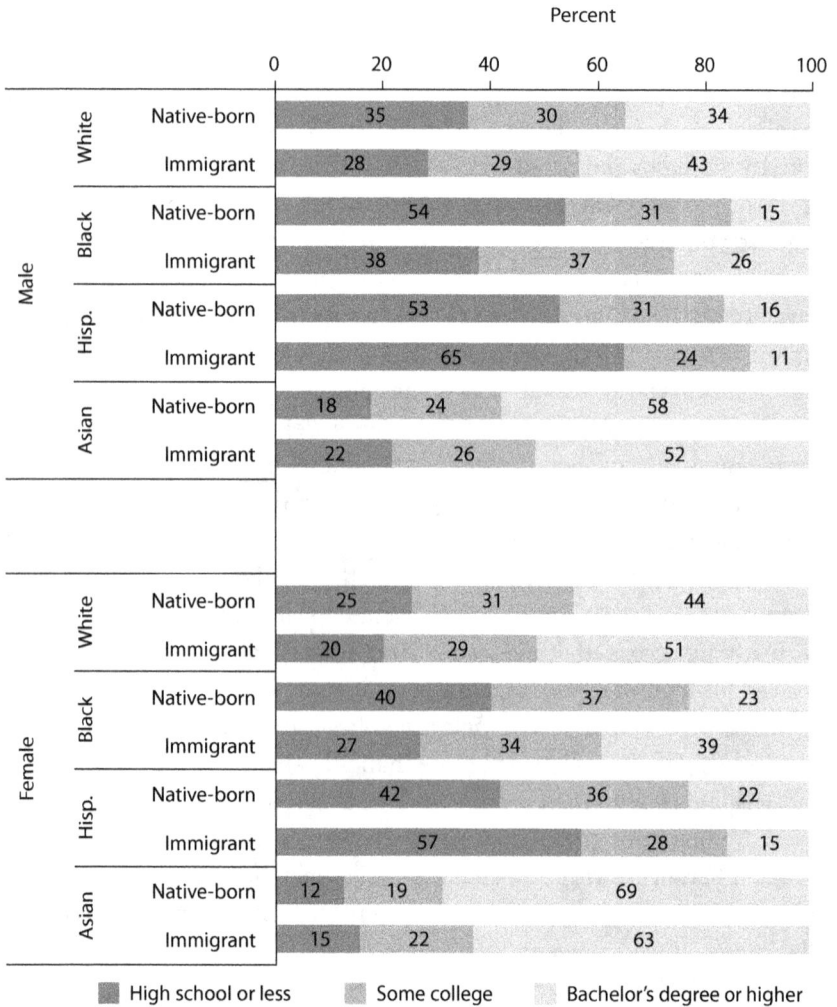

Percent

			High school or less	Some college	Bachelor's degree or higher
Male	White	Native-born	35	30	34
		Immigrant	28	29	43
	Black	Native-born	54	31	15
		Immigrant	38	37	26
	Hisp.	Native-born	53	31	16
		Immigrant	65	24	11
	Asian	Native-born	18	24	58
		Immigrant	22	26	52
Female	White	Native-born	25	31	44
		Immigrant	20	29	51
	Black	Native-born	40	37	23
		Immigrant	27	34	39
	Hisp.	Native-born	42	36	22
		Immigrant	57	28	15
	Asian	Native-born	12	19	69
		Immigrant	15	22	63

High school or less   Some college   Bachelor's degree or higher

Figure 4. Educational attainment among nonenrolled young adults (ages twenty-five to thirty-four), by gender, race and ethnicity, and nativity.

SOURCE: US Census 2017, Five-Year Estimates; Ruggles et al. 2021.

Overall, young women are more likely than their male peers to complete a bachelor's degree, a pattern that holds across race, ethnicity, and nativity. For instance, Asian young adults have the highest rates of bachelor's or higher degree attainment among both men and women but Asian women still outpace Asian men in this respect. Even among educationally disadvantaged groups, a female advantage is apparent. For example, the modal category (meaning the category with the greatest share) of educational attainment for native-born Black young women is "some college" but for native-born Black young men the modal category is "high school or less."

Educational Attainment by Nativity within Each Racial and Ethnic Group

Although patterns of racial and ethnic differences in educational attainment are similar between native-born and immigrant young adults, taking a closer look at comparisons by nativity *within* each racial and ethnic group reveals additional complexity. Among White and Black men, there is an immigrant *advantage*, with immigrants outpacing their native-born peers in bachelor's or higher degree attainment. For example, 26 percent of immigrant Black men have completed at least a four-year degree compared to 15 percent of native-born Black men. In contrast, among Hispanic and Asian men, there is an immigrant *disadvantage* in educational attainment. Compared to their native-born peers, immigrant Hispanic and Asian men are more likely to have no college experience and less likely to be college graduates. About 65 percent of immigrant Hispanic young men, for example, are in the "high school or less" category compared to 53 percent of native-born Hispanic men.

For young women, we also see a similar pattern of White and Black immigrant *advantage* and Asian and Hispanic immigrant *disadvantage*. About 20 percent of immigrant White women have no college experience (i.e., "high school or less") compared to 25 percent of native-born White women. Nearly 40 percent of immigrant Black women are college graduates (i.e., "bachelor's degree or higher") compared to 23 percent of native-born Black women. Immigrant Hispanic and Asian women, however, are less likely than their native-born counterparts to be college graduates.

KEY FINDINGS

- Compared to White young adults, Asian young adults have higher rates and Black and Hispanic young adults have lower rates of bachelor's or higher degree attainment, a pattern that holds across gender and nativity.
- Black and White immigrants have an educational advantage, outpacing their native-born peers in bachelor's or higher degree attainment, while Hispanic and Asian immigrants are at an educational disadvantage, being less likely to have earned a bachelor's or higher degree than their native-born peers.
- Young women outpace their male peers in bachelor's or higher degree attainment, a pattern that holds across race, ethnicity, and nativity.

About 15 percent of immigrant Hispanic women have at least a bachelor's degree compared to 22 percent of native-born Hispanic women. Both native-born and immigrant Asian women have the highest rates of bachelor's degree attainment among their peers but native-born Asian women still outpace immigrant Asian women (69 percent versus 63 percent).

Understanding Differences in Educational Attainment

Our discussion in this chapter has focused on educational attainment, for which data are readily available in the American Community Survey. However, we are limited in our ability to examine differences in educational experiences. Racial and ethnic inequalities as well as gender differences in education begin well before young people apply to and enter higher education. Unequal social origins and the broader social context influence the experiences of young people throughout their academic careers.[43] The persistence of educational gaps in achievement and attainment by race, ethnicity, nativity, and gender has led to continuing sociological research on the sources of these differences. For example, how do we explain the discrepancy between adolescents' near-uniform expectations that they will complete a bachelor's degree and the marked differences by race, ethnicity, nativity, and gender in the share who actually do so? Perhaps for young people today, thinking of themselves as college-goers is not just a rational choice to secure their future but also part of their construction of a "virtuous identity." Sociologist Margaret Frye suggests this is the case in Malawi, where young women with very slim chances of pursuing a university education nevertheless continue to hold such aspirations.[44] However dim the possibility, a young person can still claim they are working to improve their lot by pursuing a college degree. What we want to emphasize in this section, however, is the *structural barriers* that keep young people from reaching their aspirations, especially those young people who are entering adulthood already at a disadvantage.

Academic preparation and the cost of higher education are structural barriers that are especially likely to impact Black and Hispanic young people. As we described in chapter 1, Black and Hispanic students are more likely to attend schools that serve a greater share of poorer students and to have teachers with fewer years of experience.[45] In high school, Black and Hispanic students are less likely to earn advanced course credits and have, on average, lower GPAs than White and Asian students—indicators that they receive less academic preparation for college.[46] Research also finds that Black and Hispanic college students are more likely to require and to experience problems with financial aid and, relatedly, are more likely to work. These experiences all have adverse academic consequences.[47] Black and Hispanic students are also more likely than their White and Asian peers to experience "interrupted movement" during college, meaning they attend multiple institutions while also experiencing periods of interrupted enrollment, largely due to their lower levels of socioeconomic resources.[48]

Some institutional characteristics can also serve as structural barriers by reinforcing racial and ethnic disparities in college completion. Black and Hispanic students make up a greater share of the student population in two-year colleges than they do in four-year colleges. While two-year colleges can provide vocational certifications and a path to transferring to a four-year college, these outcomes are not guaranteed. In fact, credential completion and transfer rates are relatively low.[49] One view of two-year colleges is that such institutions serve a "cooling-out" function for students whose aspirations do not match their academic ability, through practices such as pretesting, placement into remedial coursework, and counseling students to downgrade their plans.[50] However, other research points to the transfer process rather than academic ability as a likelier obstacle—two-year college students who lose more of their credits upon transfer to four-year colleges are less likely to complete their bachelor's degree compared to students who retain more of their credits. Moreover, students who do manage to transfer to four-year colleges have comparable rates of bachelor's degree completion as their peers who began at four-year colleges.[51] Since Black and Hispanic students are more likely to be enrolled at two-year colleges, both "cooling-out" processes and transfer difficulties are more likely to affect their college outcomes than those of other racial and ethnic groups. The share of Black and Hispanic students that attend for-profit colleges is also noticeably higher than the share of their White and Asian peers who do so: 29 percent of students at private, for-profit, four-year institutions are Black and 26 percent are Hispanic.[52] These types of for-profit institutions have been sharply criticized for their low graduation rates and their relatively high costs and debt burden compared to the salaries graduates can expect to earn.[53]

How do students from different racial and ethnic backgrounds who start at four-year institutions, especially those at selective institutions, fare? In *The Source of the River* and *Taming the River*, Douglas Massey and Camille Charles, along with their colleagues, examined the background characteristics of incoming freshmen at twenty-eight academically selective colleges and universities as well as their campus experiences in the first two years. The studies show that Black and Hispanic college students are more likely to have experienced early structural inequalities in education, such as attending less integrated schools that experience more disorder and have poorer teaching quality. As a result, they tend to have less academic preparation than their White and Asian peers when they enter college. Once on campus, Black and Hispanic students also experience college differently from their White and Asian peers. For example, they are more likely to experience "stereotype threat," a psychological phenomenon that suggests individuals may underperform when faced with the possibility that their performance will confirm stereotypes about their particular group.[54] Though still an evolving area of research, some studies suggest that how underrepresented minority students perceive the "racial climate" of their college campus is related to their sense of belonging, which may have an effect on their academic outcomes.[55] While elite institutions offer students many resources, their rarefied environment may also contribute to the social isolation of underrepresented groups. Drawing on interview data from students at a highly selective university, sociologist Anthony Jack describes the challenges faced by "doubly disadvantaged" minority students—those who come from lower-income backgrounds and who attended lower-income high schools. Compared to their "privileged poor" peers (from lower-income backgrounds but who attended elite high schools) and their middle-class peers, "doubly disadvantaged" minority students expressed much more difficulty fitting into elite academic environments. Isabel, one such "doubly disadvantaged" student, says:

> I have never felt comfortable speaking to adults as equals or even asking them questions. It is something I have been cognizant of since I came here. I need to be able to talk to adults. How am I going to get some sort of recommendation? How am I going to ask for help? How am I going to build a relationship they say is "one of a kind" here? I can't even open my mouth.[56]

These differences in college experiences can impact "doubly disadvantaged" minority students' academics and future opportunities.

What are we to make of the racial and ethnic variation in educational attainment among immigrant young people? That is, why aren't immigrant young people uniformly advantaged or disadvantaged compared to their native-born peers? Overall, research suggests an educational advantage among immigrants, and theories variously attribute the success of the children of immigrants to factors such as premigration family characteristics, host-country reception, and immigrant optimism (see chapter 1).[57] However, it is also important to note that much of the quantitative research on immigrants' educational outcomes statistically adjusts for factors known to be associated with educational attainment, such as family socioeconomic status and school characteristics. These adjustments allow for comparisons between "similar" immigrant and native-born students. Given data limitations, our figures do not make these statistical adjustments. With such adjustments, we might find, for example, that family socioeconomic resources explain much of the Black and White immigrant advantage and the Asian and Hispanic immigrant disadvantage.

What else distinguishes the educational experiences of immigrant youth who arrived as children or young teens from those of their native-born peers? Language acquisition and peer relationships are important. For immigrant youth who are not native English speakers—which likely include some of the 1.5- and 1.75-generation young people in our sample—the need to gain fluency in English might hamper their academic progress. National-level data shows that elementary, middle, and high school students classified as English language learners (ELL) have lower average reading and math scores than their non-ELL peers. In high school, ELL students also earn fewer advanced course credits, placing them at a disadvantage in college readiness.[58] Students are also keenly aware of differences by immigrant generation. In a study of one California high school, Gilda Ochoa found that native-born Asian students, and to some extent native-born Latino students, draw firm boundaries between themselves and their immigrant peers, largely on the basis of English fluency and their perceived familiarity with "American" cultural norms. Immigrant students are often relegated to the bottom of the social hierarchy.[59] These peer relationships might isolate immigrant youth, contributing to poorer academic outcomes for some.[60] The experiences of Sing, a teenage immigrant featured in the documentary *I Learn America* (2013), embody many of these challenges. Though fluent in a variety of languages as a result of multiple border crossings, Sing is frustrated that he has to learn yet another new language (English). He left most of his family behind in Myanmar and is socially isolated at school, leaving him with few sources of social support. A change in residence due to economic circumstances means Sing has to make a long commute to his high school. At the end of the documentary, Sing expresses his commitment to graduating high school but despite his optimism, we are left wondering what the future holds for him.

Another important factor is the impact of undocumented status on educational outcomes. Unlike their second-generation peers, who as native-born children of immigrant parents are US citizens by birth, some of the 1.5- and 1.75-generation immigrant young people in our sample are likely to be undocumented immigrants. Undocumented status is also more likely to impact Hispanic and Asian groups since they make up the largest shares of immigrants coming to the United States. Undocumented young people face significant obstacles to completing a college degree and this may in part be reflected in the patterns of Hispanic and Asian immigrant disadvantage in educational attainment seen in this chapter. In a rare study that examined variations in educational outcomes by immigrant generation and legal status, Caitlin Patler found that compared to their second-generation peers, 1.5-generation immigrants (who, on average, arrived in the United States at age six) were less likely to enroll in college even after accounting for differences in family socioeconomic background and high school course-taking. Patler found that this was especially the case for 1.5-generation young people who were not citizens (i.e., were permanent residents or undocumented).[61] These findings suggest a need to go beyond the usual native-born/immigrant comparisons to examine forms of structural inequality by legal status. We look more closely at undocumented young people in chapter 5.

While structural factors, such as family socioeconomic status, often account for much of the difference in educational attainment between Black and Hispanic students and their White peers, they are less consistent predictors of Asian students' academic advantages.[62] Some researchers have proposed explanations based on the socioeconomic composition of Asian immigrant groups, as some Asian ethnic groups are more socioeconomically advantaged than others. However, other researchers argue that there are distinctive cultural family processes found among particular Asian groups. These include higher educational aspirations, lower rates of parental divorce, greater investment in children's educational activities, and more interdependent parent-child relationships (see *familism* in chapter 1). All of these factors might contribute to children's academic advantages.[63] Still other research suggests that cultural orientations and immigrant status combine to shape Asian American students' academic attitudes and behaviors. In one study, Amy Hsin and Yu Xie found that Asian American high school students were more likely than their White peers to believe that their parents expected them to succeed and that academic ability is something that can be developed rather than something that is innate. These beliefs—which Hsin and Xie argue constitute cultural orientations—explain some of the academic advantage Asian American students have over their White peers. However, having immigrant parents explained even more of the academic advantage, which suggests an immigrant background is more important than a particular ethnicity-based cultural orientation for understanding Asian American academic achievement.[64]

One reason it is so difficult to characterize the overall educational advantage of Asian American young people is because they are an ethnically diverse population. Both structural and cultural explanations require significant nuance in order to adequately explain patterns for each ethnic group. In chapter 1, we described the work of Jennifer Lee and Min Zhou, who argue that the positive selection of Chinese and Vietnamese immigrants (meaning that they tend to arrive in the United States with higher levels of education than non-migrants from their countries of origin) helps explain their children's educational advantage compared to the children of less positively selected immigrant groups.[65] We have seen in this chapter that Asian Americans, on average, attain bachelor's or higher degrees at a higher rate than Hispanic Americans. However, these pan-ethnic averages tend to obscure meaningful ethnic variation. For example, between 76 and 85 percent of native-born Chinese American young people have attained a bachelor's degree compared to between 52 and 66 percent of native-born Vietnamese American young people. Among Hispanic Americans, between 31 and 45 percent of Cuban American young people have attained at least a bachelor's degree compared to between 13 and 19 percent of Mexican American young people. Paying attention to such ethnic variation is useful for delineating between structural and cultural forces as influences on young people's lives. We provide a more detailed look at ethnic group differences among both Asian American and Hispanic American groups in chapter 5.

Lastly, the female advantage in educational attainment observed in this chapter is consistent with other research. In fact, for each racial and ethnic group, women now outpace men in college enrollment and completion.[66] Clearly, women today have more opportunity to pursue advanced credentials than in the past. These broadening opportunities have shifted women's priorities toward careers and educational attainment.[67] Women are less likely than men to drop out of high school and are more likely to enroll in college immediately after high school, all of which are likely to lead to better college completion outcomes.[68] Are these gender differences purely due to changes in the structures of opportunity for women? Perhaps not—indeed, some sociologists argue that sociocultural explanations also play a role. In *The Rise of Women*, Thomas DiPrete and Claudia Buchmann argue that cultural "models for masculinity" offer rewards to boys that go beyond academic achievement, such as being popular or athletic, akin to Harding's concept of *cultural heterogeneity* (see chapter 1). DiPrete and Buchmann argue that pre-adolescent and adolescent boys who see alternative pathways to success may exert less effort in their academic study early on, placing them at a disadvantage in college readiness, entry, and even completion.

LABOR MARKET TRENDS: WHY EDUCATION MATTERS FOR GOOD JOBS, CAREER POTENTIAL, AND EARNINGS

Next to the completion of formal education, being employed full-time is seen by most Americans as one of the most important indicators of adulthood.[69] However, the increasing polarization of the labor market in the United States has fundamentally changed the school-to-work transition for today's young people.[70] The current US labor market has been described as an hourglass, with a concentration of low-wage, low-skill jobs requiring less education at the bottom and better-paying professional jobs requiring significant education at the top.[71] Young people today must contend with the rise of so-called "bad jobs" characterized by low pay, few benefits, and little worker control and flexibility, and a dearth of "good jobs" that provide better pay, greater benefits, and more autonomy.[72] For young people, these changes to the labor market have created a sense of economic precariousness. A Pew Research Center report shows that in 1998, more than six in ten young adults were extremely or very confident they could find another job if they lost or left their current position. In 2012, only about four in ten young adults were that confident.[73]

Young adults are also more likely to take on additional jobs out of financial necessity. In 2009, about 5 percent of twenty-five-to-thirty-four-year-olds held more than one job (similar to the overall average for all age groups), but 28 percent of these young adults were working more than one job "to meet expenses or pay off debt," the highest rate among reported age groups. Black, Hispanic, and immigrant multiple jobholders as well as those with high school or less education were also more likely to be doing so out of financial need.[74] Some of these young multiple jobholders are likely part of the "gig" economy, which the Bureau of Labor Statistics describes as a system in which a worker is hired for a "single project or task . . . often through a digital marketplace, to work on demand." These include popular services such as rideshares (e.g., Uber, Lyft), food delivery (e.g., Grubhub, Door Dash), and pet care (e.g., Rover). By one measure available in data from the US Census Bureau, in the decade between 2003 and 2013, all industry sectors saw a growth in gig workers.[75] For younger workers, gigs might be a "side hustle," something they do in addition to a full-time job. Side hustles can be a way to pursue passions that are not well-paying, but it is also important to note that almost half of workers with side hustles interviewed by researchers and featured in a *Harvard Business Review* article were motivated to do so to increase their "pay and prestige."[76] In a *New York Times* article criticizing a 2021 Super Bowl ad that reworked Dolly Parton's hit song "9 to 5" (described as a "working-class anthem") as "5 to 9" (in a reference to side hustles that occur after the regular 9-to-5 work day), sociologist Tressie McMillan Cottom remarked, "Another word for hustle is 'survival.'"[77] In other words, the rise of gigs and side hustles cannot replace "good jobs" that provide stability and benefits.

Educational attainment is an important determinant in labor market experiences. A recent study by the Federal Reserve Bank of "opportunity employment"—jobs that are accessible to workers without bachelor's degrees but that typically pay above the median wage (meaning the top half of wages)—estimated that less than a quarter of total employment meet these criteria. We can think of such "opportunity employment" as that narrow middle in an hourglass economy. In contrast to the small share of jobs that constitute "opportunity employment," the same study estimates that more than a quarter of total employment comes from higher wage work requiring a bachelor's degree.[78] Moreover, jobs requiring college or advanced degrees are projected to grow much more rapidly than jobs requiring only a high school-level education. The Bureau of Labor Statistics predicts that jobs requiring a high school diploma at entry will grow about 5 percent between 2016 and 2026, compared to 13 percent for jobs requiring a bachelor's degree and 17 percent for jobs requiring a master's degree.[79] Whether young adults consider their current positions as "careers" is also shaped by their educational attainment: 83 percent of college graduates see their current jobs as either their career or a "stepping stone" to a career, compared to 51 percent of those without college degrees. Young adults who consider themselves in a career are also more satisfied with their jobs than are their peers who think of their current position as "just a job."[80]

Since education is a crucial determinant of the types of jobs young adults can secure, it should come as no surprise that it also affects their earnings. The link between educational attainment and earnings has become stronger over time. A recent College Board report showed that in 1975, median earnings were 19 percent and 37 percent higher for young men and women with a bachelor's or higher degree, respectively, compared to their peers who were high school graduates. By 2015, the earnings premium associated with a bachelor's or higher degree jumped to 75 percent for men and 84 percent for women.[81] To put into perspective just how much education shapes the earning potential of young people, a 2019 report from the Bureau of Labor Statistics estimated that the median weekly earnings of workers with the highest levels of education (doctoral or professional degrees) are about triple those of workers with the lowest levels of education (less than a high school diploma). As the report succinctly concludes, "the more you learn, the more you earn."[82] Consider two in-demand occupations in healthcare with different educational requirements: personal care aides and registered nurses. To be a personal care aide, one typically needs a high school-level education, while to be a registered nurse, one often needs a bachelor's degree. The two occupations also have sharply differing earnings potential. The median annual wage (meaning half of such workers will earn more and half will earn less) is just over twenty-three thousand dollars for personal care aides but about seventy thousand dollars for registered nurses.[83]

Young people today are experiencing a labor market in which career potential and earnings are highly stratified by educational attainment. How well are young people from different demographic backgrounds and with varying levels of education faring in the labor market? Figures 5 and 6 show the share of young men and women (ages twenty-five to thirty-four), respectively, who are employed full-time across levels of educational attainment. Working full-time means that the young adult is currently employed and usually working thirty-five or more hours per week. Only young adults who

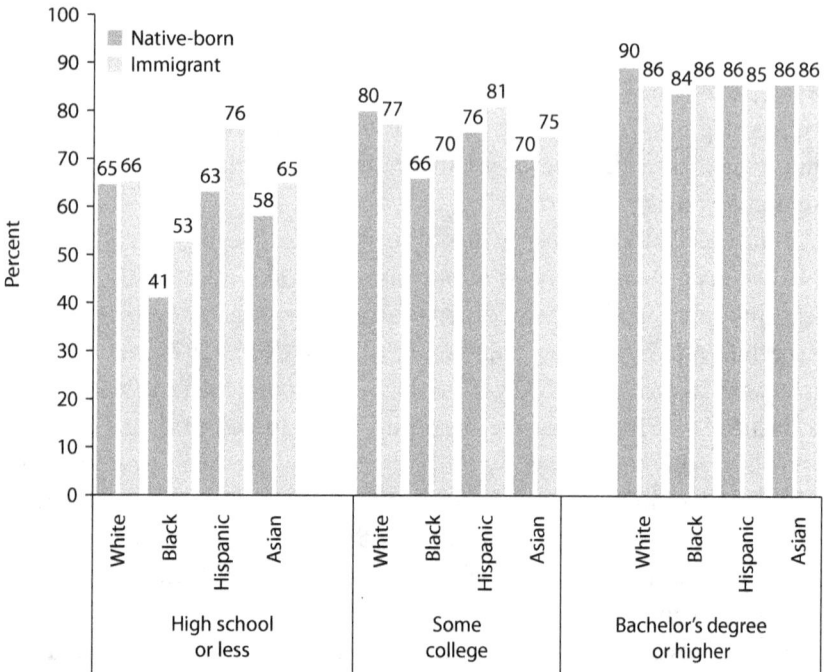

Figure 5. Percentage of young men (ages twenty-five to thirty-four) employed full-time, by educational attainment, race and ethnicity, and nativity.

SOURCE: US Census 2017, Five-Year Estimates; Ruggles et al. 2021.

are not currently enrolled in school are included, since for those who are still enrolled, the education they are currently pursuing will likely play a role in their subsequent labor market experiences. Also, we think it is less likely that those who are currently enrolled in school are working full-time. As we saw in figure 3, the majority of young adults in this age range are not currently enrolled in education, so excluding those who are enrolled will have a relatively small impact on our overall estimates.

Race, Ethnicity, and Education in Full-Time Employment

Figure 5 clearly shows the positive association between education and full-time employment among young men. Young men without any college experience (i.e., "high school or less") are much less likely to be employed

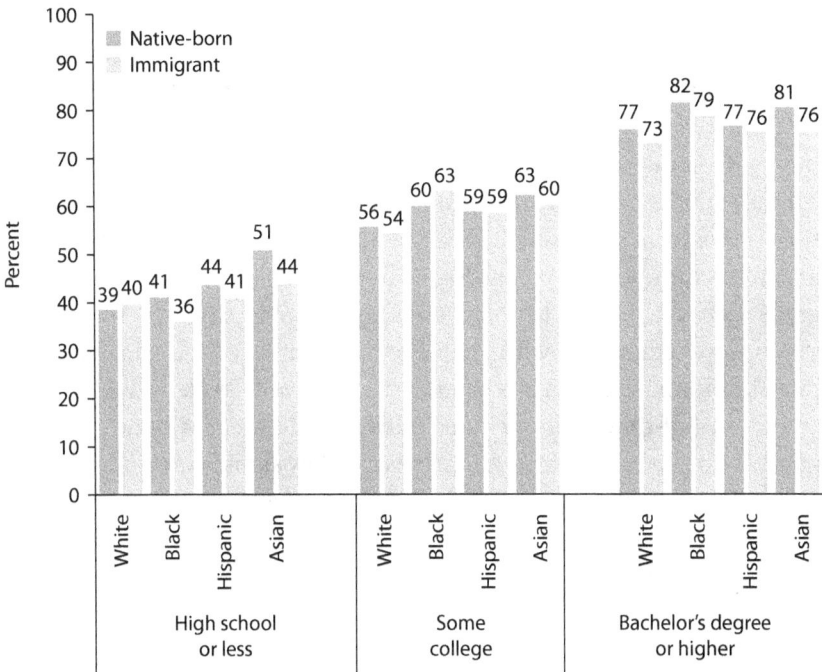

Figure 6. Percentage of young women (ages twenty-five to thirty-four) employed full-time, by educational attainment, race and ethnicity, and nativity.

SOURCE: US Census 2017, Five-Year Estimates; Ruggles et al. 2021.

full-time than those with more education. This pattern holds across racial and ethnic groups and for both native-born and immigrant young people. At the lower end of educational attainment, native-born White men have higher rates of full-time employment compared to their Black, Hispanic, and Asian peers. About 65 percent of native-born White men with no college experience are employed full-time, compared to 63 percent of native-born Hispanic, 58 percent of native-born Asian, and 41 percent of native-born Black men. Comparisons among immigrant young men with less education reveal somewhat different patterns. Immigrant White men with no college experience have higher rates of full-time employment than immigrant Black men (66 percent versus 53 percent) but similar rates compared to immigrant Asian men (65 percent) and *lower* rates compared to immigrant Hispanic men (76 percent).

Young men with some college experience but less than a bachelor's degree fare better than their peers with no college experience. A majority of these young men are employed full-time, regardless of race, ethnicity, and nativity. However, racial and ethnic differences persist among young men with some college experience. Among native-born men with some college experience, White men remain the most likely to be employed full-time (80 percent), followed by Hispanic (76 percent), Asian (70 percent), and Black (66 percent) men. Racial and ethnic patterns among immigrant men are similar to those seen among men with at most a high school–level education, with Hispanic men employed full-time at higher rates than immigrant White men and immigrant Black and Asian men employed full-time at lower rates (although differences between immigrant White and Asian men are not statistically significant).

Young men with bachelor's or higher degrees consistently outpace their peers with some college experience and far exceed their peers with no college experience in the shares that are employed full-time. For example, among native-born Black men, the rate of full-time employment among those with a bachelor's or higher degree is more than double that of their peers with at most a high school-level education (84 percent versus 41 percent). Between native-born Black men with some college experience and their peers who completed at least a bachelor's degree there remains about an 18-percentage point difference in rates of full-time employment (66 percent versus 84 percent). In fact, across all groups of young men with bachelor's degrees, the vast majority are employed full-time (90 percent of native-born White young men and more than 80 percent of native-born minority men). Comparisons among immigrant men with bachelor's or higher degrees reveal remarkably little variation, with 85 percent or more of such young men employed full-time across racial and ethnic groups.

For young women, educational attainment also plays an important role in their rates of full-time employment. Figure 6 reveals the steady rise in the shares of young women who are employed full-time as educational attainment increases. Like their male counterparts, young women with no college experience are less likely to be employed full-time compared to their peers with more education. Indeed, only a minority of such women work full-time, with the exception of native-born Asian women. However, unlike patterns among their male counterparts, native-born minority women with no college experience are actually more likely to be employed full-time than their native-born White peers. About 51 percent of native-born Asian, 44 percent of native-born Hispanic, and 41 percent of native-born Black women with no college experience work full-time, compared to 39 percent of native-born White women. However, these racial and ethnic comparisons among immigrant women do not reach statistical significance (meaning we cannot rule out that these differences are chance occurrences).

There is a fairly significant increase across the board in rates of full-time employment when moving to young women with some college experience. More than half of such women across groups are employed full-time. Similar to their peers with less education, minority women with some college experience are more likely to be employed full-time compared to their White peers. Among women with some college experience, about 56 percent of native-born White women work full-time, compared to 63 percent of native-born Asian, 60 percent of native-born Black, and 59 percent of native-born Hispanic women. Immigrant Black, Hispanic, and Asian women with some college experience also have higher rates of working full-time compared to immigrant White women.

Young women who have obtained at least a bachelor's degree are the most likely group of women to be employed full-time. Regardless of their race, ethnicity, and nativity, more than three-quarters of these young women work full-time. Once again, minority women with at least a bachelor's degree are typically more likely to be employed full-time than White women, a pattern that holds for both native-born and immigrant young adults. For example, more than 80 percent of native-born Black and Asian women with bachelor's or higher degrees work full-time, a slightly larger share than the 77 percent of native-born White women who do so.

Despite their edge in educational attainment, young women are generally less likely than young men to be employed full-time. Comparing rates of full-time employment between young men and women with similar levels of education in figure 5 and figure 6 reveals that at each level of educational attainment, young men are consistently more likely to be employed full-time. This gender gap in full-time employment tends to be larger among young adults who lack a bachelor's degree. For instance, the 26-percentage point difference in rates of full-time employment between native-born White men and women with no college experience (65 percent versus 39 percent) is about double the 13-percentage point difference between their counterparts with bachelor's or higher degrees (90 percent versus 77 percent).

Nativity and Education in Full-Time Employment

Immigrant Black, Hispanic, and Asian men routinely have higher rates and immigrant White men lower rates of full-time employment compared to their native-born counterparts. This is especially the case among young men without a bachelor's degree. Among those with no college experience, immigrant minority men have rates of full-time employment that range from 7 to 13 percentage points higher than their native-born counterparts. This immigrant minority advantage is also seen among immigrant young men with some college experience, for whom rates of employment are 4 to 5 percentage points higher than their native-born counterparts. For example, about 76 percent of native-born Hispanic men with some college experience are employed full-time compared to 81 percent of similarly educated immigrant Hispanic men. However, this immigrant minority advantage is less apparent among young men with bachelor's or higher degrees, among whom differences by nativity are not statistically significant. In contrast, immigrant White men without any college experience have fairly similar levels of full-time employment as their native-born peers. Among those with bachelor's or higher degrees, native-born White men are more likely than immigrant White men to be employed full-time.

For women, we find the inverse pattern—immigrant women are generally less likely to be employed full-time than their native-born peers. This is most clearly seen among women in the lowest category of educational attainment ("high school or less"), where native-born minority women's rates of full-time employment are 3 to 7 percentage points higher than those of immigrant minority women; the difference between native-born and immigrant White women do not reach statistical significance. At higher levels of educational attainment, native-born and immigrant women are more similar in the shares that are employed full-time. Most differences here are not statistically significant. So, while immigrant minority men with less education are more likely than their native-born peers to work full-time, their female counterparts are less likely to do so.

Gender differences in full-time employment are also larger among immigrant young adults compared to their native-born peers, though this is most evident among those without bachelor's degrees and among Hispanic and Asian young adults. For example, there is about a 19-percentage point difference in rates of full-time employment between native-born Hispanic men and women with a high school-level or less education (63 percent versus 44 percent) but a 35-percentage point difference among similarly educated immigrant Hispanic young adults (76 percent versus 41 percent). Similarly, the gender gap in full-time employment among native-born Asian young adults with some college experience favoring men is about 7 percentage points (70 percent versus 63 percent), compared to a 15-percentage point male advantage among immigrant Asian young adults (75 percent versus 60 percent).

We note that a bachelor's degree reduces racial, ethnic, immigrant, and gender differences in the odds of full-time employment. Young people who complete at least a bachelor's degree exhibit modest racial and ethnic differences in their rates of full-time employment. In contrast, for those with only a high school-level education, we see large differences by race, ethnicity, nativity, and gender. For example, the White-Black gap in full-time employment among native-born men with no college experience is about 24 percentage points (65 percent versus 41 percent) compared to 6 percentage points among their male counterparts with bachelor's or higher degrees (90 percent versus 84 percent). Likewise, the immigrant disadvantage seen among Black, Hispanic, and Asian women with less education is minimized among bachelor's degree-holders. Gender differences in full-time employment are also consistently smaller among young people with bachelor's or higher degrees. Compare, for example, the 9-percentage point difference in rates of full-time employment between immigrant Hispanic men and women with bachelor's degrees (85 percent versus 76 percent) to the 35-percentage point difference among their counterparts with at most a high school-level education (76 percent versus 41 percent). While college degrees do not by any means entirely erase significant inequalities in rates of full-time employment, they do increase the likelihood of working full-time even for otherwise disadvantaged groups.

Nonworking Young Adults

Another way of thinking about how educational attainment shapes the labor market participation of young adults is to look at the share who are nonworkers. Figures 7 and 8 show the share of twenty-five-to-thirty-four-year-olds who are nonworkers, by educational attainment. Nonworking young adults fall into two categories: out of the labor force and unemployed. Though we consider both groups nonworkers, these are distinct categories. Young adults out of the labor force are neither working nor were they seeking work in the past week. Unemployed young adults are still considered in the labor market because they were seeking work but not employed in the last week. Since a relatively small share of young adults not in school are working part-time, we can think of the numbers in figures 7 and 8 as the inverse of those in figures 5 and 6. That is, together these figures show which groups of young adults are participating fully in the labor market and which groups are experiencing marginal participation in the labor market.

Figures 7 and 8 confirm what we saw above: educational attainment is strongly related to the labor market participation of young adults. The share of young people who are nonworkers is typically higher among those with less education compared to those who completed at least a bachelor's degree. Native-born White men are less likely than native-born minority men to be unemployed or out of the labor force (figure 7). The immigrant minority advantage among men with less education is reflected in their lower rates of nonparticipation in the labor force. Native-born White women are more likely to be out of the labor market and less likely to be unemployed compared to their native-born Black, Hispanic, and Asian peers. In other words, nonworking native-born minority women are more likely to be searching for work compared to their White peers. For example, among native-born women with at least a bachelor's degree, about 10 percent of White women are out of the labor force and 2 percent are unemployed compared to 5 percent out of the labor force and 4 percent

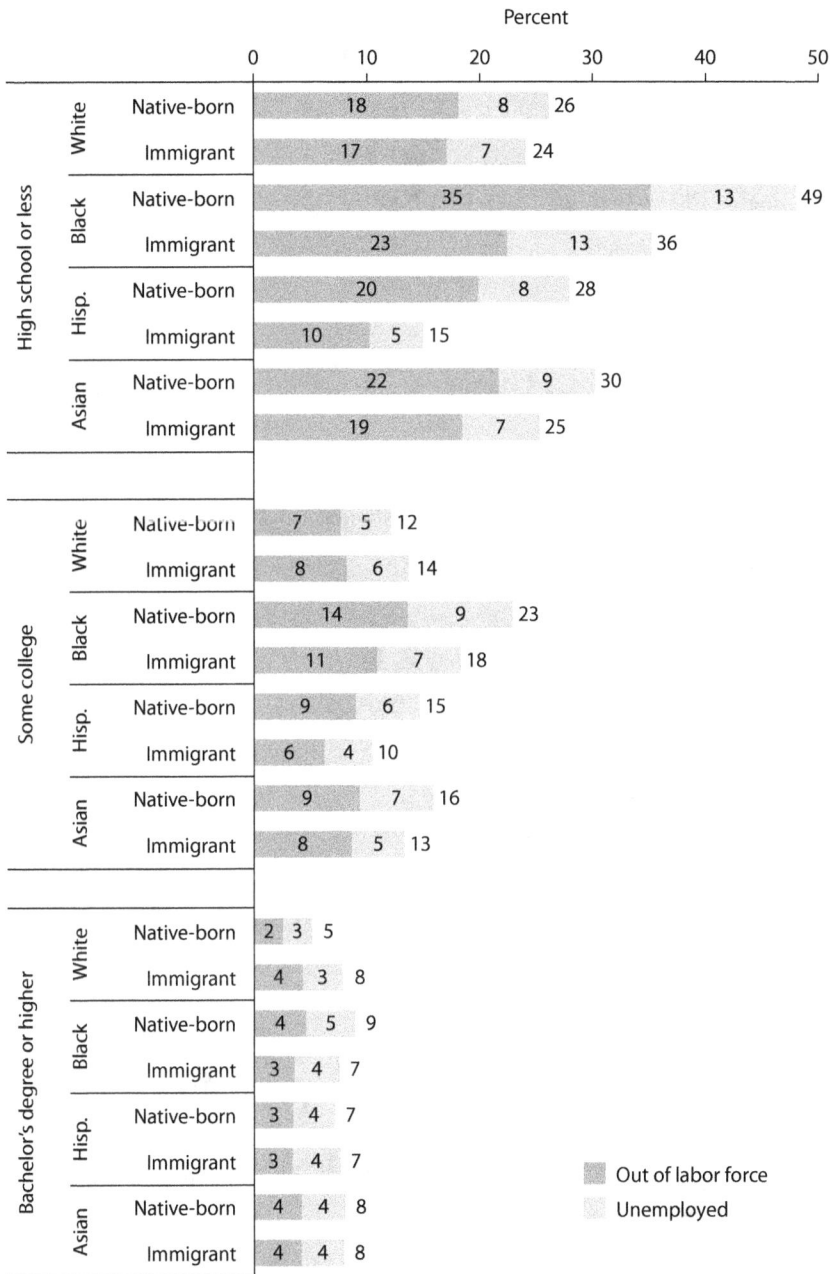

Percent

			Out of labor force	Unemployed	Total
High school or less	White	Native-born	18	8	26
		Immigrant	17	7	24
	Black	Native-born	35	13	49
		Immigrant	23	13	36
	Hisp.	Native-born	20	8	28
		Immigrant	10	5	15
	Asian	Native-born	22	9	30
		Immigrant	19	7	25
Some college	White	Native-born	7	5	12
		Immigrant	8	6	14
	Black	Native-born	14	9	23
		Immigrant	11	7	18
	Hisp.	Native-born	9	6	15
		Immigrant	6	4	10
	Asian	Native-born	9	7	16
		Immigrant	8	5	13
Bachelor's degree or higher	White	Native-born	2	3	5
		Immigrant	4	3	8
	Black	Native-born	4	5	9
		Immigrant	3	4	7
	Hisp.	Native-born	3	4	7
		Immigrant	3	4	7
	Asian	Native-born	4	4	8
		Immigrant	4	4	8

Figure 7. Percentage of nonworking young men (ages twenty-five to thirty-four), by educational attainment, race and ethnicity, and nativity. "Out of labor force" and "unemployed" may not sum to total nonworking due to rounding.

SOURCE: US Census 2017, Five-Year Estimates; Ruggles et al. 2021.

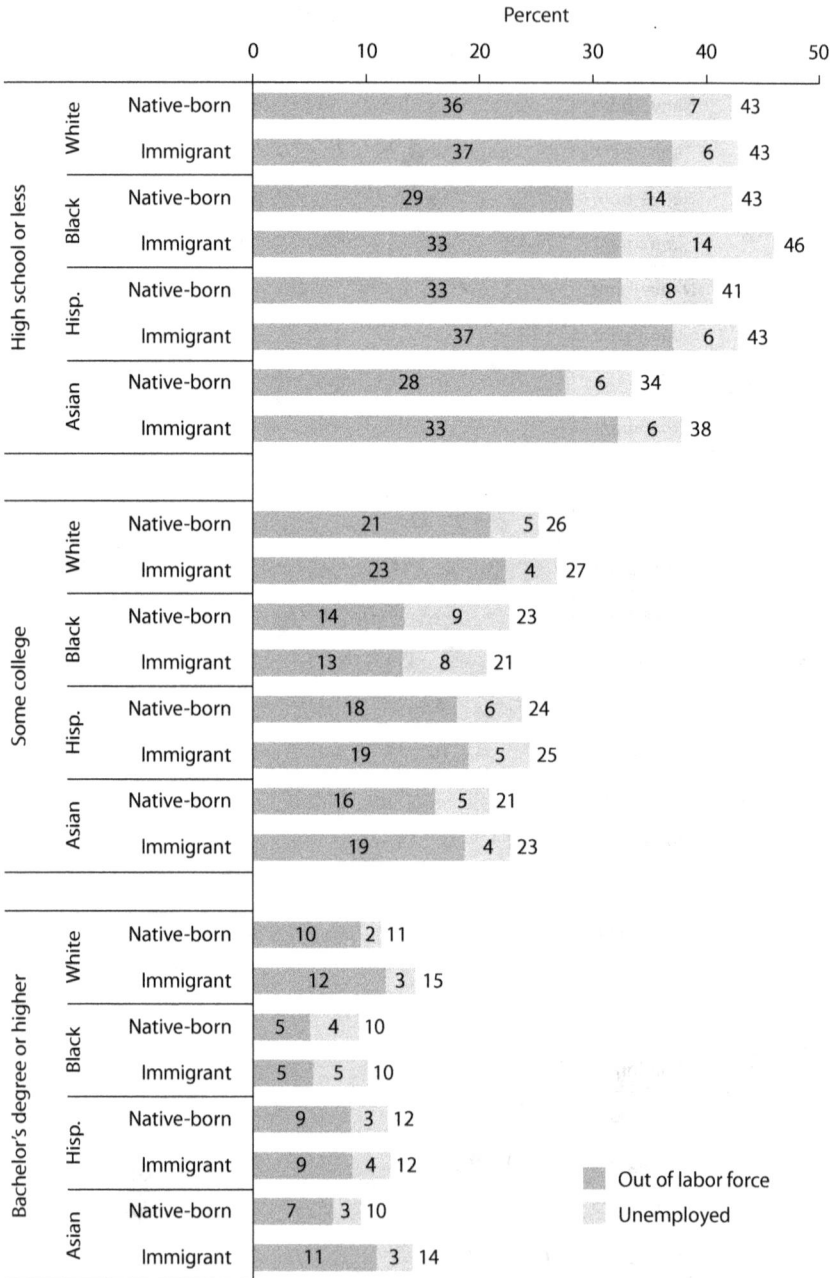

Figure 8. Percentage of nonworking young women (ages twenty-five to thirty-four), by educational attainment, race and ethnicity, and nativity. "Out of labor force" and "unemployed" may not sum to total nonworking due to rounding.

SOURCE: US Census 2017, Five-Year Estimates; Ruggles et al. 2021.

KEY FINDINGS

- Young adults with more education are consistently more likely to be employed full-time regardless of race, ethnicity, nativity, and gender.
- White young men have higher rates and White young women lower rates of full-time employment compared to their racial and ethnic minority peers.
- At the lower end of educational attainment, immigrant minority men are more likely and immigrant minority women less likely to be employed full-time compared to their native-born counterparts.
- Young women are less likely to be employed full-time and more likely to be out of the labor force compared to men.

unemployed among Black women. Immigrant women are generally more likely to be out of the labor force compared to native-born women.

Comparing figure 7 and figure 8 also shows nuances in labor market participation by educational attainment for men and women. First, for young men, their educational attainment is related to the type of nonwork they experience. Nonworking young men without bachelor's degrees are more likely to be out of the labor force than unemployed while the opposite is true for their peers with at least a bachelor's degree. For example, of the roughly 30 percent of nonworking native-born Asian men without any college experience, the share who are out of the labor force (22 percent) is more than double the share who are unemployed (9 percent). In contrast, the 8 percent of native-born Asian men with bachelor's or higher degrees who are not working is about evenly split between the unemployed and labor force nonparticipants. For young women, a different relationship between educational attainment and nonworking status emerges. Like their male peers, nonworking young women with no college experience are more likely to be out of the labor force than unemployed. However, even among women with bachelor's or higher degrees, for most groups greater shares are out of the labor force than are unemployed. For instance, of the 15 percent of immigrant White women with bachelor's or higher degrees who are currently not working, 12 percent are out of the labor force and just 3 percent are unemployed. Thus, gender continues to exert a profound influence on how young people participate in the labor market.

Understanding Differences in Labor Market Outcomes

Clearly, racial and ethnic differences in labor market outcomes are at least in part due to the distribution of educational attainment across groups. Black and Hispanic young adults, who have lower average levels of educational attainment compared to their White and Asian peers, also experience worse outcomes in terms of labor market participation. However, noticeable racial and ethnic differences even among young people with similar levels of education point to the existence of *structural inequalities*. For example, at both the upper and lower end of educational attainment—that is, among those with no college experience and among those with bachelor's or higher degrees—native-born White men have higher rates of employment than native-born minority men. Why? One reason is the social networks available to different groups of people. In their study of White and Black children growing up in highly disadvantaged neighborhoods in Baltimore, Karl Alexander, Doris Entwisle, and Linda Olson find that even though the heyday of Baltimore's unionized blue-collar economy has passed, young White men are often able to secure rare well-paying jobs that do not require college degrees through family connections. Black young men, on the other hand, are much less likely to have family members who can help them secure such work. The history of racial segregation in Baltimore labor unions meant Black workers joined labor unions only once they were in decline. As the researchers describe, "At every juncture and in every category of employment, whites have better jobs. In sales, for example, whites sell insurance, blacks sell shoes; in protective services, whites work in crime labs, blacks are security guards."[84]

Why then do labor market disadvantages persist even among young adults with high levels of education? Of course, we know that different groups face unequal treatment in the labor market. Discrimination is difficult to directly measure but audit studies, a type of experiment conducted in the field rather than in labs, have yielded important insights into how race and ethnicity intersect with education in the labor market.[85]

In one study, the sociologist S. Michael Gaddis applied to over one thousand jobs seeking entry-level workers with bachelor's degrees, using a series of carefully matched résumés that primarily differed by the selectivity of the higher education institution attended (e.g., Harvard versus the University of Massachusetts), gender, and race. Gaddis found that while all résumés from elite university graduates received more employer responses, Black résumés from elite institutions only did as well as White résumés from less selective institutions.[86] Other audit studies reveal a similar disadvantage among Hispanic job applicants. One early audit study conducted in Chicago and San Diego found that Hispanic auditors (those hired as part of the study to apply to jobs) were less likely than White auditors to be allowed to fill out a job application, to receive an interview, and to be offered a job if they received an interview.[87] Despite their high educational attainment, Asians also have a well-documented disadvantage in the labor market relative to Whites, at both higher-level positions (what some researchers term a "bamboo ceiling") and among workers with less education.[88]

Given that the young adults in our study have most likely completed most if not all of their schooling in the United States, how is it that, among men with less education, immigrant minority men maintain an advantage over their native-born peers? Research suggests two interrelated reasons: immigrant men may rely more on the availability of jobs in ethnic communities and the informal labor market and are more willing to accept such jobs compared to native-born young adults. In a study of immigrants in New York City, researchers found that for many children of immigrants, their first jobs were working for family members, often as unpaid workers. While many children of immigrants aspired to and eventually did find professional work in the formal economy, some, particularly those with less education or those who migrated at later ages, continued to work low-pay jobs in the ethnic economy.[89] So, while some immigrant minority men with low levels of education are more likely to be employed full-time, they are not necessarily working in high-paying "good jobs."

It is probably not surprising that young women are less likely to be in the labor market relative to men, but what are the reasons for such a gender gap, especially considering women's greater educational attainment relative to men? One perspective is that the payoff for working is simply lower for women than it is for men since women tend to earn less than men. Research shows that compared to male college students, female college students are concentrated in fields such as education and the humanities that are less lucrative. This accounts for a significant portion of the gender wage gap.[90] However, the more complex question of *why* women and men tend to concentrate in different fields remains. A recent comprehensive review of research on STEM (science, technology, engineering, and math) education argues that biologically "essentialist" arguments (e.g., that men and women are biologically predisposed to value different types of interactions and thus occupations) are not well supported, since interest in STEM is highly influenced by social environments. Rather, research should focus on how the broader social environment shapes gender differences in educational attainment and occupational outcomes.[91] For example, across many societies, women typically work as the primary caregivers of children, which burdens them with a greater share of household labor. As a result, different-sex couples may calculate that it costs more to replace a woman's unpaid labor at home than what she can earn in the labor market. In other words, a structural feature of society—lower pay for women compared to men—can contribute to or normalize a cultural norm for women to not seek paid work in the labor market. We will return to similar gender issues in the next chapter on family formation milestones.

GLOBAL AND COMPARATIVE PERSPECTIVES

Thus far, we have focused on the experiences of young people in the United States. However, many of the factors that shape the transition to adulthood for young people in the United States, such as the expansion of education and changes in the labor market structure, also apply to their peers in other developed countries. Table 1 provides a number of comparisons across countries on indicators similar to those we have reviewed in this chapter. We include a select number of developed countries that are part of the Organisation for Economic Co-operation and Development (OECD) to allow for comparisons to the United States on multiple dimensions, including the educational attainment of young adults, gender norms, and

Table 1 Percentage Distribution of Young Adult (Ages 25–34) Educational Attainment across Selected OECD Countries

	Males			Females		
	BELOW UPPER SECONDARY	UPPER SECONDARY	TERTIARY	BELOW UPPER SECONDARY	UPPER SECONDARY	TERTIARY
OECD Average	16	45	39	13	35	52
Australia	11	42	47	7	31	62
Canada	7	38	56	4	23	73
Chile	16	53	30	13	50	27
Denmark	20	42	39	15	29	56
France	13	41	46	11	36	53
Germany	14	52	33	12	51	36
Greece	12	52	37	9	40	51
Italy	25	52	23	20	45	35
Japan	—	—	59	—	—	64
Korea	2	34	64	2	21	76
Mexico	47	29	25	46	29	26
Netherlands	12	40	47	9	34	57
Spain	34	25	41	23	24	54
Sweden	18	42	40	14	28	58
United Kingdom	15	33	52	10	30	59
United States	6	47	47	6	38	57

NOTE: Data on Chile from 2017, data on Denmark and Japan from 2019, data for all other countries from 2020. Data on tertiary education completion in Japan include postsecondary nontertiary programs.

SOURCE: OECD 2021.

immigration policies. Countries include those in Central and South America (Mexico, Chile), North America (Canada, the United States), Eastern Asia (Japan, the Republic of Korea), Northern Europe (Denmark, Sweden, the United Kingdom), Southern Europe (Greece, Italy, Spain), Western Europe (France, Germany, Netherlands), as well as Australia.

Table 1 shows the distribution of educational attainment for young adult men and women (ages twenty-five to thirty-four) in each of the selected OECD countries. The three categories of educational attainment shown in table 1 ("less than upper secondary," "upper secondary," and "tertiary") are defined by the OECD and are not directly comparable to the categories we examined earlier for the United States. For the United States, the middle category ("upper secondary") includes those with at least a tenth-grade education and what the OECD describes as "postsecondary nontertiary programs," which in the United States are typically vocational or one-year certificate programs.[92] Tertiary education is considered the highest level of education in the OECD data, and includes programs leading to advanced research and high-skill professions as well as vocational programs.[93] For the United States, the category "less than upper secondary" includes young adults with less than a tenth-grade education and "tertiary" includes those with associate's degrees.

In the share of its young people with a tertiary-level education, the United States does better than the OECD average. Across OECD countries, about 39 percent of young men and 52 percent of young women have completed tertiary education, compared to 47 percent of men and 57 percent of women in the United States. Young people in Japan and Korea have among the highest rates of tertiary-level education among the selected OECD countries. In Korea, for example, 64 percent of young men and 76 percent of young women have completed tertiary education. In other countries—for example, Chile, Germany, Italy, and Mexico—the rates of tertiary education completion are below the OECD average. In Italy, only about 23 percent of young men and 35 percent of young women have a tertiary-level education. We made the case earlier in the chapter that going to college has become a common thread in the fabric of US society, but this is not the case for all countries.

What is consistent across countries, however, is the female advantage in educational attainment. Across the selected OECD countries shown in table 1, young adult women are more likely than their male peers to have attained tertiary education. On average, young women in OECD countries outpace their male peers in completing tertiary-level education by about 13 percentage points. In the United States, the gap is smaller than average—about 10 percentage points. The gender gap in educational attainment is especially large in Canada, Denmark, and Sweden. In Canada, for example, 73 percent of young women and 56 percent of young men have tertiary credentials, a 17-percentage point difference. The gender gaps in Germany and Mexico are among the smallest, but so are overall rates of tertiary education completion. In Mexico, young men and women complete tertiary education at nearly identical rates, but only about a quarter of men and women have done so.

Given the considerable variation across countries in the levels of education attained by young people, does this mean the payoff to education also varies across countries? To answer this, we turn to table 2, which shows the percentage of young adults who are employed, by their educational attainment, across the selected OECD countries. The measure of employment used by the OECD is whether individuals worked at least one hour in the week prior, a very broad definition of employment. Nevertheless, we can still see a clear payoff to a tertiary education in terms of employment across OECD countries. Moreover, the employment advantage associated with more education appears consistently for both young men and women, underscoring just how important education is for the labor market outcomes of contemporary young adults around the world. For example, the average rate of employment across OECD countries is 87 percent for men and 80 percent for women with a tertiary education compared to just 69 percent and 43 percent, respectively, for their counterparts with less than an upper secondary education.

In each of the selected countries, young people with tertiary education are more likely to be employed than are their peers who have attained less education. The singular exception is Mexico, where men with a tertiary education are less likely to be employed (85 percent) than those with less than an upper secondary education (88 percent). However, the high rate of employment among less-educated young men in Mexico is an outlier among the selected OECD countries. The difference in rates of employment between the least and most educated men is smaller in Greece, Italy,

Table 2 Percentage of Young Adults (Ages 25–34) Employed across Selected OECD Countries, by Educational Attainment

	Males			Females		
	BELOW UPPER SECONDARY	UPPER SECONDARY	TERTIARY	BELOW UPPER SECONDARY	UPPER SECONDARY	TERTIARY
OECD Average	69	83	87	43	66	80
Australia	67	83	86	43	64	77
Canada	62	76	85	39	65	80
Chile	77	80	88	48	59	83
Denmark	64	84	87	45	72	82
France	66	82	87	37	66	84
Germany	69	87	90	49	84	87
Greece	68	66	74	37	51	67
Italy	64	72	69	30	51	65
Japan	–	–	94	–	–	82
Korea	76	69	80	48	54	71
Mexico	88	85	85	43	53	72
Netherlands	74	87	93	53	81	91
Spain	66	68	77	47	62	73
Sweden	69	86	87	46	77	84
United Kingdom	74	90	93	53	78	88
United States	70	76	87	41	64	82

NOTE: Data on Chile from 2017, data on Denmark and Japan from 2019, data for all other countries from 2020. Data on tertiary-level completion in Japan include postsecondary nontertiary programs.

SOURCE: "Educational Attainment and Labour-Force Status: Employment, Unemployment and Inactivity Rate of 25–64 Year-Olds, by Educational Attainment," available at https://stats.oecd.org, data last accessed January 2022.

and Korea, countries where youth unemployment and underemployment are major policy issues.[94] The clear pattern of higher rates of employment among the tertiary-educated is also seen for young women. In fact, there are no instances among the selected countries in which women with tertiary education have lower rates of employment than women with less education. Put simply, education is consistently beneficial for women's employment across countries. The payoff to education is also much larger for women than men across countries, especially given the much lower rates of employment experienced by women with less education. In the Netherlands, for example, about 91 percent of women with tertiary education are employed, compared to 53 percent of women with education below the upper secondary level. For men, the corresponding education gap in employment rates is smaller (93 percent versus 74 percent).

Another consistent pattern seen across the selected OECD countries is the lower rate of employment among young women compared to men. As we saw earlier in the chapter, the overall female advantage in bachelor's degree completion among US young adults does not translate into a female advantage in employment. This pattern also holds in global comparisons—in the selected OECD countries, rates of employment for women never outpace those of their male peers with similar levels of education. However, education does help narrow the gender gap. The average difference in rates of employment between men and women in OECD countries is about 26 percentage points for those with less than an upper secondary education (69 percent versus 43 percent), more than triple the size of the 7-percentage point difference among those with a tertiary education (87 percent versus 80 percent).

SUMMARY AND CONCLUSION

We began this chapter by emphasizing the role of educational attainment in the school-to-work transition. We observe strong racial and ethnic patterns in educational attainment, in that Asian and White young adults have higher rates of bachelor's degree completion than their Black and Hispanic peers. The Asian and White advantage and Black and Hispanic disadvantage in educational attainment is apparent among native-born and immigrant young men and women, underscoring the strength of the association between race, ethnicity, and educational opportunities. Comparisons within racial and ethnic groups, however, also reveal the importance of nativity for understanding young adults' educational attainment. Among White and Black young adults, immigrants are more likely than their native-born peers to have completed a bachelor's degree, while among Hispanic and Asian young adults, the reverse is true. This pattern holds for both men and women. Another consistent finding across groups is that women outpace their male counterparts in rates of bachelor's degree completion.

The amount of education young adults complete has long-term implications for other milestones in the transition to adulthood, such as entry into and experiences in the labor market. As we have seen in this chapter, young adults with no college experience are less likely to be employed full-time compared to their college-educated peers. The gap in full-time employment by education tends to be smaller for immigrant men than for native-born men, but the education gap tends to be larger for immigrant women than for native-born women. Education thus appears to play an even more important role in determining full-time employment for native-born men and immigrant women. We also saw that the immigrant advantage in employment among men is most apparent among those with less education. That is, immigrant men with less education are more likely to secure full-time employment than their native-born peers with similar levels of education. However, we should keep in mind that the types of jobs immigrant men with no college experience are able to obtain are not likely to be the sorts of "good jobs" that ease the transition to adulthood.

In addition, the Great Recession, which occurred between 2007 and 2009, has had a tremendous impact on young people's labor market experiences around the world.[95] In the United States, the Great Recession led to rising unemployment rates, and the recovery took much longer than that of past economic downturns.[96] Research also shows that the negative effects of the Great Recession on labor market outcomes have been concentrated among younger people, Black people, and immigrants, as well as those with less education.[97] Young adults entering the labor market during and after the Great Recession face lower wages and fewer job opportunities, both of which have long-term impacts for their future employability and earnings.[98] The COVID-19 pandemic also continues to create economic uncertainty and its impact on the longer-term labor market conditions of young people remains unclear, though some researchers believe it will have at least as significant an impact as the Great Recession.[99]

Educational attainment strongly shapes the labor market participation of young adults. Young people without college credentials face enormous challenges in the labor market. And even those with bachelor's degrees are entering a challenging labor market. Now that we have a clearer picture of how diverse groups of young adults fare in the school-to-work transition, we can turn to how these experiences affect other aspects of their transitions to adulthood. In the next chapter, we will connect educational experiences to other significant adulthood milestones: residential independence, marriage, and parenthood.

3 Settling In, Settling Down

HOUSEHOLD AND FAMILY FORMATION

The parents of today's young adults come primarily from the Baby Boomer generation. These parents came of age during the 1970s and early 1980s, a period when young people sought early independence from their parents. It may be frustrating for this generation to have grown children who take longer to leave home or who leave but then return home. However, the problem of adult children not leaving the parental household in a timely manner is not new. Take, for example, the titles of two books published almost a quarter of a century apart: *Failure to Launch: Why Your Twentysomething Hasn't Grown Up and What to Do About It* (published in 2020) and *Boomerang Kids: How to Live with Adult Children Who Return Home* (published in 1987).[1] The popularity of the terms "failure to launch," referring to young adults who do not move out of their parents' homes, and "boomerang kids," referring to young people who return to their parents' homes after moving out, is indicative of changing residential patterns. A web search of these terms will yield a spate of recent articles from mainstream news sources about how parents and young people alike deal with extended periods of coresidence.[2] While we might associate these trends as characteristic of the Millennial generation (referring roughly to those born between 1981 and 2000), researchers have been studying the changing living arrangements of young adults for some time.

Establishing residential independence is often expected of young adults, and achieving this goal may be taken for granted and simply seen as a stepping stone to other, more-celebrated milestones like marriage and parenthood.[3] In the past, residential independence came hand-in-hand with marriage. Young adults left the parental home in order to establish their own households, typically with a spouse.[4] However, the marriage rate of young adults today is much lower than in the past.[5] One reason is that young people hope to be financially secure before marriage, which, as we learned in the previous chapter, has become increasingly difficult. In a 2019 *CNBC* article, twenty-seven-year-old Jessica, a minimum-wage worker who has some college experience but no degree, described her and her live-in boyfriend's marital plans: "We would be married, but that costs too . . . . Things like [marriage] get put on the back burner."[6] LaTisha, a recently married college graduate in her thirties interviewed in a 2016 report for the Pew Charitable Trusts, uses similar language to describe the delay in her marital plans: "I wanted to get married in my early 20s but I had to put it on the back burner and work on my career."[7] Both Jessica and LaTisha prioritized financial stability before marriage, but their different educational profiles have already led to differences in their marriage decisions.

The final milestone in the "traditional" pathway to adulthood, and one that in the past quickly followed marriage, is parenthood. However, the United States, like other highly developed countries, has witnessed a general decline in birth rates. Moreover, women who do have children are waiting longer to do so than in the past.[8] Marriage and parenthood are also increasingly "out of sync," with a growing share of children born outside marriage.[9] As we already mentioned, marriage is closely related to educational attainment, so it is not surprising that births within and outside the context of marriage are also closely related to maternal education: the majority of births to mothers without any college experience now occur outside of marriage while births to college-educated mothers still primarily occur within marriage.[10] Changes to marriage and parenthood are part of what social scientists call the "second demographic transition," which began in the 1960s and is characterized by "delays in fertility and marriage; increases in cohabitation, divorce, and nonmarital childbearing; and increases in maternal employment."[11]

The interrelatedness of educational attainment and milestones like residential independence, marriage, and parenthood can be seen in the experiences of Katrina Gilbert, the thirty-year-old single mother who is the subject of the documentary *Paycheck to Paycheck* (2014). Early in the documentary, Katrina, a certified nursing assistant who struggles to make ends meet, describes her separation from her husband and plans that have gone awry: "I didn't expect to be a single mom with three children. That was my biggest fear . . . . Like, I wanted a house by the time I was twenty-eight years old and I didn't get it. You know, to finish school . . . . I have nothing to show for those years besides my children. That's it." Following these themes, this chapter covers three additional milestones in the transition to adulthood: (1) residential independence, (2) marriage, and (3) parenthood. These milestones continue to be intimately linked with one another. However, as we will see, the strength of the association between these milestones varies considerably by young people's educational attainment as well as by their race, ethnicity, and nativity.

First, we focus on the share of young adults who have established their own households, by educational attainment. Next, we examine marriage among young adults with varying levels of education. We then turn to motherhood among unmarried and married young women, again by educational attainment. As we did in the previous chapter, we will attend to significant racial, ethnic, and immigrant differences in the attainment of these three milestones. Patterns of residential independence, family formation, and their variations are often treated as individual decisions driven by cultural preferences, but we argue that many of these decisions are shaped by structural constraints. Thus, throughout the chapter, we will pay close attention to how researchers characterize findings on these milestones. Finally, we will provide a brief overview of how the United States compares to countries around the world on measures of residential independence and family formation.

TRENDS IN LIVING ARRANGEMENTS: VARIABILITY IN
HOW AND WHEN YOUNG PEOPLE LEAVE HOME TODAY

Recent studies consistently show an increase in the share of US young adults who are delaying departure from the parental home.[12] In 1960, about 29 percent of young people ages eighteen to twenty-nine were living with a parent. This is the lowest rate seen in the twentieth century. In February 2020, prior to COVID-19 shutdowns of workplaces and schools, about 47 percent of young people ages eighteen to twenty-nine were living with a parent. By July 2020, as the COVID-19 pandemic spread across the United States, the share of young adults living with their parents increased to 52 percent. This means that living with a parent is the most common living arrangement among this age group. Tellingly, the only recorded period in the twentieth century that witnessed such high rates of coresidence of American young adults with their parents was in the 1940 decennial census, marking the end of the Great Depression.[13]

Does this mean that young people are simply staying put in the parental home? Not quite. Research shows that for many young people, the path out of (or back into) the parental home is more complicated. Young people might move out of the parental home initially, perhaps to attend college, only to return later for short or extended periods of time. This movement is sometimes called "boomeranging." Some young people might stay in the parental home while in college, perhaps to save on expenses, and move out only after they are financially established. Other young people do seem to be spending longer periods of time in the parental home. Though such young people are often popularly described as having "failed to launch," the reasons why they remain in the parental home are unlikely to be uniform—for example, some may lack the financial means to live on their own, while others might stay to contribute financially to their families.

The overall delay in establishing an independent household among today's young adults also obscures considerable variation by race, ethnicity, and nativity. Black, Hispanic, and Asian young adults are generally more likely to live with a parent than are their White peers. Research also finds ethnic variation among Asians.[14] Immigrant young adults tend to show higher levels of coresidence with a parent than do native-born young

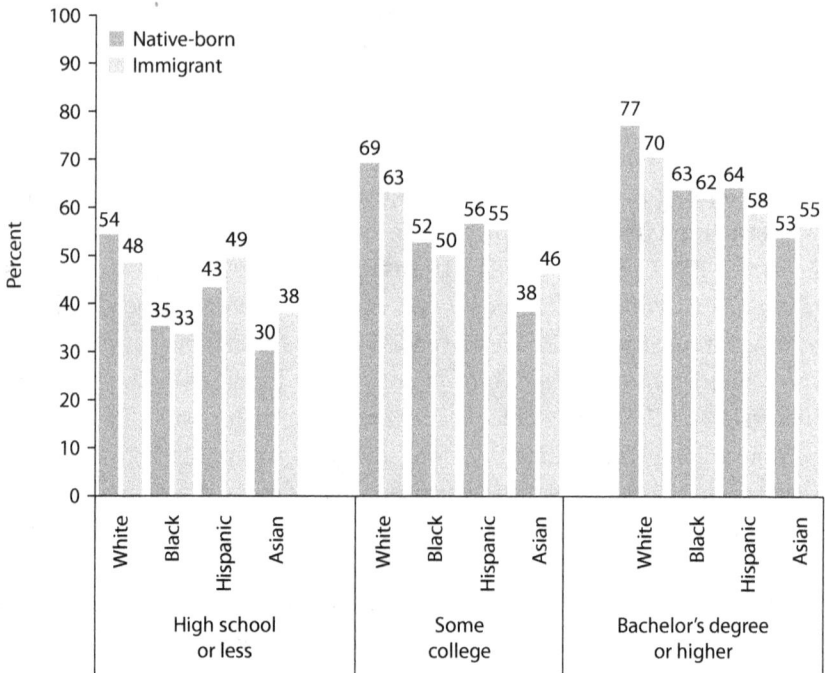

Figure 9. Percentage of young men (ages twenty-five to thirty-four) in independent households, by educational attainment, race and ethnicity, and nativity.

SOURCE: US Census 2017, Five-Year Estimates; Ruggles et al. 2021.

adults, though this also varies by race and ethnicity.[15] Existing literature suggests that socioeconomic and demographic factors all play a role in shaping young adults' living arrangements. Adding to the complexity of understanding young adults' living arrangements is that these factors interact with one another. Some studies focus on identifying the multitude of factors that influence young adults' living arrangements, but rarely do they focus simultaneously on race, ethnicity, nativity, and socioeconomic status.[16] It is also difficult to discern between the effects of cultural norms and economic constraints on young adults' living arrangements. We will return to these potential explanations below.

Perhaps residential independence is so strongly linked to adulthood in the public consciousness because it is the physical manifestation of personal and financial independence. As we discussed earlier, the likelihood

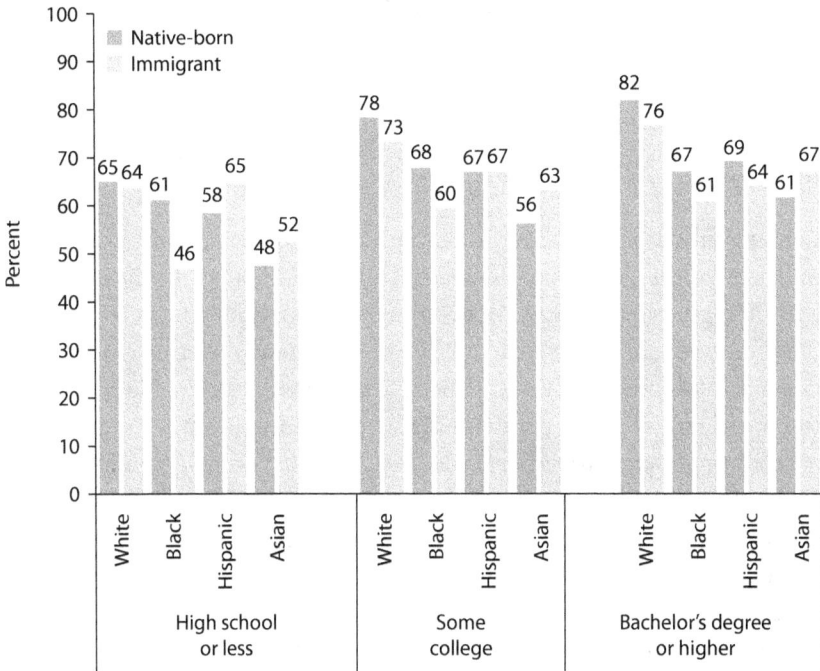

Figure 10. Percentage of young women (ages twenty-five to thirty-four) in independent households, by educational attainment, race and ethnicity, and nativity.
SOURCE: US Census 2017, Five-Year Estimates; Ruggles et al. 2021.

of working full-time (and thus having the means to support oneself) is heavily dependent on educational attainment. Hence, we expect that young adults' living arrangements are also shaped by their educational attainment. Figures 9 and 10 show the percentage of young men and women, respectively, who are in an independent household, by race, ethnicity, nativity, and educational attainment. An independent household means the young adult, aged twenty-five to thirty-four, is either the householder or the spouse/cohabiting partner of the householder ("householder" is the term used by the Census Bureau to designate the individual in whose name the housing unit is owned or rented). Only young people who are not currently enrolled in school are included in the figures. A final point we want to stress about the patterns of residential independence shown below is that they are measured at only one point in time.

Our "snapshot" does not convey movement in and out of the parental home over time, but only whether a young person is *currently* living independently.

Race, Ethnicity, and Education in Residential Independence

Looking first at patterns of residential independence among young men, in figure 9, it is clear that educational attainment is positively associated with living independently. Most young men with no college experience (i.e., "high school or less") do not live independently. At this level of educational attainment, only native-born White men are more likely than not to be residentially independent. Rates of residential independence are even lower among native-born minority men with no college experience—for example, just 30 percent of such native-born Asian men live in independent households. These racial and ethnic patterns also largely hold among immigrant men with no college experience, with the exception of immigrant Hispanic young men, who are more similar to immigrant White men in their rates of residential independence.

Young men with some college experience but without a bachelor's degree are more likely than their peers with less education to have established their own households. With the exception of Asian men, more than half of these young men live in independent households. Racial and ethnic patterns seen earlier for young men with no college experience persist—for example, native-born White men show the highest share in independent households compared to native-born minority men. Similarly, among immigrants with some college experience, White men have the highest rates of residential independence, followed by Hispanic, Black, and Asian men.

In contrast to their peers with less education, most young men with bachelor's or higher degrees are residentially independent. This pattern holds for each racial and ethnic group and for native-born and immigrant young men. Among young men with at least a bachelor's degree, 77 percent of native-born White men have established their own household. About 63 percent of native-born Black and 64 percent of native-born Hispanic young men with bachelor's or higher degrees have established their own households as well as over 50 percent of similarly educated native-born Asian men. Likewise, among immigrant young men, a majority reside in independent households across racial and ethnic groups. The importance of educational attainment for residential independence is especially evident among Black men: for both native-born and immigrant Black men, just over 30 percent of those with no college experience have established independent households compared to more than 60 percent of those with bachelor's or higher degrees.

Among young women (figure 10) with no college experience, racial and ethnic patterns are similar to those found among their male counterparts. For example, among native-born women with no college experience, White women are the most likely and Asian women the least likely to be in independent households (65 percent and 48 percent, respectively), with Black and Hispanic women falling in-between. Moreover, similar to the patterns observed for men, among immigrant women, Hispanic women are similar to their White peers, with nearly 67 percent of both residing in their own households. In contrast, about 50 percent or less of immigrant Black and Asian women are in their own households. In other words, along with their White peers, both immigrant Hispanic men and women are among the most likely to have established their own house-holds, among young people with no college experience. Overall, young women with no college experience are more likely than their male peers to be residentially independent.

As we also saw among young men, young women with some college experience are generally more likely to be residentially independent com-pared to their peers with no college experience. Again, native-born and immigrant White women lead their minority peers in residential independ-ence, with more than 70 percent living in independent households. Between 56 percent to 68 percent of native-born and immigrant Black, Hispanic, and Asian women live in independent households. The shares of residen-tially independent young women with some college education are also noticeably larger than shares among their similarly educated male peers.

A significant majority of young women with bachelor's or higher degrees have established their own households. More than 80 percent of native-born and 76 percent of immigrant White women with bachelor's or higher degrees live in independent households. Among comparably educated native-born and immigrant minority women, the share in independent households ranges from 61 percent to 69 percent. This is a pattern similar to that of their male counterparts. Once again, young women with bachelor's or higher degrees outpace their male peers in rates of residential independence. For example, comparing native-born White men and women with at least a bachelor's degree—both among the most likely of their peers to have established their own households—reveals a 5-percentage point difference in rates of residential independence that favors women (82 percent versus 77 percent).

Moreover, differences by education among women are smaller than differences among men. Comparisons between young adults at the lower end of educational attainment ("high school or less") to their peers at the upper end ("bachelor's degree or higher") reveals much larger gaps among men than women. For example, the 28-percentage point difference in rates of residential independence between native-born Black men with no college experience and those with at least a bachelor's degree (35 percent versus 63 percent) is more than four times the size of the corresponding difference seen among native-born Black women (61 percent versus 67 percent). Likewise, the shares of immigrant Hispanic women in their own households are very consistent across levels of education, unlike differences by education seen among immigrant Hispanic men. In other words, not having a bachelor's degree appears to be less of a constraint to establishing residential independence among young women than among young men.

Nativity and Education in Residential Independence

Thus far, we have seen that racial and ethnic patterns of residential independence largely hold for both native-born and immigrant young adults. How though do immigrants compare to their native-born peers within racial and ethnic groups? Are immigrant young adults more or less likely to establish independent households? How much does educational attainment—which we already know differs between native-born and immigrant young people (see chapter 2)—shape the nature of differences by nativity in residential independence?

Comparisons between the native-born and immigrants within each racial and ethnic group in figures 9 and 10 reveal a number of consistent patterns among White and Black young people. First, across levels of education and for both young men and women, native-born White young adults are more likely than immigrant White young adults to establish independent households. In fact, among White young men and women, the share of the native-born who are residentially independent exceeds that of immigrants by a steady 5 to 6 percentage points across levels of education. The only exception is White women with no college experience, where we see no differences between native-born and immigrant women in the shares who live independently. Second, native-born Black women are more likely than immigrant Black women to establish their own households. This is especially apparent at lower levels of education—for example, there is about a 15-percentage point difference between native-born and immigrant Black women with no college experience compared to a 6-percentage point difference between their counterparts with at least a bachelor's degree. Third, comparing rates of residential independence between native-born and immigrant Black men at each level of educational attainment reveals little difference.

Variations between the native-born and immigrants for Hispanic and Asian young adults, however, are unlike those of their White and Black peers. First, across levels of education, native-born Asian young adults are typically *less*, rather than more, likely to be residentially independent compared to their immigrant counterparts. These differences are especially pronounced among Asian men without bachelor's degrees, with the shares of native-born Asian young men in independent households nearly 8 percentage points below those of immigrants, among both those with no college experience and those with some college experience but no bachelor's degree. Immigrant Hispanic young adults are also more likely than their native-born peers to have established independent households, but only among young adults with no college experience. Among Hispanic young adults with some college experience, differences by nativity are minimal, and among those with bachelor's or higher degrees, native-born Hispanic young adults are more likely than immigrants to be residentially independent.

Understanding Differences in Residential Independence

Underlying much of the attention surrounding young adults' living arrangements is a normative view of residential independence as desirable.

KEY FINDINGS

- Young adults with more education are more likely to have established independent households.
- Racial and ethnic differences in rates of residential independence are mostly consistent across levels of education, with White young adults typically the most likely to live in independent households.
- Young women are more likely than young men to have established their own households and differences by education tend to be smaller among women.
- Among White and Black young adults, the native-born are as or more likely than immigrants to be residentially independent but among Asian and Hispanic young adults with less than a bachelor's degree, immigrants are typically more likely to be residentially independent than are the native-born.

The media and the public tend to frame residential independence as a universal aspiration. An episode description of the long-running show *My First Place* illustrates the power of such a narrative: "Nicole lives in her parents' basement and can't wait to get her first place and some privacy . . . . When she thinks she may have found the condo of her dreams, will she push her finances to the limit or be forced to continue living with Mom and Dad?" The description emphasizes Nicole's desire to live on her own, even if it means stretching her budget, and the apparently less-than-ideal situation of being "forced" to continue living with her parents. Yet, as we have seen, the chance that a young adult will have established an independent household is associated with their racial, ethnic, immigrant, and gender identities. What might help explain these differences?

There are two broad perspectives on what motivates young people to stay in or leave the parental home. First, a *cultural perspective* posits that minority and immigrant groups have different norms and beliefs about desirable living arrangements. For racial and ethnic minority and immigrant groups, researchers often invoke the notion of *familism*. This is the idea that individuals place the needs of the family above those of the individual. For immigrant families in particular, the theme of familial obligations, wherein children feel compelled to repay the sacrifices of their immigrant parents through contributing to the household, recurs throughout the literature (see chapter 1).[17] There is some evidence that the young adult children of immigrants do view the "American" norm of residential independence as distinctly different from their own cultural backgrounds.[18] This can be seen in two contrasting interviews with young adults from a study based in New York City. Maria, a twenty-eight-year-old West Indian woman moving into a home with her mother, daughter, and sister, says, "It's not, I guess not in my culture to push, to get away from my mother and push her away from my own life and my own family." Contrast Maria's sentiments with those of Jeff, a native-born thirty-eight-year-old man renting a two-bedroom apartment with his wife and two children. When asked if he lives with anyone else, he first responds "just a cat." When then asked about living with his parents, Jeff jokes, "No. I'd have to kill myself!"[19]

However, research also suggests that familism does not fully account for group differences in living arrangements. In one study, Marcus Britton finds that Hispanic and Asian (but not Black) adolescents were more likely than their White peers to feel it was important to live close to family, and that this sentiment was positively related to living with one's parents as a young adult. However, these feelings did not fully explain Hispanic, Asian, and Black young adults' greater likelihood of living with their parents. A young person's marital or relationship status, level of education, and personal income were stronger predictors of whether or not they were living with parents.[20] Moreover, some of our own research elsewhere challenges the idea that familism is an orientation uniformly shared by members of pan-ethnic groups. Phoebe Ho and Hyunjoon Park find, for example, that adolescents who identify as Southeast Asian or South Asian place greater importance on living close to family than do adolescents who identify as East Asian, whose attitudes are more similar to those of their Black and White peers.[21] This research, furthermore, reminds us to be cautious in interpreting the lower levels of independent living among Asian American young men and women seen in figures 9 and 10, as these averages may obscure substantial differences among different ethnic groups. Researchers also note the possibility of cultural "mismatch" between young people's feelings and those of their parents. Rather than focusing solely on adolescents' feelings, Kennan Cepa and Grace Kao looked at a combination of parents' and adolescents' senses of familism. In families where parents but not the child felt it was important to live close to home, young adults were still more likely to live with their parents compared to their peers who, along with their parents, did not place as much importance on living close to family.[22] This suggests a more complex social process beyond individual desire that shapes young people's patterns of parental coresidence.

A second perspective for understanding differences in patterns of residential independence focuses on *structural factors,* such as socioeconomic opportunities and the geography of where certain populations are concentrated. Young adults with more economic resources, often indicated by their educational attainment, occupation, and income, are more likely to be able to afford to live independently.[23] The relative disadvantage of Black and Hispanic young people in their educational attainment and their labor market participation (see chapter 2) are thought to be at least partially responsible for their prolonged residence in the parental home. Depending on where young people live, housing prices can constrain their ability to live independently, even for those with college degrees. A study of young adults in New York City, for example, notes the high cost of housing as one reason why many of the young people interviewed did not view residential independence as essential to becoming an adult.[24] The high costs of living in other areas where immigrants are concentrated—such as Los Angeles and Miami—might lead immigrant-origin young people to live with their parents in order to "pool resources and minimize expenses."[25] This practical consideration is probably less likely to cause distress when young people and their parents feel it is culturally acceptable or even preferable for parents and adult children to coreside. However, economic factors are not the entire story.[26] One early review of the literature on young adults leaving the parental home concluded that structural forces might explain differences for some groups (e.g., White and Black young adults) while cultural reasons might better explain differences for other groups (e.g., Hispanic young adults).[27] It would thus not be unreasonable to conclude that structural and cultural forces operate in tandem to shape how young adults think about and establish residential independence.

TRENDS IN MARRIAGE: DELAYS AND DIVERSITY
IN WHO MARRIES

In the United States, people now marry at lower rates and, if they do marry, they do so later than they did in the past. In 1970, the median age at first marriage in the United States for men was about twenty-three and for women about twenty-one. By 2021, the median age at first marriage had reached thirty for men and nearly twenty-nine for women.[28] Meanwhile, the marriage rate for women (calculated as the number of marriages per 1,000 unmarried women in the past year for women at least fifteen years old) decreased from nearly 77 in 1970 to 31 in 2018.[29]

The past several decades have also witnessed an increase in the importance of socioeconomic status for the likelihood of getting married. A report from the Pew Research Center found that in 1990, about 69 percent of adults in the United States ages twenty-five and older with bachelor's or higher degrees were married, somewhat higher than the 63 percent of adults with a high school-level education or less. However, the education gap in marriage has widened over time such that by 2015, 65 percent of adults ages twenty-five and older with bachelor's or higher degrees were married, compared to 50 percent of those with high school or less education.[30] In other words, the decline in marriage has been steeper among adults without bachelor's degrees.

Research has also documented the shifts in educational differences in marriage patterns by gender. For men, their educational attainment and other socioeconomic characteristics are positively associated with their odds of marriage, not just in the United States but in other countries as well.[31] For women in the United States, there has been an "educational crossover" in marriage: past patterns which showed a tenuous or even negative relationship between women's education and their odds of marriage have reversed among younger cohorts of women.[32] For example, in 1940, women (ages fifteen and older) with lower educational attainment were more likely to be married: 63 percent of women with less than a high school diploma and 58 percent of women with a high school education compared to 53 percent of women with at least a bachelor's degree. In 2018, however, just 27 percent of women (ages fifteen and older) without a high school diploma and 44 percent of women with a high school diploma were married compared to 59 percent of women with a bachelor's or higher degree.[33] The growing importance of women's socioeconomic status in determining marriage is part of what sociologist Megan Sweeney has described as the "shifting economic foundations of marriage."[34]

Moreover, race, ethnicity, and nativity are related to one's likelihood of marrying and staying married.[35] According to one recent study, almost nine out of ten White and Asian/Pacific Islander women and more than eight in ten Hispanic women were married by age forty, compared to about six in ten Black women. Black women are also more likely than White women to experience divorce, while rates of divorce tend to be lower among Asian and immigrant Hispanic women. This divergence, which began appearing in the 1970s, has widened over time.[36] Young women who immigrated as young children are more likely to be married at ages twenty-five to thirty-four than are their second-generation co-ethnic peers (who were born in the United States to immigrant parents). However, they are less likely to be married at ages twenty-five to thirty-four compared to their first-generation co-ethnic peers (who immigrated as teens or older).[37] This suggests that immigrant young people who are largely socialized in the United States are more similar to their native-born peers than are immigrants who have spent fewer of their formative years in the United States. Clearly, nativity is also an important factor to consider when examining marriage patterns among young people.

Coinciding with declines in the marriage rate among young people is the rise in the share of young people living alone. One-person households have more than doubled in the United States in the period between 1960 and 2019, from about 13 percent of all US households to 28 percent.[38] This trend is apparent not only in the United States but also across many regions of the world, largely driven by the growing share of young people who live alone.[39] Of course, this does not mean young people living alone are not involved in romantic relationships. It does seem to indicate that, at the very least, there is a prolonged delay or disinterest in getting married. As one twenty-nine-year-old lawyer featured in a web article on Millennial women living alone described, "I did not want to go into marriage or any other type of co-habitation situation in life without having a period of time where I got to live on my own. I wanted to experience the good and bad of it before I chose to live with someone and build a family."[40]

Another significant trend related to marriage is the greater share of young people who cohabit with a partner before or instead of marrying. In 1968, less than 1 percent of young people ages twenty-five to thirty-four were living with a partner outside of marriage. Fifty years later, nearly 15 percent of young people ages twenty-five to thirty-four are living with a partner who is not their spouse.[41] Explanations for the rise in cohabiting couples include those that emphasize culture (e.g., rising individualism) to those that highlight economic factors (e.g., women's increased labor force participation).[42] Cohabiting is often seen as a "stepping stone" to marriage. Today, most women who marry cohabit with a partner first. About four in ten women who married for the first time in the early 1980s lived with their spouse before marriage compared to more than seven in ten women who married in the early 2010s. However, the extent to which cohabiting leads to marriage varies by educational attainment. College-educated women are less likely to cohabit than are women with less education but college-educated women who *do* cohabit are also more likely to enter into marriage. For women with less education, "serial cohabiting" (living in a series of cohabiting relationships) is more likely.[43] Research also shows that the experience of cohabiting varies by young people's educational attainment—college-educated couples tend to have more positive experiences with cohabiting and are more likely to see marriage as the next step compared to "service-class" couples.[44]

Though living alone and cohabiting are important changes to residential patterns, researchers know less about how these shifts in behavior affect traditional adulthood milestones such as marriage and parenthood. For example, recent research suggests that rates of cohabiting have plateaued while marriage rates continue to decline in the United States, meaning that cohabiting no longer "offsets" the decline in marriage.[45] We know even less about variations by race, ethnicity, and nativity. Moreover, both solo living and cohabiting are potentially more "temporary" statuses than marriage. By this we mean that young people who are currently living alone or cohabiting are probably more likely to experience a change in these statuses as they age than are young people who are currently married.

While marriage may be delayed among younger people, it remains culturally important and widely celebrated. Marriage is, as the sociologist Andrew Cherlin describes, a "marker of prestige," a "capstone" to adulthood,

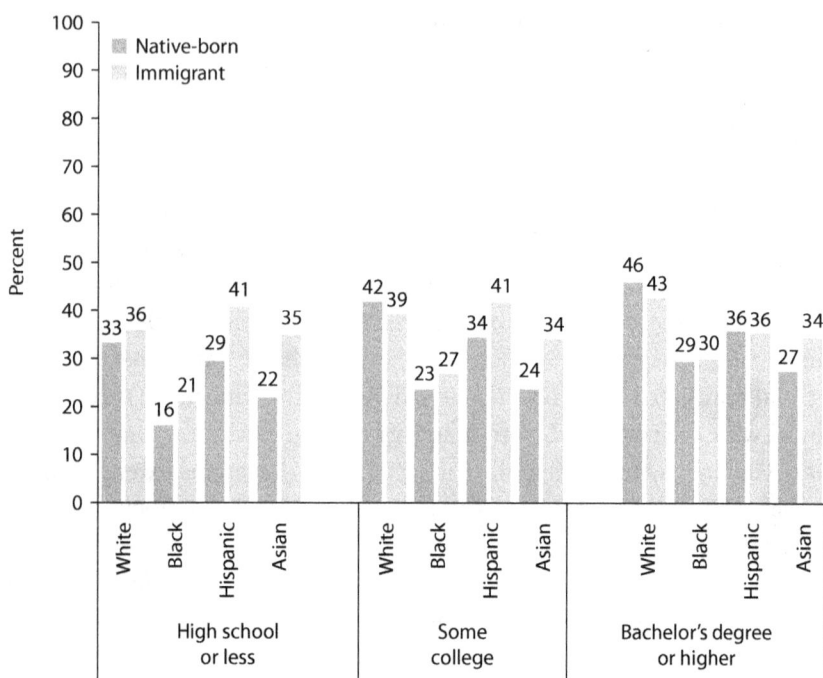

Figure 11. Percentage of young men (ages twenty-five to thirty-four) currently married, by educational attainment, race and ethnicity, and nativity.

SOURCE: US Census 2017, Five-Year Estimates; Ruggles et al. 2021.

and an individualistic "achievement."[46] As such, it remains important to understand which groups of young adults are attaining this milestone. Finally, we have data limitations. Using the American Community Survey, we would be able to measure cohabitation only in relation to the "household head" (i.e., when a young person is listed as an "unmarried partner" of the household head). This can be an unreliable measure, since a nontrivial share of cohabiting couples may be missed. For example, subfamily cohabitors (unmarried couples in which neither partner is the household head, as the couple lives with someone else who is the household head) would be omitted.[47] For these reasons, in this section we focus on the share of young people who are currently married. Figures 11 and 12 show the share of young men and women (ages 25–34), respectively, who report that they are currently married. Our measure considers those who are divorced,

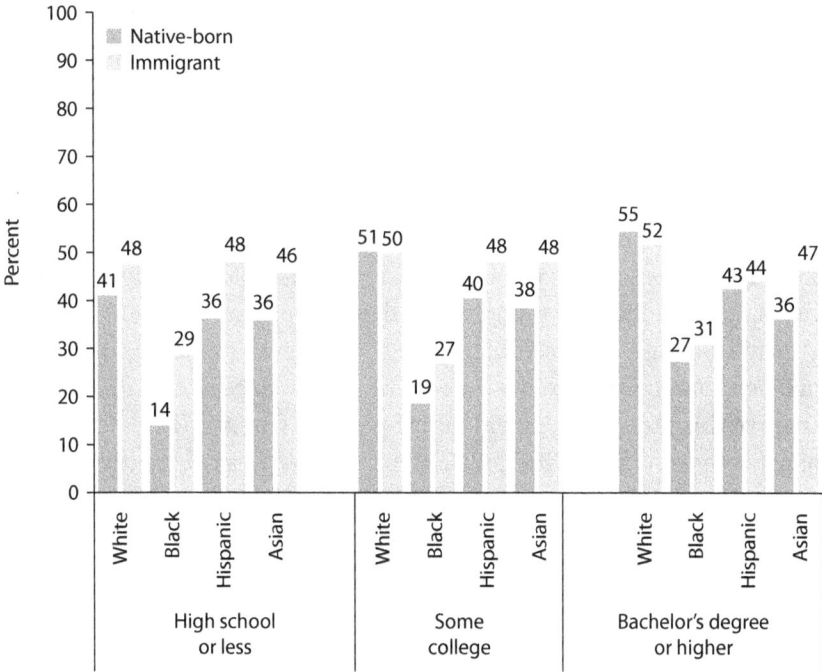

Figure 12. Percentage of young women (ages twenty-five to thirty-four) currently married, by educational attainment, race and ethnicity, and nativity.

SOURCE: US Census 2017, Five-Year Estimates; Ruggles et al. 2021.

separated, and widowed (a minority in our sample) as unmarried. In addition to presenting patterns by race and ethnicity, we distinguish between native-born and immigrant young adults and young men and women. We also show patterns by educational attainment and our estimates include only young people who are not currently enrolled in school, similar to those in previous figures.

Race, Ethnicity, and Education in Marriage

Figure 11 shows the share of young men currently married. We find a positive relationship between education and marriage, though it is not as sharply defined as we saw for labor market participation and residential independence. Among young men with no college experience (i.e., "high school or less"), only a minority are currently married. About 33 percent of White men are married, the highest share among native-born men with no college experience. In contrast, only 16 percent of native-born Black men are married, the lowest share among native-born men with no college experience. Racial and ethnic patterns among immigrant men differ in that Hispanic men are the most likely to be married among young men with no college experience and Asian men do not differ significantly from their White peers. However, Black men remain the least likely to be married among immigrant young men with no college experience.

While young men with some college experience are more likely to be married than their peers with no college experience, it is still a modest share of this group. Racial and ethnic patterns persist. About 42 percent of native-born Whites with some college experience are currently married, compared to 34 percent of native-born Hispanic men and less than 25 percent of native-born Black and Asian. Among immigrant men with some college experience, Black and Asian men are also the least likely to be married. However, differences relative to their White peers tend to be smaller than the corresponding comparisons among the native-born.

Young men with bachelor's or higher degrees are generally most likely to be married. However, we find two exceptions among immigrant men. First, the shares of married immigrant Asian men do not vary much by educational attainment—at each level of education, about one-third of immigrant Asian men are married. Second, immigrant Hispanic men with bachelor's or higher degrees are actually *less* likely to be married than immigrant Hispanic men without bachelor's degrees. However, racial and ethnic patterns remain similar among men with bachelor's degrees, with greater shares of native-born and immigrant White men currently married compared to their minority peers.

Figure 12 displays the percentage of young women who are currently married by their educational attainment. For native-born young women without any college experience (e.g., "high school or less"), the shares married are greatest among White women and lowest among Black women. Specifically, 41 percent of young White women are currently married compared to 14 percent of young Black women. The shares married are also smaller among native-born Hispanic and Asian women with no college experience compared to their White peers, with about 36 percent of such women married. Among immigrant women with no college experience, White women are also the most likely to be currently married (48 percent) and immigrant Black women the least likely (29 percent). However, there are relatively minimal differences between immigrant Hispanic and Asian women relative to their White peers. Overall, young women with no college experience are more likely than their male counterparts to be married.

Similar patterns are also seen among young women with some college experience. For example, about 50 percent of native-born and immigrant White women are currently married compared to less than 20 percent of native-born and less than 30 percent of immigrant Black women, respectively. Smaller shares of native-born Hispanic and Asian women are married relative to native-born White women. In contrast, immigrant Hispanic and Asian women are similar to White immigrant women in their likelihood of being currently married. Native-born young women with some college experience typically have higher rates of marriage than their peers without any college experience. However, among immigrant women, differences between those with no college versus some college experience are minimal.

Racial and ethnic differences among young women with at least a bachelor's degree are less pronounced. However, patterns are similar to those seen among young women with lower levels of education. Among those with at least a bachelor's degree, native-born and immigrant White women remain among the most likely and native-born and immigrant Black women the least likely to be currently married. Both native-born and immigrant Hispanic and Asian women with bachelor's or higher degrees are also less likely than their White peers to be married.

As was also the case for native-born young men, the likelihood of being married increases with educational attainment, especially for native-born women. For example, the share of married native-born Black women with at least a bachelor's degree is almost twice the share of married Black women with no college experience (27 percent versus 14 percent). However, differences by education among immigrant women are much less apparent. For both immigrant White and Asian women, about half are married across all levels of education and around one-third of immigrant Black women are married across all levels of education. Moreover, immigrant Hispanic women with bachelor's or higher degrees are actually somewhat less likely to be married compared to their peers without bachelor's degrees, a pattern that we also observe among Hispanic young men.

Nativity and Education in Marriage

Comparing the shares currently married between native-born and immigrant members of racial and ethnic groups reveals important differences by nativity. Among young men, immigrants across racial and ethnic groups are often more likely to be married compared to their native-born peers. This holds true particularly among young men with less education. For example, among young men with no college experience (i.e., "high school or less"), the extent to which the share of immigrants who are married exceeds that of native-born adults ranges from 3 percentage points between native-born and immigrant White men (33 percent versus 36 percent) to about 13 percentage points between native-born and immigrant Asian men (22 percent versus 35 percent). Native-born/immigrant differences among young men with some college experience are somewhat smaller, but minority immigrants remain more likely to be married than their native-born peers. Among those with at least a bachelor's degree, native-born/immigrant differences are minimal for Black and Hispanic young men but immigrant Asian men remain more likely to be married than their native-born counterparts.

The greater share of immigrant young adults who are currently married is even more apparent among young women. In fact, immigrant Black, Hispanic, and Asian women are consistently more likely than their native-born counterparts to be married, regardless of educational attainment. For example, across levels of education, the shares of immigrant Asian women who are currently married are a steady 10 percentage points or so higher than the share of native-born Asian women who are currently married. Only among White women with some college or more education do we see the native-born outpacing immigrants in the shares who are married. At the lowest level of educational attainment, a greater share of immigrant White women are married than native-born White women.

KEY FINDINGS

- At ages twenty-five to thirty-four, those with bachelor's or higher degrees are generally more likely to be married compared to their peers with less education.
- Greater shares of White young adults are married at ages twenty-five to thirty-four compared to shares of Black, Hispanic, and Asian young adults.
- At ages twenty-five to thirty-four, Black, Hispanic, and Asian immigrants are generally more likely than their native-born peers to be married.
- Young women are typically more likely than their male peers to be married at ages twenty-five to thirty-four, with the exception of native-born Black women.

Understanding Differences in Marriage among Young Adults

As we described earlier, educational attainment has become increasingly important for understanding marriage patterns. While the overall marriage rate in the United States has declined in the past several decades, the decline has been much greater among people with less education.[48] That is, to understand marriage and the transition to adulthood today means we need to understand the experiences of young adults with less education. One explanation, supported by a broad body of research, is undoubtedly the relationship between one's educational attainment and one's economic status (see chapter 2). Economic stability now appears to be an even more important consideration for young people deciding whether or not to marry. Given the increasing premium on higher educational attainment in the labor market, young people with less education are even less likely to achieve the type of economic security they wish for themselves and for their future spouse.[49]

Even though the positive association between educational attainment and marriage is seen for all groups of young people, racial and ethnic differences persist among similarly educated young people. Black, Hispanic, and Asian twenty-five to thirty-four-year-olds are generally less likely than their White peers to be married. In this chapter, we saw that among young women with no college experience, native-born Black women stand out in the smaller shares who are married (fewer than two in ten are married at ages twenty-five to thirty-four). Likewise, native-born Asian young men are also an outlier among young men with bachelor's or higher degrees in their lower likelihood of being married (fewer than three in ten are married at ages twenty-five to thirty-four). Focusing on the experiences of native-born Black women and native-born Asian men underscores the complexity of marriage as a social institution that cannot be solely attributed to economic decisions. Structural factors—such as residential segregation and discrimination in the labor market and criminal justice systems—explain much though not all of White-Black differences in rates of marriage.[50] However, these are not likely explanations for White-Asian differences. Rather, another structural feature—the racial hierarchy of the United States, which perpetuates stereotypes about particular minority groups—seems more relevant.[51]

In one study, researchers explored three potential explanations for the decline in marriage rates from 1969 to 2013: men's declining economic circumstances, women's growing economic independence, and incarceration (rates of which have ballooned over the same period). Among their most strongly supported findings was that mass incarceration appears to contribute to declines in marriage among Black women and women with less education.[52] This is consistent with the work of William Julius Wilson and Kathryn Neckerman, who argued that a lack of employment opportunities among and the disproportionate impact of mass incarceration on low-income Black populations have reduced the number of viable partners for Black women.[53] Even at the upper end of educational attainment, Black women must contend with what the authors of *The Source of the River* describe as the "tyranny of demography": because Black women outnumber Black men in colleges, they must either choose a non-Black partner or a partner with less education.[54] Since both the color line and the education divide are difficult boundaries to cross, highly educated Black women are less likely to be married compared to other similarly educated women. Mass incarceration and the greater shares of college-educated Black women relative to Black men impose *structural constraints* on opportunities for marriage among Black women.

For Asian men, their lower rates of marriage often serve as a prime example of how socioeconomic status alone does not translate into "marriageability." Given their high educational attainment and favorable labor market outcomes (see chapter 2), a purely economic view would place Asian men as among the most desirable partners, yet they have the lowest rates of marriage and dating. In a study of romantic relationship involvement among young adults, Grace Kao and coauthors express skepticism toward arguments that cultural norms attributed broadly to Asians drive differences between Asian men and other young adults, since their study finds no such difference between Asian and White women. Moreover, native-born and immigrant Asian men behave similarly. They conclude that their evidence best supports a racial-gender hierarchy framework, one that places Asian men in particular at the bottom in terms of romantic preferences.[55]

Though they occupy seemingly opposite social positions in terms of race, gender, and educational attainment, the similarly low rates of marriage (at ages twenty-five to thirty-four) of native-born Black women and native-born Asian men can also be understood within the context of romantic markets that are highly racialized in gendered ways. For example, White and Hispanic men and women tend to intermarry across racial lines at comparable rates. However, Black men are more likely than Black women to marry interracially and Asian women are more likely than Asian men to do so.[56] Other research shows that Black women and Asian men are among the least likely to experience romantic involvements as young adults.[57] This can be seen in the dating experiences of twenty-nine-year-old Jason, an Asian man, and twenty-eight-year-old Ari, a Black woman, shared in a 2018 *NPR* segment entitled "Least Desirable." The segment's title is a reference to the popular dating website OkCupid's findings that Black women and Asian men are the least preferred dating partners on the site.[58] Describing the experience of being rejected on the basis of race, Jason says, "It was hurtful at first. But I started to think, I have a choice: Would I rather be alone, or should I, like, face racism?" Ari remarks that people should be able to express dating preferences but also wonders, "If racism weren't so ingrained in our culture, would they have those preferences?" The two "extreme" cases of native-born Black women and native-born Asian men are illustrative examples of how race, ethnicity, and education intersect with romantic relationships and marriage.

Racial and ethnic patterns in marriage are more muted among immigrants. Moreover, minority immigrant young adults are generally more likely to marry than their native-born counterparts, with native-born/immigrant differences in the shares who are married most apparent at lower levels of educational attainment. That is, even though young adults with less education are typically less likely to be married, immigrants still have a greater chance of being married than the native-born. This is consistent with research showing that 1.5-generation immigrant young people (who immigrated as children) are generally more likely than their second-generation peers (who were born in the United States to immigrant parents) to be married at ages eighteen to twenty-four.[59] As sociologist Zhenchao Qian writes, "Clearly, marriage is prevalent and not seen as a status symbol among immigrants, regardless of race-ethnicity and educational attainment."[60] In other words, for some immigrant young adults, marriage may be a more pivotal milestone and educational attainment may play a less important role in influencing their decision to marry. In interviews with the children of immigrants in San Diego, for example, researchers found that immigrant parents place more emphasis on marriage and children, which may affect how their own children think about marriage and parenthood.[61]

On the other hand, research on 1.5- and second-generation immigrants suggests that their views on marriage and romantic partners do not necessarily align with those of their parents.[62] Rather than think of immigrant young people as holders of static cultural values inherited from their parents, it is more useful to consider how they integrate the cultural norms held by their parents and the US norms that they experience within the context of opportunities available to them. For immigrant young men who are already working, marriage may seem like a logical next step while for immigrant young women, who are less likely to be working, marriage may be a more viable pathway than work to establishing their own households. These "traditional" roles of male breadwinner and female homemaker may be supported by their immigrant parents and peers, making such decisions preferable to alternatives.

Most research on immigrant populations and marriage tends to focus on older adults and broader demographic implications. There is a considerable body of literature examining patterns of whom immigrants marry (such as the extent to which immigrants marry across racial, ethnic, and generational lines) that has provided important insight on an array of trends, from the growth of the multiracial population to assimilation processes.[63] There is also a tradition of examining gender norms in immigrant families, including factors related to marriage such as immigrant parents' attitudes toward dating and sexual behavior.[64] These bodies of research tell us that nativity plays a role in marriage patterns, but there is surprisingly little research that focuses on how immigrant young people think and feel about marriage as a part of the transition to adulthood.

Lastly, we want to point out that the American Community Survey (ACS), our source of data on young people's marriage patterns, does not contain information about the sexual orientation of young people. In fact, it was not until 2019 that the Current Population Survey (CPS), a widely used source of data in studies of family life, began explicitly collecting information about opposite-sex and same-sex couples (both married and unmarried). CPS data shows that there were more than half a million same-sex married couple households in the United States.[65] Some of the young people in our sample who are married may be married to a same-sex partner, but we are unable to precisely identify them in the ACS. It is also important to mention that our data covers a time period during which same-sex marriage was legalized in the United States (through a 2015 Supreme Court ruling). Although marriage is seen as a significant milestone in the transition to adulthood, it is only very recently that people who wish to marry a same-sex partner have been able to so. In chapter 5, we cover research on the transition to adulthood among sexual minority young people.

TRENDS IN PARENTHOOD: MODERN SINGLE MOTHERHOOD AND MARRIED MOTHERHOOD

Family structure and parenthood as experienced by young people today also look very different from in the past. The marriage, divorce, and childbirth trends that have taken place since the 1960s mean that depending on their socioeconomic and racial and ethnic backgrounds, young people today are more likely to have been raised by single parents and to be single parents themselves. In the last half-century, the share of unmarried parents in the United States has grown from less than 10 percent in 1968 to

25 percent in 2017. While more unmarried parent households now include cohabiting parents (parents who live together but who are not married), the majority of unmarried parent families remain headed by single mothers, as they were in past.[66]

However, the growth of single motherhood has not been experienced equally across all groups of women. Rates of single motherhood have increased dramatically among the least educated women but have not changed much among the most educated women.[67] Single mother households and cohabiting parent households are both much more likely to have parents with no college experience than parents with a bachelor's or higher degree.[68] College-educated young adults typically delay parenthood until later in adulthood and then have fewer children.[69] This aligns with the trends in marriage rates we discussed earlier, in which we saw that more-educated women delay marriage but are more likely to eventually marry.

The higher rates of unmarried motherhood among socioeconomically disadvantaged women have generated considerable policy and research debate. Some argue that unmarried motherhood places children and families at risk and undermines the institution of marriage.[70] There is evidence that children from single-parent families do experience adverse outcomes compared to children from two-parent families. For example, sociologist Sara McClanahan argued that the large-scale societal trends associated with the second demographic shift—including delays in marriage and childbirth and increases in rates of divorce, cohabitation, and childbirth outside of marriage—have disparately affected women with varying levels of education. While benefits such as greater employment and lower divorce rates have accrued to women with more education, women with less education have experienced sharp losses in family resources, including a rise in single motherhood. As a result, children born to more-educated mothers and those born to less-educated mothers come to experience "diverging destinies."[71]

Single and married motherhood are both clearly shaped by educational attainment, but we can also imagine how the context of motherhood influences other adulthood milestones. For example, unmarried mothers with lower levels of education might be less likely than married mothers to attain residential independence since they may have fewer financial resources from which to draw.[72] Unmarried mothers of young children who lack the social support or financial resources for reliable childcare might be unable to enter the labor market. There is also persistent social stigma attached to single motherhood in the United States—a Pew Research Center survey in 2018 found that fully two-thirds of adults surveyed viewed the trend of single women having children without a partner as "bad for society."[73] Though the stigma may not be so overt today as it was in the past, it is clear that public attitudes and restrictions to social welfare benefits can make single motherhood difficult for young women.

While there is extensive literature on and formal demographic methods for measuring fertility, birth rates, and other statistics related to parenthood, *defining* parenthood is not always straightforward. We primarily rely on the ACS, which has two measures of fertility and parenthood: (1) a measure of whether or not women experienced a birth in the previous year and (2) the number of "own children" residing with an individual. The first option is limited to a particular population (women), time period (within the past year), and form of parenthood (biological births), so we have opted for the latter. The measure of "own children" includes stepchildren and adopted children, so we consider it more a measure of parenthood than fertility.

However, there are limitations to our choice of measure. Since this measure only captures parenthood among young adults (ages twenty-five to thirty-four) with at least one child of their own in their households, in instances where parents of a child do not coreside and where the child primarily resides with only one parent (as might be the case for divorced, separated, or never married parents, among other situations), we would be able to observe parenthood only for the primary parent. This is especially a problem when measuring fatherhood, as the majority of single-parent households in the United States are headed by women rather than men.[74] That is to say, because children of parents who do not coreside are much more likely to reside with their mothers rather than their fathers, we have a clearer picture of motherhood among young adults than we do of fatherhood. For this reason, figures 13 and 14 focus on unmarried and married *motherhood*. The figures show the share of young women who have children of their own in their household, first for women who are currently unmarried (figure 13) and then for women who are currently married (figure 14). Both figures show rates of motherhood by young

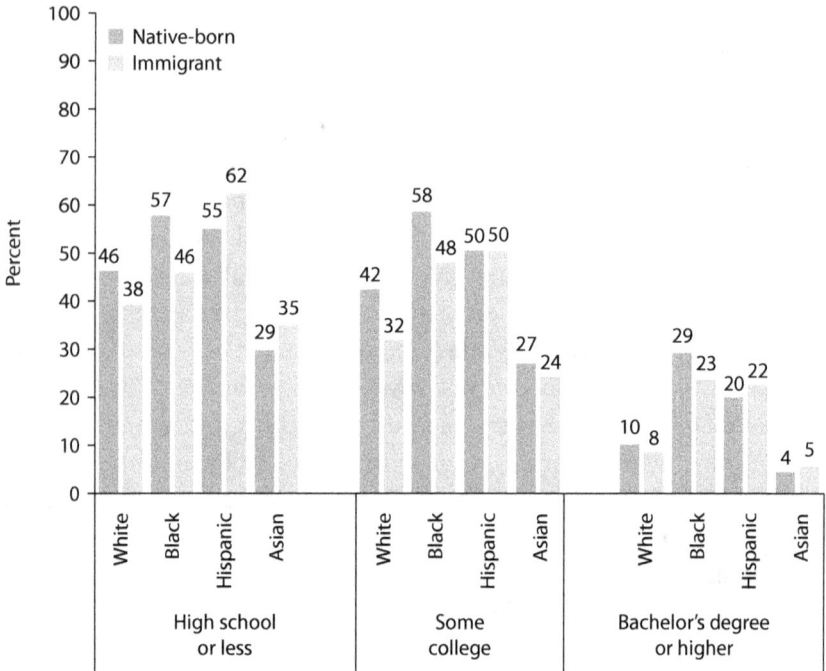

Figure 13. Percentage of unmarried young women (ages twenty-five to thirty-four) with own children in household, by educational attainment, race and ethnicity, and nativity.

SOURCE: US Census 2017, Five-Year Estimates; Ruggles et al. 2021.

women's educational attainment since we know rates of single mother-hood vary by maternal education. Once again, we show patterns for young people who are not currently enrolled in school.

Motherhood among Unmarried Women

Figure 13 focuses on unmarried young women (recall from figure 12 that about half or more of young women ages twenty-five to thirty-four are not currently married). It is immediately apparent that educational attainment is negatively associated with motherhood among unmarried women. The share of unmarried women who are mothers declines significantly with more education. Between 29 percent and 62 percent of unmarried young

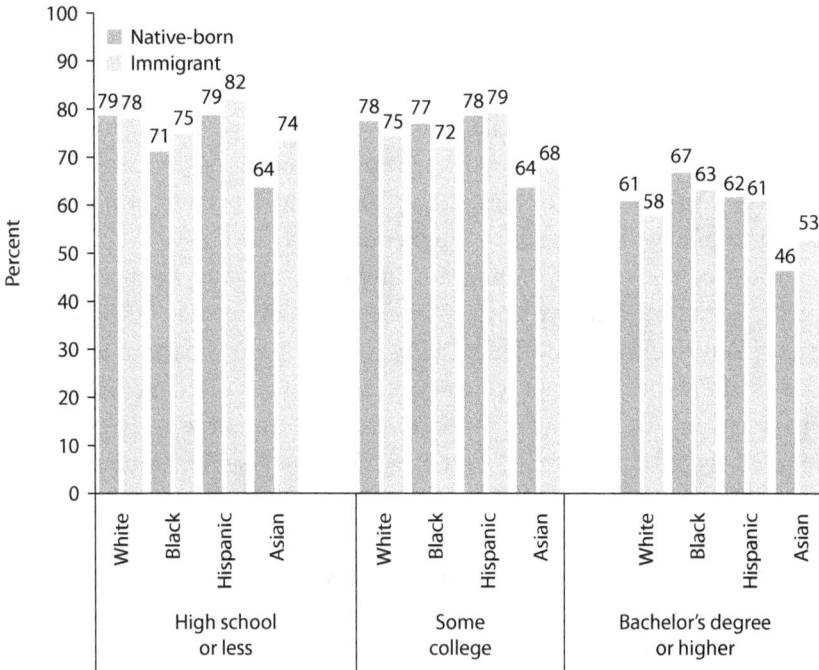

Figure 14. Percentage of married young women (ages twenty-five to thirty-four) with own children in household, by educational attainment, race and ethnicity, and nativity.

SOURCE: US Census 2017, Five-Year Estimates; Ruggles et al. 2021.

women without any college experience are mothers and 24 percent to 58 percent of unmarried young women with some college experience are mothers. In contrast, rates of unmarried motherhood range from 4 percent to 29 percent among young women with bachelor's or higher degrees.

Regardless of their race, ethnicity, or nativity, unmarried young women with more education are less likely to be mothers compared to their peers with less education. However, comparisons among women with similar levels of education also reveal specific racial and ethnic patterns. At every level of educational attainment, a greater share of unmarried Black and Hispanic young women and a smaller share of unmarried Asian young women are mothers compared to their unmarried White peers, a pattern that holds for both native-born and immigrant women. For example, among the unmarried, 57 percent of native-born Black and 62 percent of native-born Hispanic women with no college experience have children of their own compared to 46 percent of native-born White and 29 percent of native-born Asian women. Likewise, more than 20 percent of immigrant Black and Hispanic women with bachelor's or higher degrees are mothers compared to 8 percent of immigrant White and 5 percent of immigrant Asian women with bachelor's or higher degrees.

Note that native-born/immigrant differences also vary by race and ethnicity. Unmarried native-born White and Black women are generally more likely than their immigrant peers to be mothers, a pattern that holds across different levels of education. In contrast, among unmarried Hispanic and Asian women, immigrants rather than the native-born are more likely to be mothers. This is especially the case for women without any college experience and less so among women with some college and a bachelor's degree or higher. Keep in mind, though, that the share of twenty-five-to-thirty-four-year-old women who are unmarried is smaller among immigrants than the native-born, especially among those with at most a high school-level education (see figure 12).

Motherhood among Married Women

Now turning to motherhood among married women, in figure 14, two patterns are readily apparent. First, the share of married women who are mothers is substantially higher than the share of unmarried women. Though our measure does not indicate whether these women became mothers before or after marriage, we can nevertheless take the greater shares of mothers among married women as an indication that for young women, marriage and motherhood are still closely linked. Second, as we also observed among unmarried women, the share of married women who are mothers is lowest among those with bachelor's or higher degrees and highest among women with no college experience. For example, close to 80 percent of married White and Hispanic young women with no college experience are mothers compared to about 60 percent of their peers with bachelor's or higher degrees (among both the native-born and immigrants). Another way of considering these patterns is that for women without college experience, marriage and motherhood are more likely to go hand-in-

KEY FINDINGS

- Unmarried and married young women with greater educational attainment are less likely to be mothers at ages twenty-five to thirty-four.
- Among the unmarried, Black and Hispanic women have higher rates of motherhood at ages twenty-five to thirty-four than White and Asian women, but among the married, racial and ethnic differences in rates of motherhood are less apparent.
- Unmarried native-born White and Black women are more likely than their immigrant counterparts to be mothers at ages twenty-five to thirty-four, while the opposite is typically the case for unmarried Hispanic and Asian women.
- Native-born/immigrant differences in motherhood among married women tend to be smaller than the corresponding differences among unmarried women for most racial and ethnic groups.

hand than for women with bachelor's or higher degrees, who, even if married, are less likely at ages twenty-four to thirty-four to be mothers.

Racial and ethnic differences among married women in the shares who are mothers also tend to be less pronounced than those found among unmarried women. Recall that among unmarried women, a greater share of Black and Hispanic young women and a smaller share of Asian young women are mothers compared to White young women. Among all married women, Asian young women are still generally less likely to be mothers compared to White young women. However, among married women with no college experience, native-born White women and native-born Hispanic women are the most likely to be mothers (79 percent each) and native-born Black women have lower rates of motherhood in comparison (71 percent).

Differences by nativity in the shares of married women who are mothers tend to be less pronounced than those among unmarried women. The shares of married immigrant White, Black, and Hispanic young women with children of their own in their households are similar to the shares among their native-born counterparts across levels of educational attainment. For example, about 80 percent of native-born and immigrant married Hispanic women with less than a bachelor's degree are mothers and about 60 percent of such women with at least a bachelor's degree are mothers. It is only among Asian young women that native-born/immigrant differences are more pronounced among married versus unmarried women. Among married Asian women, immigrants are consistently more likely than their native-born counterparts to be mothers, across all levels of education.

Understanding Differences in Unmarried and Married Motherhood

Educational attainment plays a central role in understanding contemporary motherhood. Young women with more education are consistently less likely to be mothers by ages twenty-five to thirty-four, regardless of their marital status. Some of these women may eventually become mothers, since the median age at first birth for women with bachelor's degrees is about twenty-eight (meaning half of such women experience their first birth before this age and half after), while for women with no college experience, the median age at first birth is twenty-four.[75] Increased educational attainment seems to delay motherhood among young women, since becoming a parent may be at odds with higher educational and occupational aspirations.[76]

Among young women with less education, rates of unmarried motherhood vary by race and ethnicity. Tracing trends in young people's accomplishment of adulthood milestones over a century, Elizabeth Fussell and Frank Furstenberg note that while the share of young women who are single mothers has increased across racial and ethnic groups as well as for both native-born and immigrant women, it has increased the most among native-born Black women and the least among native-born White women and immigrant women.[77] These patterns, not surprisingly, mirror those of marriage rates. If some groups of women are less likely to marry then it follows that they are at greater "risk" of having children outside of marriage given the same fertility rates. However, the question of why women today are more likely to have children outside of marriage and why this is more common for less-advantaged women is difficult to answer. Part of the explanation might be that low-income mothers perceive less social stigma attached to single motherhood, at least within their neighborhood contexts.[78] As we described in chapter 1, ethnographic research by

Kathryn Edin and Maria Kefalas reveals that low-income single mothers have not given up on marriage. Rather, they maintain an idealized image of marriage, one that emphasizes financial stability. Since socioeconomic circumstances make it difficult to realize this ideal, women instead turn to something they feel confident they can accomplish: becoming good mothers.[79] In contrast, women with more education might continue to delay motherhood until they are established in their careers and feel they can afford to have children.[80]

Attitudes about marriage and motherhood may also fit what we consider to be *cultural values*. Research suggests that attitudes about motherhood and marriage among low-income women may vary by ethnicity and nativity. In one study, researchers found that Dominican American (mostly immigrants), native-born Mexican American, and immigrant Mexican American low-income mothers, but not low-income native-born White mothers, were less likely than low-income native-born Black mothers to support having children before marriage.[81] This suggests the possibility of cultural norms tied to ethnic and immigrant identity. Certain structural conditions—such as economic precarity and the lack of marriageable partners—might increase rates of unmarried motherhood among young women with less education, regardless of their race, ethnicity, or nativity. However, this does not mean that these women share similar beliefs about unmarried motherhood.

Since immigrant women are not consistently more likely than their native-born peers to be mothers across different racial and ethnic groups, we cannot simply assume that immigrants have more "traditional" gender norms that emphasize motherhood. On the one hand, at ages eighteen to twenty-four, 1.5-generation immigrant women (who immigrated as children) are typically more likely than their second-generation peers (who were born in the United States to immigrant parents) to be mothers. However, this gap narrows considerably by ages twenty-five to thirty-four, suggesting that 1.5-generation immigrant women are less likely to delay motherhood compared to their U.S.-born peers. On the other hand, they are more likely to delay motherhood compared to first-generation immigrant women (who immigrated as teens or older).[82] This is at least suggestive of acculturative processes, whereby immigrant young people who are largely socialized in the United States come to resemble their native-born peers more than they do their immigrant peers who arrived at older ages.[83]

Differences by nativity highlight the intersection of cultural values and structural factors in producing divergent routes to marriage and parenthood. In a large sociological study of the experiences of young adult children of immigrants in New York City, researchers found that while some immigrant groups did hold beliefs about premarital sex and marriage that differed from those of their native-born peers, these beliefs did not always align with actual behavior. For example, a majority of the adult children of Dominican immigrants interviewed agreed that girls should stay in the parental home until marriage and that girls should not engage in premarital sex. However, these young adults also had high rates of residential independence and unmarried parenthood.[84] So, even if young people from immigrant families might report more traditional views of family behavior, they might not always act consistently with such beliefs. In some cases, beliefs may give way to or change in the face of structural conditions—such as educational and employment opportunities—that are stratified by race, ethnicity, nativity, and gender.[85]

GLOBAL AND COMPARATIVE PERSPECTIVES

Are the broad trends in leaving the parental home, marriage, and parenthood seen in the United States also apparent in other countries? In terms of young adults living with parents, the United States falls somewhere in the middle among developed countries. Statistics from the OECD (Organisation for Economic Cooperation and Development), an international organization with relatively developed countries as its members, shown in table 3 reveal that the share of young adults (ages twenty to thirty-four) in the United States who were residing with at least one parent in 2011 was about 30 percent. This is below the OECD average of 35 percent. While this is higher than in some European countries such as Denmark, where only 11 percent of young adults lived with a parent, it is lower than some Southern European countries. In Greece and Spain, for example, nearly half of young adults lived with a parent and in Italy, more than half did so. Although comparable OECD data on Japan and Korea are not available, pejorative terms such as "parasitic singles" and "kanga-roo tribe" have been used in these countries to describe the growing share of young adults who continue to reside with their parents.[86] Katherine Newman has described how related structural conditions, such as the rise of part-time and temporary employment along with expensive housing markets, have hampered the ability of young people across Europe and Japan to leave the parental home. Newman also argues that because such structural conditions affect large segments of the young adult population, they can lead to increased social acceptance of living at home with parents for an extended period of time.[87]

Compared to other developed countries, the average age at which young men and women in the United States first marry—age thirty for men and age twenty-seven for women—is lower than the OECD average (age thirty-two for men and age thirty for women). In fact, the average age at first marriage in the United States is one of the lowest among the selected countries shown in table 3. For example, the average age at first marriage in Sweden is thirty-seven for men and thirty-four for women, more than half a decade older than corresponding averages in the United States. Of course, the later mean age at first marriage in some countries does not necessarily mean that young people in those countries are not forming romantic relation-ships. Instead, young people in developed countries may instead be cohab-iting with a partner outside of marriage (relationships sometimes referred to as "de facto" or "common law" marriages). For example, taking Sweden again as a point of comparison, the share of twenty- to thirty-four-year-old Swedish young adults cohabiting with a partner outside of marriage is about 29 percent, more than double the 12 percent of US young adults doing so.[88] Another point to note is the consistent age gap between men and women in the average ages at first marriage across countries, with women typically marrying at a younger age than men.

The United States also stands out from selected OECD countries because of the relatively younger age at which women first become moth-ers. In the United States, the mean age at which women first give birth is about twenty-seven, younger than the 2016 OECD average of twenty-nine, and younger than all the selected OECD countries in table 3 for which data were available. Moreover, the average age at which women in the United States experience their first birth tracks closely with the

Table 3   Young Adult Residential Independence, Marriage, and Motherhood across
Selected OECD Countries

	Percentage of Young Adults (Ages 20–34) Living with at Least One Parent (2011)	*Mean Age at First Marriage, by Gender (2016)*		*Mean Age of Women at First Birth (2016)*
		MALE	FEMALE	
OECD Average	35%	32	30	29
Australia	—	30	29	—
Canada	—	—	—	29
Chile	—	32	31	—
Denmark	11%	35	32	29
France	22%	34	32	29
Germany	28%	34	31	29
Greece	45%	33	30	30
Italy	53%	35	32	31
Japan	—	31	29	31
Korea	—	33	30	31
Mexico	—	30	28	—
Netherlands	24%	34	31	30
Spain	45%	35	33	31
Sweden	22%	37	34	29
United Kingdom	25%	33	31	29
United States	30%	30	27	27

NOTE: Data not available for all countries.

SOURCES: Residence data from OECD 2016b, "Cohabitation Rate and Prevalence of Other Forms of Partnership"; marriage and motherhood data from OECD 2019.

average age at which women first marry, suggesting the two milestones of marriage and parenthood are still tied to one another. However, the link between marriage and parenthood has loosened compared to the past. Research shows that starting in the 1990s, there has been a "crossover" in the median ages at which women in the United States first experience marriage (age 27.4 in 2016) and birth (age 26.9 in 2016).[89] This is also the case in many other OECD countries, particularly in Europe, where the mean age at women's first birth is often younger than the mean age at first marriage. For example, in Denmark and France, women typically marry around age thirty-two but have their first child around age twenty-nine. In countries such as Japan and Korea, women typically marry at a younger age than they first experience birth. Thus, unlike in many other highly developed countries in Europe, in Japan and Korea childbearing comes after, and remains tightly linked to, marriage. In a 2018 report from the OECD, Japan and Korea rank at the very bottom in the share of births that occur outside marriage, the United States ranks in the bottom half, and Mexico, France, and Sweden rank toward the top.[90]

The adulthood milestones we have examined matter not only to the young people experiencing the transition to adulthood, but also to national economies. In developed countries, milestones such as educational attainment, labor market participation, and birth rates are often treated as measures of a country's current and future economic health. Countries where few young people can find secure, stable employment and where young people appear to have given up on starting their own families face the prospect of diminished economic growth and aging populations. Concerned governments in more developed regions of the world have adopted various policies to incentivize childbirth. Nearly all countries in developed regions have some form of maternity leave, child or family allowances, and publicly subsidized healthcare. According to a recent report from the United Nations, more than two-thirds have policies supporting paternity leave, baby "bonuses," flexible work hours, or tax credits.[91] However, the effectiveness of such policies varies and critics have argued that policies that do not address related broader social issues, such as gender norms that make it difficult for women to work and have children, are not likely to succeed.[92]

SUMMARY AND CONCLUSION

In this chapter we have looked at how young people in the United States fare on three related milestones strongly associated with adulthood: establishing an independent household, getting married, and becoming parents. We have shown that educational attainment is positively associated with the likelihood of being residentially independent and married.

For young women, educational attainment is also important for understanding motherhood in early adulthood—young women with college degrees are typically less likely to be mothers by ages twenty-five to thirty-four and very unlikely to be unwed mothers. As we saw in chapter 2, educational attainment is closely associated with full-time employment and thus, in all likelihood, to the financial means needed to establish one's own household and one's attractiveness in the dating market.

That is not to say that only college-educated young people are establishing their own households and families. In fact, there is significant variation by race, ethnicity, and nativity in how educational attainment shapes household and family formation. White young people, for example, typically have the highest rates of residential independence, a pattern that holds across levels of educational attainment. Black, Hispanic, and Asian immigrant young people are typically more likely than their native-born peers to be married, regardless of level of education. There is also racial and ethnic variation in rates of unmarried motherhood. Unmarried motherhood is less common among Asian young women at all levels of educational attainment compared to other racial and ethnic groups. Since some racial, ethnic, and immigrant differences persist across levels of education, it is possible that groups vary in their beliefs and values regarding particular milestones. Racial and ethnic minority young people might feel differently than their White peers about residing with their parents. Immigrant young people might believe in or be subjected to different gender norms than their native-born peers (for example, attitudes about whether and when a woman must marry and have children). Racial and ethnic groups might vary in their general acceptance of "nontraditional" family forms, such as unmarried motherhood. Though these cultural explanations are beyond the scope of the data we rely upon, they are potentially important for understanding the racial, ethnic, and immigrant differences we observe in this chapter. In the next chapter, we bring together all five milestones that we have examined thus far in order to better understand their interconnections in creating distinct profiles of adulthood.

4 Connecting Milestones

PROFILES OF ADULTHOOD

In previous chapters, we separately examined five key adulthood milestones. We focused on racial, ethnic, immigrant, and gender differences among young adults' experiences in terms of educational attainment, full-time employment, residential independence, marriage, and parenthood. We provided comparisons by educational attainment and showed that educational attainment is strongly related to labor market participation and household and family formation outcomes across different groups of young adults. However, we did not examine how all five of these milestones are interrelated. Hence, we do not have a full view of the prevalence of certain patterns of milestones, and how they might vary by race, ethnicity, nativity, and gender. As sociologists Ross Macmillan and Scott Eliason point out, one of the limitations of looking at single milestones is that such an approach "ultimately dissects the life course into various components and focuses attention solely on these components . . . . This, in turn, limits our efforts to understand the life course as biographical, multi-faceted phenomenon and to understand the consequences of life chances in a multiplex of domains."[1] Thus, in this chapter, we seek to provide a multi-dimensional view of the transition to adulthood that goes beyond the attainment of individual milestones.

Whether a young person reaches a particular milestone is closely linked with completing other milestones—that is, milestones in adulthood are not independent of one another. Rather than thinking of the transition to adulthood as a single sequence of steps, instead we argue there exist multiple profiles of adulthood, each with different patterns of milestones attainment. For example, the adulthood profile of a young person who has attained at least a bachelor's degree is likely to include a full-time job and residential independence (as we saw in previous chapters) while a young person without a college education is less likely to have achieved these milestones. Depending on the milestones they have attained, young people are likely to eventually have different socioeconomic and lifestyle outcomes. In other words, the patterns in milestones attainment experienced by young people have important long-term consequences.[2]

Previous studies have considered multiple patterns that describe the contemporary transition to adulthood. However, the measurements of milestones and the importance attached to each vary across studies. To illustrate how research studies can share very similar conceptualizations of adulthood milestones but come to somewhat different characterizations depending on their samples of young adults, we summarize conclusions from a few such studies below.[3] Each of these studies draws on different samples of young people, which has implications for their conclusions since different populations are likely to exhibit varying probabilities of attaining each adulthood milestone. For example, data samples that include younger populations (such as those ages eighteen to twenty-four) will show different proportions who have completed a bachelor's degree, married, or become parents, compared to data samples of older populations (such as those ages twenty-five to thirty-four).[4]

In a study included in the edited volume *On the Frontier of Adulthood*, published in 2005, Gary Sandefur and coauthors used markers of adulthood that were very similar to those covered in this book (i.e., educational attainment, employment, residential independence, ever married, and ever had a child) to examine two nationally representative cohorts of young adults (those who were around age twenty-eight in 1992 and those who were approximately age twenty-six in 2000). Their characterization of the four different paths to adulthood for young men include: (1) "limited postsecondary education/family," (2) "limited postsecondary education/no family," (3) "BA (bachelor's degree)/no family," and (4) "BA/ family." The authors also found four distinct patterns for young women, of which three were also apparent among men ("limited postsecondary education/family," "BA/no family," and "BA/family"). However, for young women, the study found a "limited postsecondary education/children" pattern instead of the "limited postsecondary education/no family" pattern seen among young men.[5] Similar to our approach, the Sandefur et al. study emphasized the role of educational attainment in characterizing particular patterns in the transition to adulthood.

Another study in the same volume by D. Wayne Osgood and others examined a more specific population of young people who were around age twenty-four in 1999 and who had been sixth-graders in suburban schools in the Detroit metropolitan area when the data were first collected. Although their data were not nationally representative, Osgood et al. had more detailed categories of adulthood milestones. They also examined five similar milestones (education, employment, residential independence, marriage, and parenthood) but measured different outcomes within each of these milestone categories. For example, in terms of employment, Osgood et al. determined not just whether a young adult was working but also the type of job they had (e.g., short-term, long-term, career). For residential independence, their measure included whether respondents lived with parents or relatives, were renting on their own, or if they were homeowners. They also examined romantic relationships outside marriage, such as "steady dating" and cohabiting. Using these measures, Osgood et al. identified six different paths to adulthood, which they termed (1) "fast starters," (2) "parents without careers," (3) "educated partners," (4) "educated singles," (5) "working singles," and (6) "slow starters."[6] While educational attainment clearly played a role in how Osgood et al. viewed certain paths (e.g., "educated partners"), they also emphasized the number of milestones young adults had attained. For example, "fast starters" had reached many adulthood milestones while "slow starters" had not.

In their book *The Long Shadow*, Karl Alexander and colleagues examined the transition to adulthood for a cohort of mostly disadvantaged children who, in 1982, were starting first grade in Baltimore public schools. The researchers followed these children into their late twenties.[7] Their focus was on whether, as young adults, study members had experienced four milestones: working, living apart from parents, establishing unions (marriage or partnership), and becoming parents. Using these four milestones, the authors found six common patterns in how Baltimore youth experienced the transition to adulthood. The most common pattern, seen in nearly half of their sample, was a "fast track" to adulthood in which young people had already experienced each of the four milestones by their late twenties. The second most common pattern, characterizing the experiences of nearly one in five of the study participants, was one in which parenthood was delayed but other milestones (including work, residential independence, and union-formation) had been experienced. Less common were patterns in which the young adults were still living with parents (with a varied mix of reaching other milestones) and patterns in which young people were working and residentially independent but were not currently in unions (with variations in whether they had become parents). Notice, however, that educational attainment is not factored into these patterns. This is because Alexander et al. viewed educational attainment as open-ended since many of the young adults in their study expressed a desire to continue education, even though it was unclear how many would ultimately go back to school.

There are also numerous studies of the transition to adulthood that examine how young adults' socioeconomic background (such as parental education and family income) and demographic characteristics (such as race, ethnicity, nativity, and gender) are associated with particular adulthood milestones.[8] However, few studies look at combinations of milestones in relation to young adults' background and individual characteristics. The studies we described above are exceptions. After identifying their four different patterns through latent class analysis, a statistical method used to identify underlying patterns of interconnection among different markers, Sandefur et al. found that the likelihood of experiencing specific patterns systematically differed by parental education, family structure (e.g., whether respondents grew up in a two-parent household), race and ethnicity, and the type of high school attended.[9] Similarly, Osgood et al. examined the role of young people's family background (including their parents' income, education, and marital status) as well as young people's own characteristics, such as gender and race, in their chances of taking one of the six different paths to adulthood they identified.[10] Alexander et al. also showed that particular patterns—such as the "fast track"—are more likely to be taken by young people from disadvantaged backgrounds, while patterns in which family milestones like parenthood are delayed are more likely to be taken by young people from more advantaged family backgrounds.[11]

Our research goes beyond these existing studies in that we compare profiles of adulthood across racial and ethnic groups, for native-born and immigrant young adults, and for men and women across different levels of educational attainment. We believe this approach offers a consistently detailed focus on group differences that is rare in social science research. As we stated earlier, it is more common to find studies that focus on particular adulthood milestones—such as educational attainment or marriage—and less common to find studies that show interconnections among milestones. Rarer still are studies that show connections between milestones for multiple racial and ethnic groups or studies that distinguish between native-born and immigrant young people. Other research sometimes includes chapters that focus on racial and ethnic groups or even immigrant-origin young people, but these shorter pieces are often limited to particular cities or regions.[12] A study by Rubén Rumbaut and Golnaz Komaie is one of the few to focus on adulthood milestones among immigrant-origin young people using a national sample and even distinguishes groups by country of origin (see introduction).[13] Although their study covers a number of milestones, including residential independence and full-time work, the milestones are examined separately and as a result, we do not gain a clear sense of patterns of milestone attainment. Our aim is to systematically compare patterns of milestone attainment across race, ethnicity, nativity, and gender in order to highlight why these characteristics are relevant for young people's experiences with transitions to adulthood.

Since our data is cross-sectional and not longitudinal (meaning we have data for one point in time rather than data that follows the same young people over time), we can only demonstrate the interdependence of milestones among a cohort of young people ages twenty-five to thirty-four at a given time point. We can think about the data as a "snapshot" of a particular group of young adults (twenty-five-to-thirty-four-year-olds) and their attainment of adulthood milestones at the time data were collected (between 2013 and 2017). This snapshot would likely look different at

younger ages (such as among young people ages eighteen to twenty-four)
as studies have shown that the interconnections between milestones like
education, employment, living arrangements, marriage, and parenthood
vary across ages.[14] When researchers have longitudinal data that track the
same young people over time, they can show how patterns of interconnections among adulthood milestones change across ages leading to trajectories into adulthood.[15] In our case, we reveal the interconnections among
adulthood milestones captured at a relatively later stage of young adulthood. The advantage of our data is that we have a large number of respondents and the data are nationally representative. We use the term *profiles of
adulthood* to describe the prominent patterns of milestones attainment
captured in this snapshot of young people.

IDENTIFYING PROFILES OF ADULTHOOD

As we have stressed throughout the book, educational attainment clearly
influences the likelihood of reaching other adulthood milestones. Even
though educational attainment can be considered an open-ended outcome
(since people can continue their education at any point throughout their
lives), it is a milestone that most Americans believe should be completed by
their early twenties.[16] Moreover, the level of education a young person has
attained by ages twenty-five to thirty-four is of importance for other milestones such as marriage and parenthood, which are likely to occur during
this age range. Thus, we consider educational attainment to be a significant
dividing line in young people's experiences. Simply stated, young people
who have completed college are likely to have very different profiles of
adulthood compared to young people who have not completed college.

Educational attainment aside, if we were to count all the possible combinations of the remaining four milestones, we would have a total of sixteen different patterns (which we can calculate by multiplying the two
possible outcomes each for whether or not one attained full-time employment, residential independence, marriage, and parenthood: $2\times2\times2\times2 =$
16). These patterns are summarized in table 4. Pattern 1, for example, is
one in which all milestones have been attained while pattern 16 is one in
which none of the milestones (besides educational attainment) have been

Table 4   Patterns of Milestone Attainment

	Working Full-Time	Residentially Independent	Currently Married	Has Own Children at Home
Pattern 1	✓	✓	✓	✓
Pattern 2	✓	✓	✓	✗
Pattern 3	✓	✓	✗	✓
Pattern 4	✓	✓	✗	✗
Pattern 5	✓	✗	✓	✓
Pattern 6	✓	✗	✓	✗
Pattern 7	✓	✗	✗	✓
Pattern 8	✓	✗	✗	✗
Pattern 9	✗	✓	✓	✓
Pattern 10	✗	✓	✓	✗
Pattern 11	✗	✓	✗	✓
Pattern 12	✗	✓	✗	✗
Pattern 13	✗	✗	✓	✓
Pattern 14	✗	✗	✓	✗
Pattern 15	✗	✗	✗	✓
Pattern 16	✗	✗	✗	✗

KEY: ✓ represents a milestone attained, ✗ represents a milestone not attained.

attained. Patterns 2 through 15 cover the remaining possibilities of milestones attainment. Notice that in this chapter we are also counting fatherhood as a milestone for young men, which we did not consider in chapter 3. As we pointed out in chapter 3, the measure of parenthood we use (whether or not a young person is living with a child of their own) is much more likely to underestimate parenthood for young men than women. However, to maintain consistency in measures for pattern 1 (all milestones) and pattern 16 (no milestones) between young men and women, we have opted to include parenthood as a milestone in describing profiles of adulthood for young men in this chapter.

Displaying each of the sixteen patterns for every one of the racial, ethnic, and immigrant groups and for both young men and women complicates the presentation of data (these estimates are available in the appendix). However, some patterns are more prevalent than others among young adults and other patterns, though theoretically possible, are rarely present in our sample. For example, pattern 10—in which a young person is residentially independent and married but not working full-time nor a parent—is exceedingly rare (less than 5 percent of young people across groups fit this pattern). Since some patterns are experienced by relatively modest shares of young people, we focus on patterns that are the most substantively meaningful, such as having attained all of the milestones or none of the milestones, as well as those that are most common among young people. One challenge, of course, is to find patterns that are meaningful and common across groups of young people from different racial, ethnic, and immigrant backgrounds as well as patterns that are important for both young men and women. The patterns and combinations of patterns we have chosen to highlight are especially relevant for understanding the importance of educational attainment, race, ethnicity, nativity, and gender in shaping young people's transitions to adulthood.

Profiles of Adulthood among Young Men

Figure 15 shows the primary profiles of adulthood seen among young men with different levels of education. Two of the profiles—All Milestones and No Milestones—correspond directly to pattern 1 and pattern 16, respectively, in table 4. Young men who fit the No Milestones profile are not working full-time, not residentially independent, not married, and not living with a child of their own. Beyond their educational attainment, these young men have not met any of the traditional markers of adulthood. Young men with the All Milestones profile are working full-time, in independent households, married, and have children of their own at home. They are adults in the traditional sense, having met the requirements most Americans consider important for being an adult. The remaining three profiles we have chosen to highlight for young men are combinations of patterns. The Working Childless Single profile combines patterns 4 and 8. These are young men who are working full-time and neither married nor living with a child of their own but who may or may not be residentially independent. The Working Childless Husband profile combines patterns 2 and 6. Young men with this profile are working full-time and married and most, but not all, have established their own

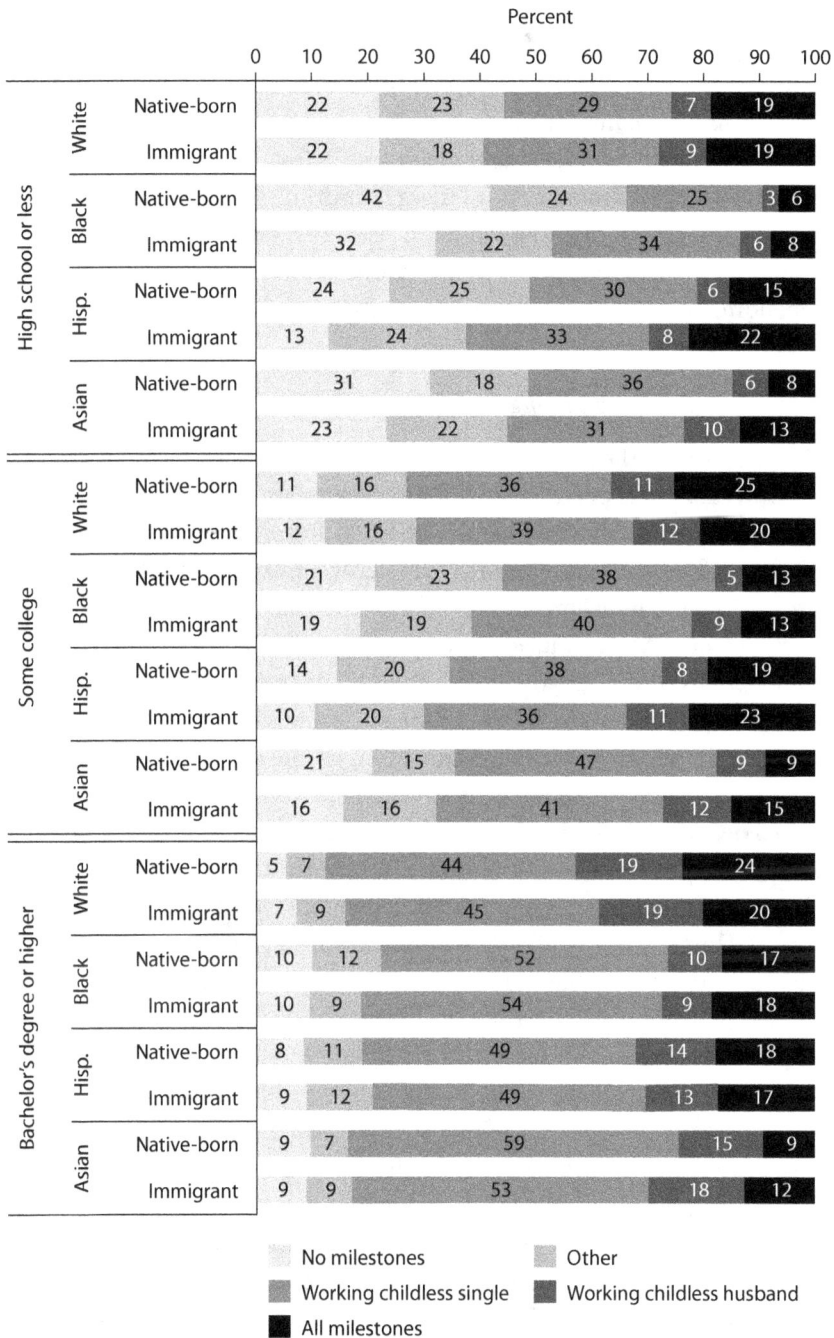

Figure 15. Major profiles of adulthood for young men (ages twenty-five to thirty-four), by educational attainment, race and ethnicity, and nativity.

SOURCE: US Census 2017, Five-Year Estimates; Ruggles et al. 2021.

Education	Race	Nativity	No milestones	Other	Working childless single	Working childless husband	All milestones
High school or less	White	Native-born	22	23	29	7	19
High school or less	White	Immigrant	22	18	31	9	19
High school or less	Black	Native-born	42	24	25	3	6
High school or less	Black	Immigrant	32	22	34	6	8
High school or less	Hisp.	Native-born	24	25	30	6	15
High school or less	Hisp.	Immigrant	13	24	33	8	22
High school or less	Asian	Native-born	31	18	36	6	8
High school or less	Asian	Immigrant	23	22	31	10	13
Some college	White	Native-born	11	16	36	11	25
Some college	White	Immigrant	12	16	39	12	20
Some college	Black	Native-born	21	23	38	5	13
Some college	Black	Immigrant	19	19	40	9	13
Some college	Hisp.	Native-born	14	20	38	8	19
Some college	Hisp.	Immigrant	10	20	36	11	23
Some college	Asian	Native-born	21	15	47	9	9
Some college	Asian	Immigrant	16	16	41	12	15
Bachelor's degree or higher	White	Native-born	5	7	44	19	24
Bachelor's degree or higher	White	Immigrant	7	9	45	19	20
Bachelor's degree or higher	Black	Native-born	10	12	52	10	17
Bachelor's degree or higher	Black	Immigrant	10	9	54	9	18
Bachelor's degree or higher	Hisp.	Native-born	8	11	49	14	18
Bachelor's degree or higher	Hisp.	Immigrant	9	12	49	13	17
Bachelor's degree or higher	Asian	Native-born	9	7	59	15	9
Bachelor's degree or higher	Asian	Immigrant	9	9	53	18	12

Legend:
- No milestones
- Working childless single
- All milestones
- Other
- Working childless husband

households. They also do not live with children of their own. With these four profiles (encompassing six patterns), we cover the vast majority of young men's experiences—more than three in four men across groups and educational attainment fit one of these four profiles. Lastly, the Other profile combines the remaining ten patterns, which are all fairly uncommon, since altogether these patterns cover one-fourth or less of young men depending on their race, ethnicity, nativity, and educational attainment.

Profiles of Adulthood among Young Women

Figure 16 shows the profiles of adulthood most common to young women with varying levels of education. Some profiles are identical to those seen among young men. These include the No Milestones, All Milestones, and Working Childless Single profiles. However, unlike for men, parenthood tends to play a more prominent role in the transition to adulthood for young women. As a result, young women tend to have more varied profiles than men. In addition to the three profiles that are also seen among young men, for young women a Single Mom profile and a Married Stay-at-Home Mom profile are relevant. The Single Mom profile combines patterns 3, 7, 11, and 15. What these patterns have in common is that they all include unmarried women living with a child of their own; they differ in whether or not the women are working full-time (which tends to vary by educational attainment) or residentially independent (most are). The Married Stay-at-Home Mom profile is comprised of patterns 9 and 13. Young women with this profile are married and have children of their own at home but do not work full-time. Most are in independent households but some are not. Together, the gendered Single Mom and Married Stay-at-Home Mom profiles are shared by a considerable proportion of young women across the spectrum of racial, ethnic, and immigrant diversity and educational attainment, whereas the share of young men with comparable profiles (i.e., being a single dad or a married stay-at-home dad) are negligible. For young women, the five profiles described (encompassing ten patterns) cover approximately three in four young women across groups and levels of education. The need for a total of five profiles to capture the experiences of a majority of young women, rather than the four we identified for young men, reflects how demographic, socioeconomic, and

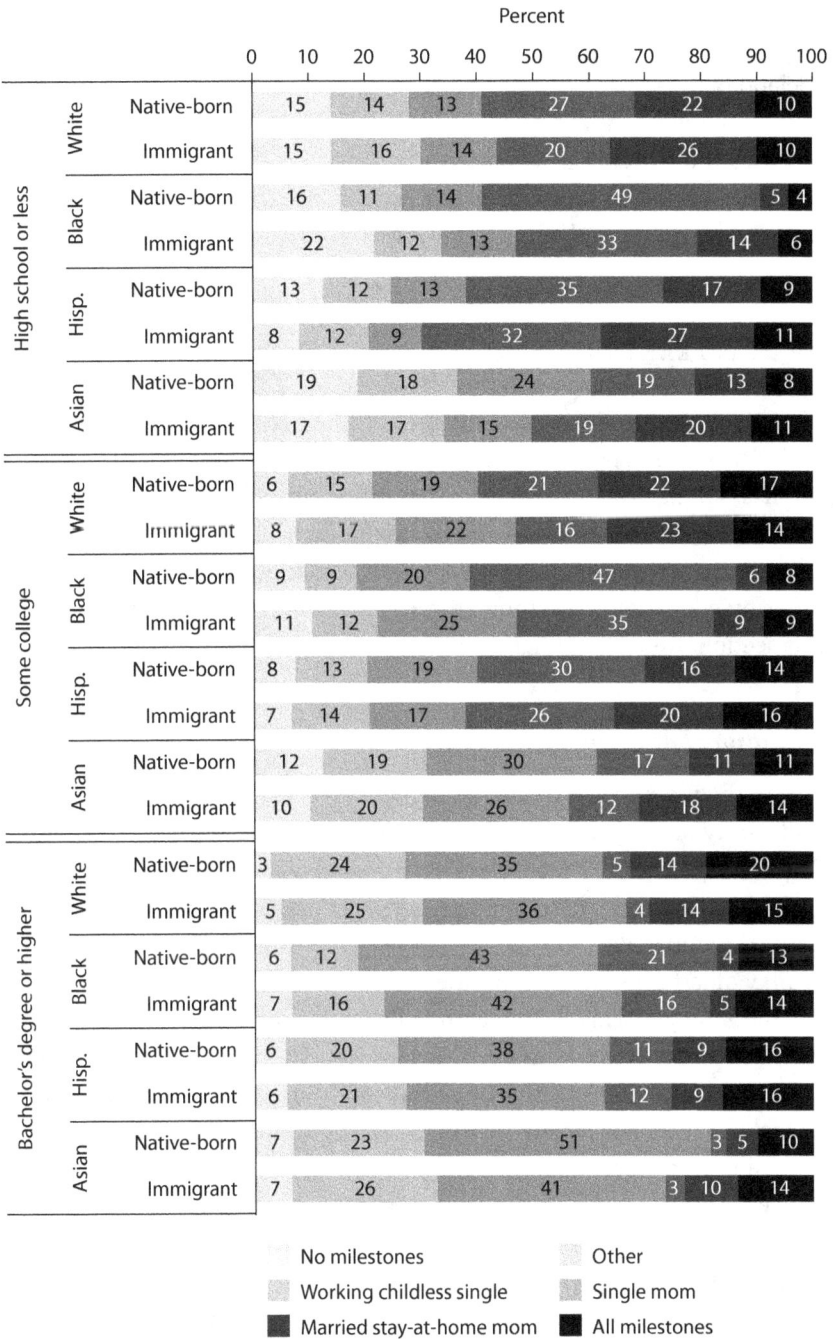

Education	Race	Nativity	No milestones	Working childless single	Married stay-at-home mom	Other	Single mom	All milestones
High school or less	White	Native-born	15	14	13	27	22	10
		Immigrant	15	16	14	20	26	10
	Black	Native-born	16	11	14	49	5	4
		Immigrant	22	12	13	33	14	6
	Hisp.	Native-born	13	12	13	35	17	9
		Immigrant	8	12	9	32	27	11
	Asian	Native-born	19	18	24	19	13	8
		Immigrant	17	17	15	19	20	11
Some college	White	Native-born	6	15	19	21	22	17
		Immigrant	8	17	22	16	23	14
	Black	Native-born	9	9	20	47	6	8
		Immigrant	11	12	25	35	9	9
	Hisp.	Native-born	8	13	19	30	16	14
		Immigrant	7	14	17	26	20	16
	Asian	Native-born	12	19	30	17	11	11
		Immigrant	10	20	26	12	18	14
Bachelor's degree or higher	White	Native-born	3	24	35	5	14	20
		Immigrant	5	25	36	4	14	15
	Black	Native-born	6	12	43	21	4	13
		Immigrant	7	16	42	16	5	14
	Hisp.	Native-born	6	20	38	11	9	16
		Immigrant	6	21	35	12	9	16
	Asian	Native-born	7	23	51	3	5	10
		Immigrant	7	26	41	3	10	14

Legend: No milestones; Other; Working childless single; Single mom; Married stay-at-home mom; All milestones.

Figure 16. Major profiles of adulthood for young women (ages twenty-five to thirty-four), by educational attainment, race and ethnicity, and nativity.

SOURCE: US Census 2017, Five-Year Estimates; Ruggles et al. 2021.

societal factors interact differentially to shape the transition to adulthood for young men and women.[17] Finally, the Other profile for young women includes the remaining six patterns, which are generally less common as together they cover one-fourth or less of women across racial, ethnic, or immigrant groups and educational levels.

THE PATTERNING OF PROFILES OF ADULTHOOD

Now that we have identified distinct profiles of adulthood shared by a majority of young people, we turn to the question of who fits each of these profiles. Though we have sought to identify the profiles that encompass the majority of young men and women's experiences, it is clear from figures 15 and 16 that the shares of young people across these profiles substantively differ by educational attainment, race, ethnicity, nativity, and gender. In this section, we will highlight some of these important variations.

Educational Attainment and Profiles of Adulthood

One of the most striking patterns to emerge from figures 15 and 16 is the uniformity of experiences among young people with bachelor's or higher degrees regardless of race, ethnicity, or nativity, compared to the wide variability of experiences among young people with less education. For both young men and women with at least a bachelor's degree, the modal profile of adulthood (the profile with the largest share) is Working Childless Single. This is true across all racial and ethnic groups and for both native-born and immigrant young men and women. Between more than one-third to more than one-half of young men and women with bachelor's or higher degrees are working full-time, unmarried, and without children of their own at home. For example, more than half of both native-born Asian women and immigrant Black men with at least a bachelor's degree fit the Working Childless Single profile (51 percent and 54 percent, respectively).

In contrast, there is no single modal profile for young people with no college experience (i.e., "high school or less"). Among these young men, we see considerable variability in the share with the No Milestones profile across race, ethnicity, and nativity. Among young women with no college education, there is a wide range of patterns by race, ethnicity, and nativity as well—for example, in the varying shares who fit the Single Mom or Married Stay-at-Home Mom profile. For young women with no college experience, the Working Childless Single profile is usually among the least common. Even among exceptions to this pattern, the share who have the Working Childless Single profile is still far smaller than the share among their counterparts with bachelor's or higher degrees. Take native-born Asian women with no college experience: nearly one quarter fit the Working Childless Single profile (24 percent), making it their modal profile, but this is still less than half the share of native-born Asian women with bachelor's or higher degrees with this profile (51 percent). This is in part because a much larger share of native-born Asian women with no college experience fit the Single Mom or Married Stay-at-Home Mom profile compared to their counterparts with at least a bachelor's degree (19 percent versus 3 percent for the Single Mom profile and 13 percent versus 5 percent for the Married Stay-at-Home Mom profile).

Among young men with no college experience (i.e., "high school or less"), the Working Childless Single profile is fairly common—it is actually the modal profile for all but native-born Black men. However, even for such men, the Working Childless Single profile is still less common compared to their peers with bachelor's or higher degrees. For example, less than one-third of native-born Hispanic men with no college experience fit the Working Childless Single profile compared to nearly half of native-born Hispanic men with at least a bachelor's degree. Moreover, we expect that men and women without college degrees who work full-time are more likely to be doing so in occupations with lower pay and fewer benefits. Given the growing share of young people who are college-educated and the significant shifts in the economic structure of the United States toward an information and knowledge-based economy over the past decades, the economic security and stability of young people without a college degree has likely deteriorated.[18] The smaller share of young men with no college experience who fit the Working Single Childless profile is in part due to the much larger share who fit the No Milestones profile, compared to their peers with bachelor's or higher degrees, which we discuss further below. It is also relatively more difficult to capture the experiences of a

larger majority of young men with no college experience in just a few profiles: anywhere from one-fifth to one-fourth of such young men have
Other profiles, meaning they do not fit one of the distinct profiles we have
identified for young men, compared to about one-fifth or less of young
men with bachelor's or higher degrees.

Young people with more education are also more likely to fit the All
Milestones profile than the No Milestones profile, while the opposite is
generally true for young people with less education. For example, among
native-born Black men with no college experience (i.e., "high school or
less"), about 40 percent fit the No Milestones profile and less than 10 percent fit the All Milestones profile. Among native-born Black men with at
least a bachelor's degree, however, only about 10 percent fit the No
Milestones profile and closer to 20 percent fit the All Milestones profile.
Likewise, among native-born White women with no college experience, 15
percent fit the No Milestones profile and just 10 percent fit the All
Milestones profile, but among their counterparts with at least a bachelor's
degree, only 3 percent fit the No Milestones profile and 20 percent fit the
All Milestones profile. There are some notable exceptions to this general
pattern among those with the highest and lowest levels of educational
attainment. First, larger proportions of immigrant Hispanic men and
women with no college experience fit the All Milestones profile than fit the
No Milestones profile. Second, the proportions of native-born Asian men
with bachelor's or higher degrees that fit the All Milestones or No
Milestones profiles are about equal, but both these profiles are less common to begin with for them.

The picture we painted of educational attainment as a significant divide
in experiences during the transition to adulthood is especially apt here.
From a theoretical perspective that emphasizes role transitions, young
people with no college experience and who have yet to complete other
major milestones deviate most from the normative view of adulthood.
With their lower levels of educational attainment and the fact that they
are not working full-time, such young people likely face serious challenges
in securing economic independence, making their prospects for stable
employment, independent living, and romantic relationships less promising. Given the level of financial and social precarity attached to their current state, we consider these young people to be on very uncertain footing

as they transition to adulthood. In contrast, for the college-educated, having either the Working Childless Single or the All Milestones profile suggests a clearer path to a middle-class life. Though there is concern that even "a college degree is no longer a ticket to the middle class," considerable evidence supports the substantial economic and social benefits that come with a college degree.[19] While a bachelor's degree is not a guarantee of a middle-class life, it increases the odds that young adults will be able to achieve economic stability or upward mobility. The pursuit of a college or advanced degree is also likely to delay some adulthood milestones, including marriage and parenthood.

Educational attainment is also crucial for understanding the gendered profiles of adulthood. For women, both the Single Mom and Married Stay-at-Home Mom profiles are more common among women with no college experience (i.e., "high school or less") than among women who have attained at least a bachelor's degree. Between 32 and 54 percent of young women with no college experience fit either the Single Mom or the Married Stay-at-Home Mom profile, compared to 25 percent or less of their peers with bachelor's or higher degrees. Differences in family formation patterns by educational attainment among women can be quite large. For example, about 35 percent of native-born Hispanic women with no college experience fit the Single Mom path, more than triple the 11 percent of native-born Hispanic women with at least a bachelor's degree with this profile. With few exceptions, the shares of young women with bachelor's or higher degrees who fit the Married Stay-at-Home Mom or All Milestones profile are almost always greater than the shares who fit the Single Mom profile. Put another way, motherhood experiences among young women with less education are more likely to come with a varied mix of other milestones while for more educated women, motherhood is more likely to include full-time work and marriage.

Racial and Ethnic Variation in Profiles of Adulthood

As we have seen, young people with bachelor's or higher degrees have similar profiles as they transition to adulthood. In contrast, racial and ethnic differences are much more pronounced among young people with less education. Racial and ethnic differences among native-born young men in the lowest category of educational attainment (i.e., "high school or less") are illuminating in this regard. Among this group of men, only about 22 percent of native-born White men fit the No Milestones profile, compared to about 24 percent of native-born Hispanic men, 31 percent of native-born Asian men, and 42 percent of native-born Black men. Native-born White men with no college experience are also more likely to be fit the All Milestones profile compared to their native-born Black, Hispanic, and Asian peers. For example, the 19 percent of native-born White men with no college experience who fit this profile is more than triple the 6 percent of their native-born Black peers with this profile. These racial and ethnic differences tend to be more modest among young men with bachelor's or higher degrees (native-born Asian men are an exception).

Racial and ethnic differences are somewhat less consistently patterned by levels of education among native-born women. This can be seen when focusing on the gendered Single Mom and Married Stay-at-Home Mom profiles. On the one hand, racial and ethnic differences in the share of young women with the Single Mom profile tend to be more pronounced among those with no college experience. For example, 49 percent of native-born Black women with no college experience fit the Single Mom profile, compared to about 35 percent of native-born Hispanic, 27 percent of native-born White, and about 19 percent of native-born Asian women with no college experience. Among young women with bachelor's or higher degrees, however, the corresponding differences by race and ethnicity are smaller. On the other hand, racial and ethnic differences in the share of women with the Married Stay-at-Home Mom profile are fairly consistent, regardless of level of education. Even though the share of women with the Married Stay-at-Home Mom profile varies across levels of education, White women are the most likely among native-born women to fit this profile across all levels of educational attainment. Overall, it appears that racial and ethnic differences among young women are less consistently influenced by educational attainment. This may reflect competing and strongly gendered demands—for example, balancing the necessity and desirability of full-time work with expectations about marriage and motherhood—that differentially influence young women across racial, ethnic, and educational backgrounds.

Nativity and Variation in Profiles of Adulthood

Differences between native-born and immigrant young people are also more visible among those with less education. Among men with no college experience (i.e., "high school or less"), immigrant minority men are less likely than their native-born peers to fit the No Milestones profile and more likely to fit the All Milestones profile. For example, about 13 percent of immigrant Hispanic men and 23 percent of immigrant Asian men with no college experience fit the No Milestones profile, lower than the 24 percent and 31 percent, respectively, of their native-born peers with comparable levels of education. Likewise, about 22 percent of immigrant Hispanic men and 13 percent of immigrant Asian men with no college experience fit the All Milestones profile, compared to only about 15 percent and 8 percent, respectively, of their native-born counterparts. The corresponding comparisons among young men with bachelor's or higher degrees, however, show minimal or smaller differences. Moreover, counting young men who fit the Working Childless Husband profiles and those who fit the All Milestones profile among young men with no college experience reveals that greater shares of immigrant young men than native-born young men have profiles of adulthood that involve family formation, whether that be marriage, fatherhood, or both. Thirty percent of immigrant Hispanic men and 23 percent of immigrant Asian men with no college experience fit either the Working Childless Husband or the All Milestones profile, compared to only 21 percent and 14 percent of their respective native-born counterparts.

Differences between native-born and immigrant young women in the share who fit either the Single Mom or Married Stay-at-Home Mom profile are also apparent. At all levels of education, native-born women are generally more likely to fit the Single Mom profile than are immigrant women. However, the differences tend to be more visible among women with less education. For example, about 27 percent of native-born White women with no college experience fit the Single Mom profile, compared to about 20 percent of similarly educated immigrant White women. In contrast, among White women with bachelor's or higher degrees, the share of native-born and immigrant women who fit the Single Mom profile are almost identical (5 percent versus 4 percent). Immigrant women are also generally more likely than native-born women to fit the Married Stay-at-Home Mom profile, a pattern seen at all levels of education. Again, though, nativity differences tend to be larger among women with less education. About 27 percent of immigrant Hispanic women with no college experience fit the Married Stay-at-Home Mom profile, for example, compared to 17 percent of native-born Hispanic women. Yet no such difference is seen between native-born and immigrant Hispanic women with bachelor's or higher degrees, with about 9 percent of both fitting the Married Stay-at-Home Mom profile. Coupled with the greater share of immigrant young men with less education who fit the Working Childless Husband and All Milestones profiles, this suggests that immigrant young people with less education are more likely than their similarly educated native-born peers to take on traditional adulthood roles that involve family formation, including marriage and parenthood.

SUMMARY AND CONCLUSION

In this chapter, we have brought together five measures of milestones considered important for the transition to adulthood (educational attainment, full-time employment, residential independence, marriage, and parenthood) and examined how patterns of attaining such milestones coalesce around several major profiles of adulthood for young men and women in the United States. The profiles we have identified in this chapter will, we believe, result in divergent socioeconomic outcomes that are likely to have significant consequences throughout a young person's life course.

College-educated young people with full-time employment are on their way to establishing a middle-class lifestyle. For some highly educated young people, this might mean focusing on educational and career opportunities before or instead of starting a family (i.e., Working Childless Singles) while for others, their identities as married parents have already been established (i.e., All Milestones). What characterizes these two paths for young people with bachelor's or higher degrees is the sense of *choice*—for example, choosing to delay or to start a family. On the other hand, young people who have not completed a college degree are more likely to experience highly variable paths to adulthood, with their race, ethnicity, nativity, and gender playing a much stronger role in shaping their outcomes. Some might find full-time work alongside establishing families, providing clear adulthood roles. Yet challenges seem likely for such young people. Their lower levels of education likely preclude them from higher-paying jobs with good benefits. They may feel greater financial pressure from the expenses associated with maintaining independent households and raising children. Depending on how early they marry and have children, this "fast track" to adulthood might even have potential downsides, giving such young people less freedom to pursue personal development.

Other young people without a college education are less likely to have any of the traditional markers of adulthood. Those who have attained few milestones or no milestones face a more precarious future relative to their peers who fit profiles of adulthood that involve the attainment of more milestones. *Coming of Age in the Other America*, a study of the transition to adulthood among disadvantaged young people, conducted by sociologists Stefanie DeLuca, Susan Clampet-Lundquist, and Kathryn Edin, provides additional insight. Through interviews with 150 Black young people from disadvantaged neighborhoods in Baltimore, most of whom were between the ages of nineteen and twenty-four in 2010, the researchers sought to understand why these young people often end up experiencing less favorable educational and occupational outcomes. The authors point out that from an intergenerational perspective—that is, comparing young people to their parents—the young people they followed do experience improvements in life outcomes, in that they are more likely than their parents to have completed high school and to be employed. They also find that many of these highly disadvantaged young people have "mainstream" aspirations that involve college and stable employment. Yet even the most promising of these young people found their aspirations curtailed by disordered neighborhood environments and lack of resources. For example, Bob, one of the young people in the study most prepared for college, found little support for his college goals from his high school, saying, "If anything, [they push you] to a community college, if that at all." Though he graduated high school with honors, Bob immediately entered the labor force and was eager to live on his own, in part to escape his neighborhood and tense relationships with family members. Each time he was interviewed, Bob mentioned a desire to return to school, but costs always weighed heavily in his decision and he was often constrained by the unpredictable nature of the low-wage work available to him. As Bob described, "I have a plan, I know what I wanna do in life . . . but I can't get there."[20]

In this chapter, we have also shown that greater educational attainment—specifically attaining at least a bachelor's degree—diminishes but does not completely erase racial, ethnic, immigrant, and gender differences in profiles of adulthood. Racial and ethnic differences in the share of young people with less education who fit the All Milestones profile consistently point to an advantage among White young people, especially White men, who are more likely than their Black, Hispanic, and Asian peers to attain milestones associated with adulthood, even without a college degree. The White advantage persists, to a lesser degree, even among the most highly educated young people. Immigrants also maintain somewhat of an advantage among young people with less education in terms of family formation milestones, in that immigrant men are more likely than native-born men to fit the All Milestones profile and immigrant women are more likely than native-born women to fit the Married Stay-at-Home Mom profile. Yet this immigrant tendency to fit more "traditional" profiles of adulthood that include earlier family formation is not very apparent among young people with bachelor's or higher degrees. This again suggests the importance of educational attainment for life trajectories—immigrant young people without college degrees who have started their own families may be headed towards working-class jobs and lifestyles.

The Single Mom and Married Stay-at-Home Mom profiles that are common among young women underscore the relevance of gender in the transition to adulthood. However, these profiles tend to be more relevant among women with less education, further showing how a college education tends to produce more uniform experiences in the transition to adulthood for men and women. On the whole, educational attainment provides a clear division in profiles of adulthood, with profiles tending to be more varied by race, ethnicity, nativity, and gender among young people without a bachelor's degree.

A final note on our characterization of profiles of adulthood: they are based on quantifiable measures of milestones—with our data, we cannot reflect on how young people feel about their lives. In *The Long Shadow*,

Alexander and colleagues share the story of Bess, a young woman who dropped out of high school in order to care for her children. When interviewed in her early twenties, Bess described her future plans as, "I just want to get a home for my kids, and get me a car, and just work and pay my bills, that's it." Five years later, Bess was still without a house or car and was working for minimal pay at a convenience store. Bess nevertheless reported that her children were the high point in her life and that her life has gotten much better since high school. As the authors point out, "Who is to say otherwise?"[21]

Our intention is not to cast any normative judgement on which paths into adulthood young people should take or which paths are "good" and which are "bad," but rather to demonstrate that the likelihood of fitting certain profiles of adulthood depends largely on educational attainment as well as on race, ethnicity, nativity, and gender. We do believe that having certain profiles in early adulthood may lead to more economic hardship in the future. It is very likely that the profiles that most depart from societal norms regarding milestone attainment can lead to more adverse socioeconomic outcomes for young people.[22] Nevertheless, the profiles we have defined are based on young people's attainment of milestones at one point in time: some young people who seem to be on uncertain footing now might be on a clearer path later in their life, just as some young people who seem to be on surer paths to the middle class might experience setbacks (such as job loss or divorce). In other words, our profiles show possibilities, not destinies.

In their opening summary of *On the Frontier to Adulthood*, a volume of research on the transition to adulthood, the editors wrote, "The timing and sequencing of traditional markers of adulthood—leaving home, finishing school, starting work, getting married, and having children—are less predictable and more prolonged, diverse, and disordered."[23] In *Coming of Age in America*, a more recent volume on the transition to adulthood, the editors attribute some of these changes in the transition to adulthood to evolving gender norms, increasing amounts of time spent in education, and challenging labor markets.[24] In this chapter, we have touched on the relevance of these factors for understanding the profiles of adulthood seen among contemporary young people. But beyond considering some of the major profiles of adulthood that are common today, we also show how fitting into particular profiles is strongly related to characteristics such as educational attainment, race, ethnicity, nativity, and gender. That the transition to adulthood is becoming less predictable and more varied for young people today is, we believe, related to the racial, ethnic, and immigrant diversity among younger generations. These differences are all the more apparent once focus shifts beyond the minority of young people who complete college to include young people with less or no college experience. Thus, one of the primary contributions of this book is that it foregrounds race, ethnicity, and nativity in the study of the transition to adulthood—characteristics that are all the more relevant as the composition of the US population continues to change (see chapter 1). In the next chapter, we will focus on additional aspects of diversity among young people—from ethnicity to legal status to sexual orientation—and the implications of these identities for their transitions to adulthood.

5 Exploring a Mosaic of Experiences

ETHNICITY, IMMIGRANT STATUS, AND
SEXUAL ORIENTATION

Thus far, we have looked at racial diversity in the United States as well as at nativity and gender differences. Using these broad brushstrokes, we have discerned significant variation in how young people experience the transition to adulthood. In this chapter, we will focus on how three additional dimensions of diversity, namely ethnicity, undocumented immigrant status, and sexual orientation, are associated with the benchmarks of adulthood.

Ethnicity

While *race* and *ethnicity* are often used interchangeably in the United States, social scientists draw distinctions between the two terms. Many people might think of race as having a biological basis but most social scientists consider race to be a social construction, since racial categories change according to societal and historical contexts. Ethnicity, on the other hand, is described by John Iceland as referring to "a group of people who are differentiated by *culture* rather than by perceived physical or genetic differences central to notions of race."[1] The US government, for example, considers Hispanic to be an ethnicity, not a racial group, but considers White, Black, and Asian to be racial groups. If you have ever filled out a decennial US Census form, you may recall that separate questions ask whether you identify as Hispanic and how you identify racially. Thus, when we referred to "race and ethnicity" in previous chapters, we were in part acknowledging this distinction.

Within the broad categories of race and ethnicity we have used so far, we can conceive of further distinctions by ethnicity and national origin for White (e.g., Irish, Ukrainian, Lebanese), Black (e.g., Haitian, Nigerian, Barbadian), Hispanic (e.g., Mexican, Guatemalan, Colombian), and Asian (e.g., Filipino, Korean, Malaysian) young people. While in previous chapters we showed the shares of young adults who achieved each milestone for four different racial and ethnic groups (White, Black, Hispanic, and Asian), below we will compare different Hispanic and Asian ethnic groups in their completion of each adulthood milestone. As we will discover in this chapter, there can be significant diversity in outcomes related to the transition to adulthood within groups that are often viewed as sharing the same race and cultural beliefs.

Undocumented Young Adults

In previous chapters, we found that native-born/immigrant differences tended to vary by race and ethnicity. However, there is one important structural feature that sets apart a specific population of immigrants, regardless of their racial and ethnic background: a lack of legal status as permanent residents or citizens. For such undocumented young people, disadvantages compared to their native-born peers and to immigrant peers who are documented are numerous. However, research also finds extraordinary resilience among undocumented young people, many of whom remain committed to fulfilling their educational and professional dreams despite significant legal obstacles. Information on undocumented status is sensitive and difficult to collect. Much of our knowledge of this population comes from indirect measures in large data sources, such as immigration and school enrollment records, and through interview studies with smaller and more localized samples. Like many other large-scale data sources, the American Community Survey (ACS), does not have information on the legal status of immigrants, so in this chapter we instead review some of the sociological literature on how undocumented young people experience the transition to adulthood. In particular, we will emphasize the importance of local, state, and federal policies in affecting their well-being.

Sexual Minorities

Young adults today are also coming of age during a period that has witnessed profound changes in public perceptions of and policies toward sexual minorities, to say nothing of evolving gender labels and identities. These topics are deeply relevant for young people, yet there is comparatively little research on the transition to adulthood among sexual minorities. Moreover, the study of events such as marriage and parenthood—which are traditionally considered important milestones in the transition to adulthood (including in this book)—is often defined by heteronormative or biological frameworks, such as measuring only different-sex marriages or measuring parenthood by births to women. These approaches sometimes reflect societal norms but are also a result of data limitations. Yet with the legalization of same-sex marriage in the United States and the rise in alternative means of becoming a parent (e.g., adoption, surrogacy), it is increasingly clear that research must develop broader definitions and measurements of family-formation milestones. A growing share of young adults identify in ways that mark them as sexual minorities, including lesbian, gay, bisexual, transsexual, and queer (LGBTQ) young people as well as those whose gender identities do not conform to the traditional male/female gender binary. However, the ACS lacks data on the gender and sexual identities of individuals. To better highlight how sexual minorities contribute to the diversity of experiences in the transition to adulthood today, we review some of the scholarly literature on young people's sexual identities and how such identities impact their transitions to adulthood.

ETHNIC DIVERSITY AND THE TRANSITION TO ADULTHOOD

It would be difficult to provide a full portrait of the transition to adulthood for each of the numerous ethnic groups identifiable in the ACS. For

Hispanic and Asian respondents, the ACS allows them to choose their ethnic subgroup(s) from either a set of choices listed or to write in their own ethnic identity. Respondents who identify as only White or only Black/African American can also write in their ethnic identity. Even focusing just on ethnic diversity among Hispanics and Asians is a daunting task, with over twenty Hispanic subgroups and nearly thirty Asian subgroups one could choose from in the ACS data. We have chosen to focus on the five largest Hispanic-origin (Mexican, Puerto Rican, Cuban, Salvadoran, and Dominican) and five largest Asian-origin (Chinese, Filipino, Asian Indian, Vietnamese, and Korean) subgroups in the United States. For these ten ethnic subgroups, we consider only young people born in the United States, who make up the majority of our sample. We do this because there are relatively small numbers of immigrant young people in our sample (since we only include 1.5- and 1.75-generation immigrant young people). Disaggregating them by ethnic groups and gender would lead to small samples and thus yield unreliable estimates.

Hispanic Ethnic Groups

Figure 17 shows, by gender, the share of native-born young adults from the five largest Hispanic subgroups in the United States (Mexican, Puerto Rican, Cuban, Salvadoran, and Dominican) who have reached each of the adulthood milestones we have focused on throughout this book: completion of a bachelor's degree, full-time employment, living independently, currently married, and living with a child of their own. However, following the logic of chapter 3, we show the share living with a child of their own only for young women (i.e., motherhood). We also only include young people who are not currently enrolled in school, consistent with previous chapters. Our presentation highlights how the experiences of young adults from the other four Hispanic subgroups compare to Mexican Americans. One reason for this is that Mexican Americans comprise the single largest Hispanic-origin group in the United States. Among the Hispanic young people ages twenty-five to thirty-four in our sample, nearly two in three identify as Mexican in origin. A second reason is that in the United States, Mexican Americans are often used to represent the larger and more diverse Hispanic population in public and political conversations and

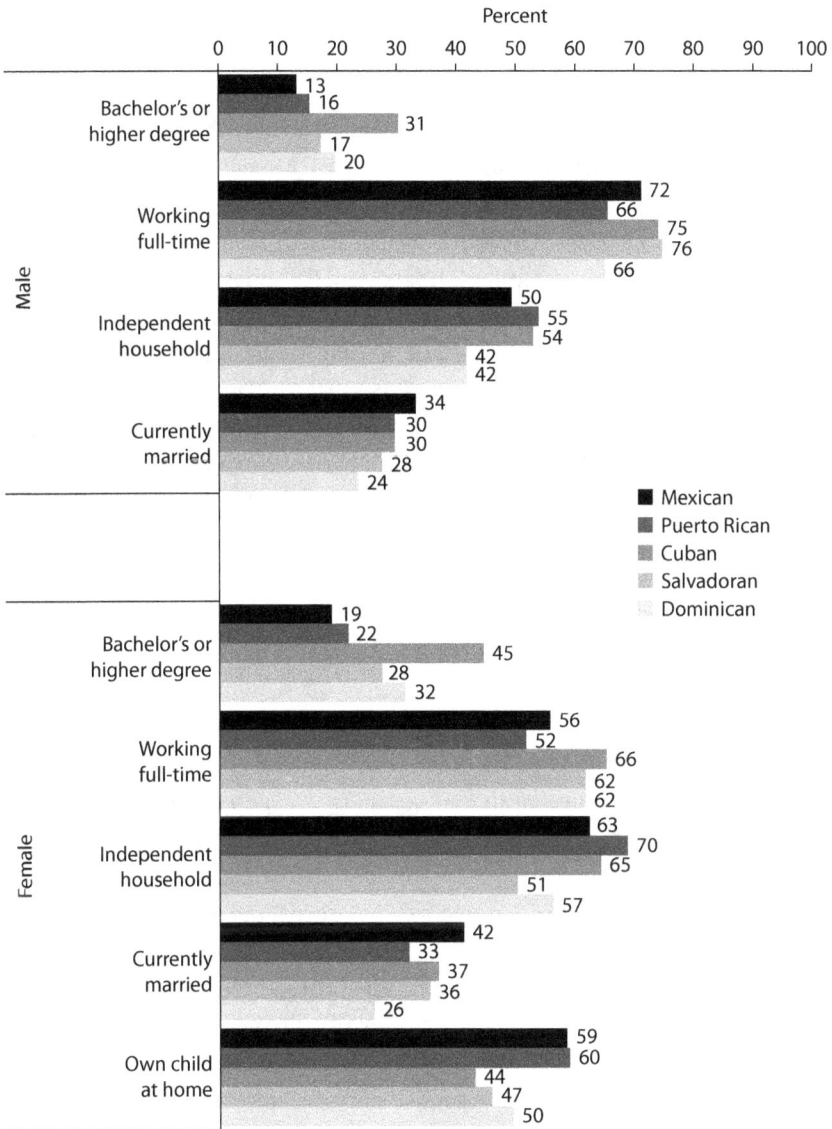

Figure 17. Percentage of native-born young adults (ages twenty-five to thirty-four) reaching milestones, selected Hispanic ethnic groups, by gender.

SOURCE: US Census 2017, Five-Year Estimates; Ruggles et al. 2021.

debates. In choosing Mexican-origin young adults as a reference group, we can better understand how a large share of the native-born Hispanic young adult population in the United States is faring, while also noting important ethnic differences in the transition to adulthood.

As shown in figure 17, smaller shares of Mexican American young adults have attained at least a bachelor's degree compared to their non-Mexican Hispanic peers. The gap is especially apparent between Mexican- and Cuban-origin young adults. The share of Cuban American young men and women with at least a bachelor's degree (31 percent and 45 percent, respectively) is more than double that of their Mexican American counterparts (13 percent and 19 percent, respectively). Young adults of Puerto Rican, Salvadoran, and Dominican origins also maintain an educational advantage over their Mexican American peers, though not to the extent of Cuban American young adults. These ethnic patterns are very similar among both Hispanic men and women, and we again see that young women across the selected Hispanic subgroups are more likely than their male peers to have completed at least a bachelor's degree.

Although Mexican-origin young men in the United States have lower rates of bachelor's degree attainment, they have higher rates of full-time employment compared to some of their peers from more educationally advantaged groups. Nearly 74 percent of Mexican American young men are employed full-time compared to about 67 percent of their Puerto Rican and Dominican American peers. Young adults of Cuban and Salvadoran origins, however, have higher rates of full-time employment than their Mexican American peers (75 percent and 76 percent, respectively). Mexican American young women, on the other hand, outpace only their Puerto Rican peers in terms of full-time employment (56 percent versus 52 percent) and have lower rates of full-time employment compared to their Cuban, Salvadoran, and Dominican American counterparts. Consistent with broader gender patterns we covered in chapter 2, Hispanic young women's higher rates of bachelor's degree attainment across ethnic groups relative to their male peers do not result in higher rates of full-time employment. Only between Dominican American young men and women are gender differences in full-time employment relatively minimal and not statistically significant (66 percent versus 62 percent), due in part to the comparatively lower rates of full-time employment among Dominican American men.

The share of Hispanic young adults who have established independent households also varies across ethnic groups. Half of Mexican American young men live in independent households compared to only about 40 percent of their Salvadoran American and Dominican American peers. However, more than half of Puerto Rican and Cuban American young men are in independent households. These ethnic patterns also persist among Hispanic young women, with Salvadoran American and Dominican American young women behind their Mexican American peers in the shares who live in independent households (51 percent, 57 percent, and 63 percent, respectively) and Cuban American women ahead (70 percent). Across each of the ethnic groups, young women live in their own households at a greater rate than their respective male counterparts. The gender gap in the share of Hispanic young people who are in independent households is especially apparent among Puerto Rican and Dominican American young people. For example, about 70 percent of Puerto Rican women are in independent households compared to about 50 percent of Puerto Rican men.

A significantly greater proportion of Mexican American young adults are currently married compared to their peers from other Hispanic groups. About 34 percent of Mexican American young men are married compared to 30 percent of both Puerto Rican and Cuban American young men, 28 percent of Salvadoran American young men, and 24 percent of Dominican American young men. Approximately 42 percent of Mexican American women are currently married, a larger share than the 26 percent of Dominican American, 33 percent of Puerto Rican, 37 percent of Cuban American, and 36 percent of Salvadoran American women.

Figure 17 shows the share of young women who are living with a child of their own (recall from chapter 3 that data for men living with children of their own are likely to be underestimates). Once again, ethnic differences are apparent. While more than half of Mexican American and Puerto Rican young women reside with a child of their own, only about half or less than half of young women of Dominican, Cuban, and Salvadoran origins do so.

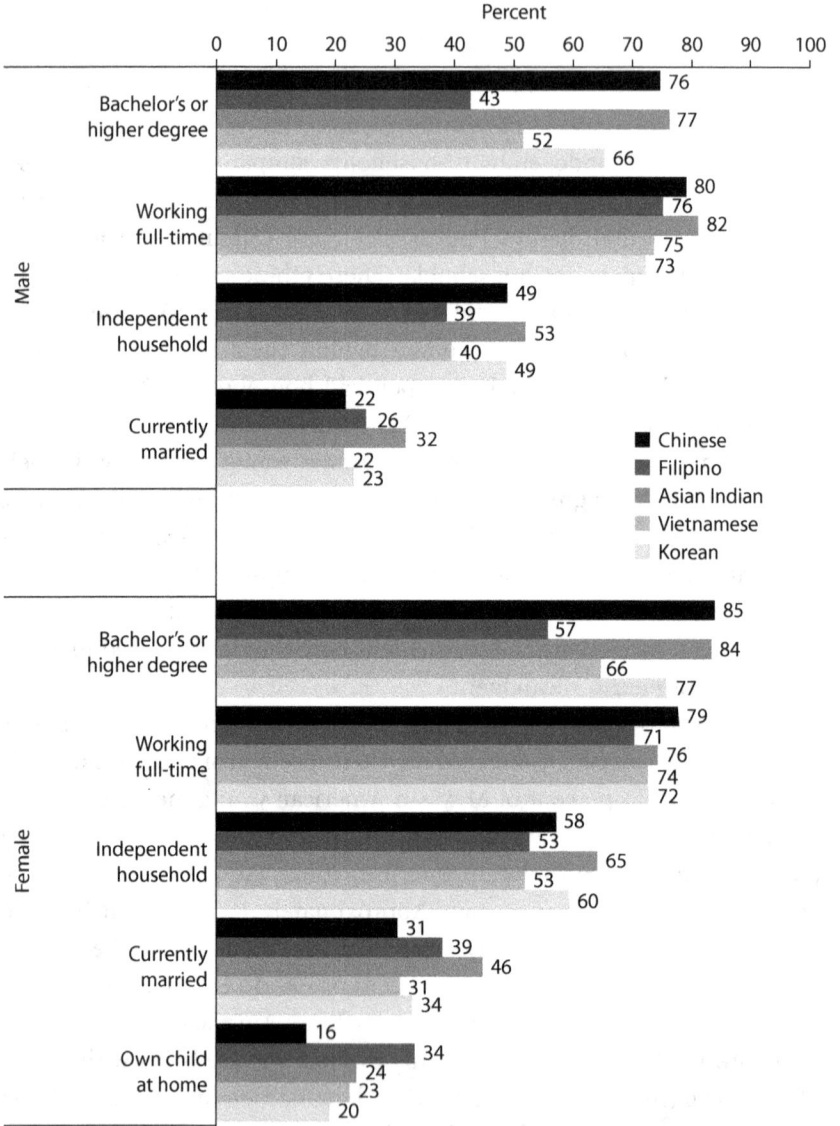

Figure 18. Percentage of native-born young adults (ages twenty-five to thirty-four) reaching milestones, selected Asian ethnic groups, by gender.

SOURCE: US Census 2017, Five-Year Estimates; Ruggles et al. 2021.

Asian Ethnic Groups

In figure 18 we show the share of young adults from the five largest Asian ethnic groups in the United States (Chinese, Filipino, Asian Indian, Vietnamese, and Korean) who have reached the five milestones traditionally associated with adulthood (although parenthood is shown only for young women). For figure 18, Chinese Americans, who are the largest single Asian ethnic group in the United States, serve as the reference group to which other Asian ethnic groups are compared. However, unlike Mexican Americans, who comprise a majority of Hispanic young adults in our sample, Chinese Americans make up less than a quarter of Asian young adults in our sample. In other words, there is no single Asian ethnic group whose experiences drive the average experiences of Asian Americans. Nevertheless, given the relative size of the Chinese American population and their long history in and continued migration to the United States, their experiences can provide a useful point of comparison to other Asian ethnic groups.

In chapter 2, we saw that native-born Asian young adults have the highest rates of bachelor's degree attainment among their peers. However, figure 18 reveals that the Asian category masks significant ethnic variation in educational attainment. While the vast majority of Chinese American and Indian American young adults have completed at least a bachelor's degree, rates of bachelor's degree completion among their Filipino American, Vietnamese American, and Korean American peers are significantly lower. For example, among young men, more than 75 percent of Chinese Americans have attained at least a bachelor's degree compared to less than 50 percent of Filipino Americans. Among young women, 85 percent of Chinese Americans have at least a bachelor's degree compared to 66 percent of Vietnamese Americans.

Ethnic variations among Asian American young adults in rates of full-time employment are somewhat similar to patterns of educational attainment, but the differences are modest. Seventy-six percent or less of Filipino American, Vietnamese American, and Korean American young men are working full-time compared to 80 percent of Chinese American young men. Only Indian American young men have rates of full-time employment that are comparable to Chinese Americans (82 percent).

Differences among Asian American young women closely resemble those among their male counterparts. Chinese American young women have the highest rates of full-time employment, with nearly 80 percent working full-time, compared to less than 75 percent of Filipino American, Vietnamese American, and Korean American young women. Indian American young women also have lower rates of full-time employment (76 percent) compared to their Chinese American peers. Gender differences in full-time employment among Asian American young adults also vary by ethnicity: among Chinese Americans, Vietnamese Americans, and Korean Americans, young women work full-time at rates comparable to those of their male peers while Filipino American and Indian American young women have lower rates of full-time employment compared to their male peers.

Asian American young adults also exhibit ethnic variation in the share who have established independent households. Close to 50 percent of Chinese American and Korean American young men live in independent households as do more than 50 percent of Indian American young men. In contrast, just 39 percent of Filipino American young men and 40 percent of Vietnamese American young men live independently. Close to or more than 60 percent of Chinese American, Korean American, and Indian American young women live in independent households. In comparison, just over 50 percent of Filipino American and Vietnamese American young women have established their own households.

As we saw in chapter 3, the share of Asian American young adults who are currently married ranks among the lowest across racial groups. This is also reflected in the low rates of marriage across Asian ethnic groups shown in figure 18. Yet ethnic variation remains visible. Slightly more than 20 percent of Chinese American, Vietnamese American, and Korean American young men are currently married, compared to 24 percent of Filipino American young men and 33 percent of Indian American young men. Vietnamese American and Korean American young women are more similar to their Chinese American peers—among each of these groups, only between 31 percent and 34 percent are currently married. Filipino American young women are more likely than their Chinese American peers to be married (39 percent) as are Indian American young women (46 percent).

Like marriage rates, the share of Asian American young women who live with a child of their own varies significantly by ethnicity. Only about 16 percent of Chinese American young women reside with a child of their own compared to 20 percent of Korean American young women, 23 percent of Vietnamese American young women, 24 percent of Indian American young women, and 34 percent of Filipino American young women. In fact, the share of Filipino American young women living with children of their own is more than double that of their Chinese American peers.

Understanding Ethnic Variation

Among Hispanic ethnic groups, Mexican Americans stand out from their peers in their relatively lower rates of bachelor's degree completion and in their higher rates of marriage and parenthood. Cuban Americans, on the other hand, are distinct in their higher rates of bachelor's degree completion, full-time employment, residential independence, and lower rates of marriage and parenthood compared to Mexican Americans. Among Asian ethnic groups, Chinese Americans differ from almost all other groups in their larger shares of bachelor's degree holders and full-time workers as well as their smaller shares of young people who are married or live with children of their own. In contrast, Filipino Americans generally have lower rates of bachelor's degree completion, full-time employment, and residential independence but higher rates of marriage and parenthood. Indian Americans are roughly similar to Chinese Americans in educational attainment, but outpace them in terms of marriage and parenthood. As these examples show, there is significant ethnic variation in the share of young people reaching various adulthood milestones, even among groups typically considered part of the same racial or pan-ethnic groups.

How do we account for these ethnic differences? One area in which there is significant overlap between the experiences of Hispanics and Asians in the United States is the share who have more recent immigrant origins. Many of the young people of Hispanic and Asian origins in our sample are descended from the post-1965 wave of immigrants we discussed in chapter 1. Even though we are focusing on native-born Hispanic and Asian young adults in this chapter, many of them have immigrant parents and are thus affected by the contexts under which their families or larger co-ethnic communities migrated. Below, we describe theories of immigrant assimilation that are relevant for understanding the transition to adulthood for young people from different Hispanic and Asian ethnic groups.

The contexts under which various ethnic groups migrate to the United States affects their socioeconomic status outcomes. Work by sociologist Cynthia Feliciano shows that all immigrant groups from top-sending countries are positively selected on education—that is, they tend to have more education than non-migrants from their home countries (see chapter 1)—but the degree of selectivity varies considerably across groups. Among Hispanic groups, Dominicans and Cubans are more positively selected on education than immigrants from El Salvador and Mexico as well as individuals from Puerto Rico (Puerto Ricans are US citizens by birth). Immigrants from India and China are more positively selected than immigrants from the Philippines, Vietnam, and Korea.[2] The level of selectivity present among different immigrant groups is important for understanding the variation in resources of immigrant families. In a study of second-generation immigrant children and their families, sociologists Alejandro Portes and Rubén Rumbaut find variation by country of origin in the level of English fluency among immigrant parents. Cuban parents' English fluency outranked those of Dominican, Mexican, and Salvadoran parents. Indian parents' English fluency ranked the highest among immigrant parents from Asia. Immigrant parents' English fluency matters for communicating with their second-generation children, many of whom do not retain fluency in their parents' native languages. Parents' English skills also affect their ability to successfully navigate mainstream institutions such as schools on behalf of their children.[3] These ethnic differences in human capital among the immigrant parent generation likely play a significant role in shaping educational outcomes among the second generation.[4]

Variations in the socioeconomic status of different ethnic groups also have implications for other adulthood milestones beyond educational attainment. In a study of how immigration impacts the transition to adulthood, Rubén Rumbaut and Golnaz Komaie emphasize how expectations that grown children will "give back" to their families are common among young people from immigrant families, a finding echoed in other research (recall in chapter 1 our discussion of the "immigrant bargain").[5] "Giving back" might entail financial assistance to parents and/or younger siblings, which could delay young people's departure from the parental home. However, the need to provide such financial assistance is likely to vary by the socioeconomic status of the family. Young people from families with fewer economic resources might be compelled to forgo postsecondary education in favor of entering the labor market early in order to help provide financial support to their families.[6] In other research, two of the coauthors of this book find that both family socioeconomic status and the level of importance attached to living close to family are related to differences in residential independence for young adults among Asian ethnic groups. Young adults from East Asian groups tended to differ from their Southeast Asian and South Asian peers on two factors positively associated with attaining residential independence in young adulthood: (1) their families were on average more socioeconomically advantaged and (2) they placed relatively lower importance on living close to family as adolescents. The study also found limited evidence that suggests similar ethnic variations among Hispanic young adults in the roles of socioeconomic status and cultural factors in explaining rates of residential independence.[7]

Hispanic Americans and Asian Americans from different ethnic groups might also vary in their experiences of racialization. Sociologist Eduardo Bonilla-Silva, for example, has argued that some ethnic groups with origins in Mexico, Puerto Rico, and the Dominican Republic are predominantly comprised of "dark-skinned" people and are more likely to fall into a disadvantaged "collective Black" racial category in the United States. In contrast, groups with origins in Argentina, Chile, Costa Rica, Cuba, and other countries comprised primarily of "light-skinned" individuals are more likely to fit into a more advantaged "honorary White" racial category. Based on variations in socioeconomic indicators (e.g., income, occupation) as well as social indicators (e.g., out-marriage rates), Bonilla-Silva argues that some Southeast Asian groups such as Vietnamese Americans, Hmong Americans, and Laotian Americans are also likely to be absorbed into the "collective Black" category while other Asian ethnic groups such as Chinese Americans, Japanese Americans, Korean Americans, Filipino Americans, and Asian Indian Americans are more likely to become "honorary Whites."[8] Research by Robert Teranishi shows that although typically grouped together as Asian Americans, Chinese American and Filipino American high schoolers in California have different schooling experiences, with the former feeling that they are treated as "model minorities" and the latter feeling that they are treated as less academically capable.[9] Such research underscores the variations in experiences by ethnicity, even among groups categorized within the same racial or pan-ethnic category.

UNDOCUMENTED STATUS AND THE TRANSITION TO ADULTHOOD

Of the nearly twelve million undocumented immigrants estimated to be living in the United States, nearly half are children and young adults ages thirty-five and under.[10] The transition to adulthood for these undocumented young people is particularly challenging. As they move from adolescence into adulthood, they lose many of the protective benefits afforded to minors while simultaneously facing constraints in taking on adult roles. Even seemingly routine aspects of adolescence and young adulthood—obtaining a driver's license, getting a part-time job, and applying to college—become critical turning points for undocumented young people, some of whom are discovering their legal status for the first time. Alongside their transition to adulthood, undocumented young people "learn to be illegal," a process the sociologist Roberto Gonzales discovered often results in young people curtailing their plans and aspirations.[11] As Cory, an undocumented young man interviewed by Gonzales, poignantly states, "I'm stuck at 16, like a clock that has stopped ticking. My life has not changed at all since then. Although I'm 22, I feel like a kid. I can't do anything adults do."[12]

Undocumented young people have garnered considerable media and political attention through the Deferred Action for Childhood Arrivals Program (DACA) initiated under the Obama administration and the proposed Development, Relief, and Education for Alien Minors (DREAM) Act. These efforts aim to provide protections and opportunities for undocumented youth who complete educational requirements (defined as completion of high school or its equivalent).[13] As we have already seen, the level of education young adults attain is a key factor in their likelihood of reaching other milestones in the transition to adulthood. The stipulations of DACA and the DREAM Act make educational attainment an especially crucial aspect of the transition to adulthood for undocumented young people. However, due to the sensitive nature of collecting data on undocumented status, it is difficult for researchers to gain a full picture of how well undocumented young people fare in the transition to adulthood. Much of the research on undocumented young people relies on small samples of individuals willing to reveal their status.[14]

Some states have adopted policies allowing undocumented students to attend colleges and universities at in-state tuition rates. The implementation of these policies as well as the administrative records of students who fall under the policy have provided additional data on undocumented college students. Research by Stella Flores shows that when Texas began offering in-state tuition rates to undocumented students, the share of foreign-born Hispanic noncitizens enrolled in college in the state increased relative to states that did not have such a policy.[15] In other research with Catherine Horn, Flores found that Hispanic students at the highly selective University of Texas at Austin who benefitted from the in-state tuition bill persisted in their studies at rates similar to those for their Hispanic citizen and documented peers.[16] In a study of undocumented students attending City University of New York (CUNY), one of the largest public university systems in the United States, Amy Hsin and Holly Reed found that college-going undocumented students are "hyper-selected"—meaning they tend to enter college more academically prepared and have higher college GPAs and graduation rates than their documented peers.[17] These studies show that undocumented young people succeed in higher education when afforded the same opportunities to enroll as those who are documented.

Unfortunately, research has also shown that some undocumented young people, even those with college plans, eventually drop out of high school or give up their pursuit of college. Some do so as a result of academic challenges that arise from fear and anxiety, others because of limited access to financial aid, and still others after witnessing undocumented relatives confront limited opportunities.[18] In a study of California community college attendees, sociologist Veronica Terriquez found that undocumented students are more likely to "stop out" (withdraw from school for a period of time while intending to re-enroll). Undocumented students were more likely than their documented and citizen peers to cite financial challenges, such as the need to contribute to family finances and inflexible work schedules that interfere with classes, as reasons for stopping out of college.[19] Undocumented students may even be restricted from attendance. As Diana, an undocumented community college student interviewed by sociologist Alexis Silver, describes: "They told me that I couldn't study there anymore because I didn't have a Social Security number or a green card. And after, I cried because all of my dreams and everything, they just disappeared."[20] On the whole, research findings consistently show that undocumented young people face significant challenges when pursuing higher education.

In chapter 2, we saw how educational attainment shapes the labor market experiences of young adults. For undocumented young people, even a college degree is no guarantee of a stable economic future because their legal status often prevents them from obtaining well-paid, secure jobs. Many end up working in the informal economy at jobs similar to those of older undocumented adults with less education.[21] Undocumented young adults who find themselves in such positions are often left feeling hopeless. In one study, Margarita, an undocumented young woman who cleans homes for a living, voices her disappointment over the jobs available to her:

> I graduated from high school and have taken some college credits. Neither of my parents made it past fourth grade, and they don't speak any English. But I'm right where they are. I mean, I work with my mom. I have the same job. I can't find anything else . . . . Why did I even go to school? It should mean something.[22]

Esperanza, another undocumented young adult in the study, graduated from college and aspired to become a journalist but was only able to find employment in restaurants and factories. Esperanza described feeling out of place for having to work at the same jobs as teenagers and older workers with less education and limited English skills.

The limited educational and occupational opportunities available to many undocumented young adults mean they are more likely to face challenges in establishing independent households. Relatively little research has focused on the household arrangements of undocumented young adults. Research that focuses on undocumented adults more broadly, however, hints at experiences that differ from both documented immigrants and native-born individuals. Based on an indirect measure of undocumented status from the Census Bureau's Survey of Income and Program Participation (SIPP), researchers found that undocumented Mexican and Central American immigrant adults are less likely to be living with their parents compared to their documented and native-born peers. However, they are more likely to live with extended family members, such as cousins. In addition to more complex household compositions, undocumented Mexican and Central American immigrants also experience less stability in their households in terms of size and members, compared to their documented and native-born peers. The household instability of these immigrants has potential deleterious consequences for their health and wellbeing.[23]

Like their peers, undocumented young people think of young adulthood as a time to explore and develop personal relationships. However, their undocumented status makes romantic relationships challenging. In a personal essay revealing his undocumented status, journalist and activist Jose Antonio Vargas confessed, "I have been unwilling, for years, to be in a long-term relationship because I never wanted anyone to get too close and ask too many questions."[24] This experience is likely shared by many undocumented individuals.[25] Experiences with dating are also affected by gendered expectations and norms. Undocumented young men, for example, have more freedom in setting the terms of dating activities and can avoid settings that might raise questions about their status. As Cruz, an undocumented young man, explained to sociologist Laura Enriquez, "Let's say some girl wanted to go somewhere . . . I'll just convince them . . . [to go where] I know I can go."[26] Yet undocumented young men are also bound by gendered norms that they be able to drive and to pay for meals and activities, even though their limited access to driver's licenses and job opportunities means they are sometimes unable to fulfill such expectations. As a result, they are more likely to struggle with fulfilling the traditional breadwinner role and thus more likely to delay milestones such as marriage and parenthood.[27] Undocumented women, on the other hand, may feel less pressure than men to contribute financially to relationships and are less likely to delay such milestones.[28] However, their reliance on their partners and the sense that they are a "burden" can create tensions in relationships that lead to breakups.[29]

The challenges associated with studying the undocumented population mean we know less about how they experience the transition to adulthood than we do about the experiences of their native-born and documented counterparts. The majority of research on undocumented young adults has focused on Hispanics, and much less is known about how undocumented young people from other racial and ethnic groups fare. For example, in 2015, five of the top ten countries of origin among undocumented immigrants were in Asia (India, Philippines, China, Korea, and Vietnam), yet considerably less research has examined undocumented Asian youth.[30] There is some comparative work on undocumented Hispanic and Asian young people, however, that reveals the continued salience of race and ethnicity in determining their life chances. Research comparing the labor market experiences of college-educated undocumented Mexican and Korean young adults demonstrates how larger structural forces such as ethnic labor markets are highly relevant for employment opportunities. Undocumented Korean young adults benefit from the availability of better-paying jobs in primary labor market businesses owned by other Koreans, such as tutoring centers and law firms, compared to similarly educated undocumented Mexican young adults, who often find themselves in lower-paying jobs in the restaurant and construction sectors.[31]

The focus on undocumented immigration from Latin America also means there is less outreach to undocumented Asian immigrant populations. Just two years after DACA was first implemented, government officials were already aware of the lower uptake among undocumented Asian immigrants. They sought to address this problem by translating DACA materials into various Asian languages and securing assistance from nongovernmental service providers.[32] In 2015, three years after DACA was implemented, the Migration Policy Institute estimated that only about two in ten eligible undocumented young people from Asia had applied for DACA compared to nearly eight in ten eligible applicants from Latin America.[33] Unlike the Spanish language shared by the majority of immigrant groups from Latin America, the diversity of languages spoken across Asian immigrant groups makes outreach and community-building more difficult.[34] Writing on the passage of a California bill in 2013 that allowed undocumented immigrants access to driver's licenses, researchers surmised that undocumented immigrants from Latin America were best poised to take advantage of the new law. The longer history and larger size of the population of immigrants from Latin America in the state meant there were more organizations that could advocate for them and provide outreach, while undocumented immigrants from other regions, such as Asia and Africa, had fewer such community resources.[35]

Undocumented young adults have also played a significant role in movements for immigrant rights, often drawing on their experiences as activists in other issues. Researchers have, for example, drawn parallels between narratives of "coming out" as LGBTQ (lesbian, gay, bisexual, transgender, and queer/questioning) and "coming out" as undocumented.[36] In one study, Veronica Terriquez surveyed and interviewed undocumented youth activists (also known as DREAMers) in California, finding that nearly 13 percent of those surveyed identified as sexual minorities. For "undocuqueer" (undocumented and queer) activists, the act of "coming out" in multiple ways can heighten their commitment to creating more inclusive social movements.[37] Another interview study of undocumented Asian young people found that South Asian Muslim youth were able to use their activism against racial profiling and surveillance post-9/11 to inform their activism for immigrant rights more broadly.[38]

As with other marginalized groups, how undocumented young adults fare in the transition to adulthood depends heavily on federal, state, and local policies. Without a clear pathway to citizenship for undocumented young people, their fates are often determined by the changing winds of electoral politics. At the federal level, the Trump Administration sought to end the DACA program in 2017. The Biden Administration has worked via executive action, to "preserve and fortify" DACA, which may provide some relief for undocumented young people.[39] Yet DACA is itself a temporary solution that does not provide a pathway to citizenship. Moreover, it does not permanently resolve the legal uncertainties for undocumented young people in their everyday lives.[40] The recurring legal battles over DACA only serve to underscore the precarious position of undocumented young people in the United States.

The painful impact of policy changes on the lives of undocumented young people is keenly felt in the story of the Miralrio brothers, featured in a *New York Times* article. As children, Jack and Owen were brought by their mother from Mexico to the United States. Jack, the twenty-year-old elder brother and a DACA beneficiary studying to become a mechanical engineer, was able to get a work permit, a driver's license, and financial aid for college. Owen, the younger seventeen-year-old brother, was preparing to apply for DACA when the Trump administration rescinded the program. Unable to apply for the same benefits as his brother, Owen moved out of the college-prep track he had been on in high school and was resigned to becoming a mechanic, saying, "I don't see a reason to get my hopes up."[41] Perhaps the Biden Administration's support for DACA will allow Owen to fulfill his college aspirations.

SEXUAL ORIENTATION AND THE TRANSITION TO ADULTHOOD

The role of sexual orientation in the transition to adulthood, in particular the experiences of sexual minorities, such as lesbian, gay, bisexual, transgender, and queer/questioning (LGBTQ) youth, is relatively understudied. Large-scale data collection efforts have not kept pace with evolving gender identities and labels. Thus, it is difficult for researchers to examine, on a national level, how the transition to adulthood might vary by a more expansive array of gender and sexual identities. For example, it was only in 2019 that estimates of same-sex couples first became available in the Current Population Survey, a widely used source of data from the US Census Bureau.[42] Despite these data limitations, it is clear from existing research that sexual minority young adults face unique experiences and challenges as they navigate the transition to adulthood.

Much of the research on young people who are sexual minorities focuses on the negative consequences of their identities. One can more easily find studies that track rates of mental health issues or bullying among LGBTQ youth than studies that examine how such young people feel about their careers or navigate their first serious romantic relationship. While research on the challenges faced by sexual minority youth is certainly necessary for understanding those in especially vulnerable situations, this limited perspective risks casting all sexual minority young people as an at-risk population beyond the normative bounds of young adult experiences. In fact, understanding the broader experiences of sexual minority young people as they transition to adulthood helps illuminate the changing forms and definitions of adulthood today.

Collecting data on the sexual orientation of young people, particularly children and youth, is difficult not only because of the sensitive nature of the topic but also because young people's awareness of and willingness to disclose their sexual identities evolves over time. Hence, it is challenging to capture the experiences of sexual minority young people in schooling and the labor market. At least one study using nationally representative longitudinal data that tracked adolescents into young adulthood found that at ages twenty-four to thirty-four, just over 7 percent of the sample identified as sexual minorities ("bisexual," "mostly homosexual," or "100 percent homosexual"). Sexual minority young women were less likely than their heterosexual peers to complete college and were more likely to be unemployed and to experience economic hardships, including having utilities shut off or being evicted. Sexual minority young men were more likely to complete college than heterosexual young men but had lower incomes and were less likely to be homeowners. Taking into account differences in educational attainment actually widened the disparities between sexual minority and heterosexual young men, indicating that at any given level of education, sexual minority young men are more vulnerable to economic risks.[43]

One reason sexual minority youth are more likely to experience hardships as young adults may be due to a lack of family support. Parental support has been shown to be an important protective factor for LGBTQ youth, but parents' reactions to their children's sexual minority identities can range from full support to rejection of their children.[44] A study of high school students in Massachusetts found that about 25 percent of lesbian and gay adolescents experienced homelessness, compared to just 3 percent of their heterosexual peers. Moreover, compared to homeless youth who do not identify as sexual minorities, homeless sexual minority youths were less likely to be homeless and with their parents (i.e., family homelessness) than they were to be homeless *without* their parents. This suggests that sexual minority youths experience heightened likelihoods of running away from or being unwelcome in their family home.[45] Thus, at critical points in the transition to adulthood, sexual minority youths are more likely to lack the financial and emotional resources from their families necessary for a successful transition to adulthood.

There is a dearth of research on intimate relationships and family formation among young people who are sexual minorities.[46] Indeed, a recent comprehensive review of sociological research on sexual and romantic relationships in young adulthood concluded that "we still know little about the prevalence of same-sex relationships or trends in the relationship behavior of LGBT individuals."[47] The lack of research is especially surprising given how important sexual orientation is to understanding marriage and parenthood, two traditional adulthood milestones. Understanding marriage among sexual minorities is hampered by both a paucity of representative data as well as legal restrictions. The first state to legalize same-sex marriage in the United States was Vermont in 2009, and same-sex marriage was not legalized in all US states until a 2015 Supreme Court ruling. Prior to that, it was difficult for same-sex relationships to enjoy legal recognition or the rights and benefits that come with marriage.[48] In other words, until very recently, many sexual minority young people were restricted from attaining what is seen by many as a significant adulthood milestone.

The discovery and disclosure of complex and nontraditional sexual and gender identities can be important life events.[49] These experiences are not well understood within existing frameworks of the transition to adulthood. Research has shown that romantic relationships among sexual minority young people cannot be fully understood using typical frameworks for heterosexual relationships.[50] An interview study of young LGBT couples in the Midwest found that these couples shared many of the same interpersonal relationship processes as those found in the literature on heterosexual couples—for example, expressing hesitation about progressing into more serious relationships. However, the researchers also pointed out several meaningful differences for LGBT couples. Most of the interviewed couples initially met through LGBT social networks, which not only required them to be "out" to some extent but also sometimes constrained the contexts in which they might meet potential partners. Moreover, some reported family disapproval of their relationships, which sometimes led to moving out of their parents' home or cohabiting early in the relationship.[51] Much more could be learned about the social context of dating and the progression of "adult" relationships among sexual minority young people.

Another traditional milestone in the transition to adulthood—parenthood—must also be reassessed with the inclusion of experiences of sexual minority youth. Much of the research on the transition to adulthood has an implicitly biological view of parenthood. Recall, for example, how the data used in this book compelled us to focus on young women living with their own children as an imperfect measure of motherhood. Considering parenthood among sexual minority young people allows for a broader conception of contemporary parenthood. Recent estimates from the Census Bureau show that nearly two hundred thousand children live with same-sex parents.[52] Sociologists Mignon Moore and Michael Stambolis-Ruhstorfer identified four primary ways through which same-sex couples become parents: (1) by birth with a prior different-sex partner, (2) through adoption, (3) using assisted reproductive technology (e.g., in vitro fertilization, surrogacy), and (4) partnering with someone who has experienced any of the former. Each form of parenthood requires varying levels of resources and can result in different family dynamics that shape the experience of parenthood.[53] A survey conducted by Family Equality, a nonprofit organization focused on equality for LGBTQ families, showed that more than half of LGBTQ people planning to have children intended to use methods that entailed additional costs, navigating societal barriers (e.g., reluctance from foster and adoption agencies), and even legal risks (e.g., securing parental rights in cases of surrogacy or sperm donors). Despite this, more than 40 percent of LGBTQ young people making less than twenty-five thousand dollars a year planned to become parents, comparable to the share of LGBTQ young people making more than one hundred thousand dollars a year who planned to become parents.[54] As thirty-seven-year-old Jonathan explained to NBC, he and his husband Kerry were willing to commit to spending more than one hundred thousand dollars on hiring a surrogate even though they could not really afford to do so, because, as Jonathan says, "I knew I wanted to be a child's father. I really just wanted to go through and enjoy bringing up this wonderful child who is a part of our family."[55]

Sexual minority status also intersects with other aspects of young people's identities, including race and ethnicity. Attending to these intersections often provides additional insight into how minority statuses complicate the transition to adulthood among young people. One study of interracial friendships and romantic relationships in adolescence and young adulthood, for example, found that same-sex relationships among young people were generally more likely to be interracial than were different-sex relationships.[56] Young people in such relationships must grapple with societal prejudices on two fronts: as sexual minorities and as an interracial couple. A 2019 *Nightline* report documented the disproportionate amount of violence experienced by trans women of color, whose deaths went largely ignored by the broader public until activists in LGBTQ and racial justice movements brought attention to them.[57] We also previously described how undocumented immigrant status and sexual minority identities intersect to inform the activism of "undocuqueer" young people.[58]

A fuller view of the transition to adulthood should also consider the subjective criteria by which young people themselves gauge their "success" as adults and acknowledge that criteria are likely to vary by groups. In interviews and focus groups with young people aging out of access to an LGBTQ youth organization, for example, researchers asked respondents what "success" looked like for them and about what steps they were taking to successfully become adults. The LGBTQ respondents mentioned goals that are familiar to most young people—for example, developing "close relationships" or obtaining a "fulfilling job"—but that also included considerations specific to their identities as sexual minorities, such as living in a "queer-friendly space," finding a job that is "trans-friendly," and emphasizing resilience in the face of adversity.[59] In many ways, sexual minority youth are at the forefront of ideas about identity that can inform our understanding of the transition to adulthood. As a youth programs manager who identifies as a queer, nonbinary, transgender person confidently told the *New York Times* in a piece celebrating World Pride, "As we grow into our identities, we're finding new ways to talk about it because we're allowed to."[60]

SUMMARY AND CONCLUSION

Throughout this book, we have emphasized how the diverse demographics of today's young people are critical for understanding the transition to adulthood. While we have chosen five traditional markers (educational attainment, full-time employment, residential independence, marriage, and parenthood) by which to assess the transition to adulthood, we have also pointed out that such markers may no longer fully represent the myriad experiences of young people today nor how they think about adulthood. This is particularly true for the populations of young people covered in this chapter—ethnic minorities, the undocumented, and sexual minorities. Demographic profiles that cover race, nativity, and gender provide some context for their experiences but do not tell the entirety of these young people's stories.

Through research that pays specific attention to ethnic variation, we clearly see that differences between broad racial groups in reaching particular adulthood milestones cannot solely be attributed to simplistic cultural explanations. Significant variation among young people within racial and pan-ethnic groups exists. Research on undocumented young people reveals how legal status can play an outsized role in shaping transitions to adulthood—from constraining young people's ability to pursue higher education to limiting labor market and even romantic opportunities. Likewise, the experiences of sexual minority youth challenge conventional conceptions of and methods for measuring marriage and parenthood as adulthood milestones. Paying attention to the diversity of experiences among young people—especially among groups that are understudied or outside of mainstream conversations—is not just an academic exercise. Rather, their experiences are a growing part of what it means to be a young adult in the United States today. In the concluding chapter, we further reflect on what the increasing diversity of young people means today, and what it will mean in the future, for the transition to adulthood.

6 Envisioning the Transition to Adulthood Today and in the Future

We began this book by thinking about the typical narrative in coming-of-age stories. Most children imagine that once they are adults, they will have completed school (most likely college), obtained a full-time job, moved out of their parents' homes, gotten married, and perhaps had some children of their own. Certainly, these are common themes for the fictional and real-life young people we have described throughout this book. But in reality, and despite the norms surrounding the idea of adulthood, the routes by which individuals move from childhood to adulthood are not straightforward. A primary motivation for this book was to address the lack of systematic research on how racial and ethnic minority and immigrant young people experience the transition to adulthood. This is more important than ever as the United States becomes increasingly diverse along these lines.[1]

In chapter 1, Understanding the New Face of America: Racial and Ethnic Diversity and Immigration, we describe the growing racial and ethnic diversity of the United States, in large part due to relatively recent waves of immigration from Asia and Latin America. Such demographic changes provide an important context for this book and form the basis of our focus on racial, ethnic, and immigrant diversity in young people's pathways to adulthood. We also discuss pervasive racial and ethnic socio-economic inequalities in the United States and how such inequalities structure the educational opportunities of young people. For example, racial and ethnic minority students, especially Black and Hispanic students, are more likely to be in high-poverty schools. Likewise, immigrants arrive to the United States with very different levels of education. Due to the complex interaction of immigration policies, histories, and the context of sending countries, immigrant adults from Asia tend to arrive in the United States with higher and immigrant adults from Latin America with lower levels of human and social capital. These differences translate into differences in family-level and community-level resources as well as opportunities related to the educational outcomes of their children. This means that many young people begin the transition to adulthood with inequalities in opportunities based on their race, ethnicity, and nativity.

Our results suggest that racial and ethnic minority and immigrant young people's experiences differ from those of their White and native-born peers. However, one of the central findings of this book is that experiences in the transition to adulthood especially differ between those who are college-educated and those who are not; while there is substantial racial, ethnic, and immigrant diversity in these pathways to adulthood, these differences are less apparent among young people with bachelor's or higher degrees than among young people who did not complete college. Below, we revisit major patterns of milestone attainment we reviewed in previous chapters in light of these two overarching themes.

TRANSITIONING TO ADULTHOOD WITH OR WITHOUT A COLLEGE DEGREE

Sociologists sometimes think of educational attainment as a "great equalizer." While family background plays an important role in affecting one's educational attainment, for those who obtain a college degree, their own socioeconomic outcomes are no longer as strongly dictated by their family origins.[2] Similarly, we see a college degree as a "great equalizer" in terms of racial, ethnic, immigrant, and gender differences in the transition to adulthood. We see much stronger influences of race, ethnicity, nativity, and gender on the completion of adulthood markers among those without a college degree. The importance of a college education is uniformly felt by Ana, Malcolm, and Ellie, the respective protagonists of *Real Women Have Curves, Dope,* and *The Half of It,* the three contemporary coming-of-age movies we described at the outset of this book. Ana fights with her immigrant mother over her reluctance to work at her sister's clothing factory and her desire to attend college across the country. Malcolm sees an escape from his disadvantaged neighborhood to an Ivy League school, as he feels out of place with his peers at home. Ellie has to decide between attending a public university close to home, which would mean remaining in the hometown she finds stifling, or attending an out-of-state small liberal arts college and moving away from her widowed immigrant father. For Malcom, Ana, and Ellie, their ideals of adulthood all involve college. As we have seen throughout this book, a college degree does profoundly shape the transition to adulthood for young people.

However, as we described in chapter 2, Getting Ahead, Falling Behind: Education and Employment, there are clear racial and ethnic differences in educational attainment. Although the sequence across transition markers has become increasingly diversified and complicated, completing education is often the first milestone in the path to adulthood for the majority of young people and the time spent completing one's education for those who pursue a bachelor's degree or graduate education contributes to the delay in achieving other milestones. Among twenty-five-to-thirty-four-year-olds who are no longer enrolled in school, Asian and White young people have higher rates of bachelor's degree completion than their Black and Hispanic peers. White and Black immigrant young people are more likely than their native-born counterparts to have attained at least a bachelor's degree, while the opposite is the case among Hispanic and Asian young people. These patterns suggest that immigrant White and Black young adults occupy a more privileged position and immigrant Hispanic and Asian young adults a less privileged position relative to their native-born counterparts. Young women are also more likely than young men to have completed at least a bachelor's degree. Although it is beyond the scope of this book to fully address all the possible factors that account for such differences in young people's educational attainment, we highlight studies of how inequalities in early educational experiences contribute to their eventual educational attainment.

In chapter 2, we also examined labor market participation as a marker of adulthood, in relation to educational attainment. Full-time employment is much more prevalent among young people with bachelor's or higher degrees than for their peers with less education. Rates of full-time employment among young men with bachelor's or higher degrees are universally high—ranging from 85 to 90 percent across race, ethnicity, and nativity. Among young men with no college experience, rates of full-time employment are both lower and more varied, ranging from 41 to 76 percent. Given the shifting labor market towards greater demand for college-educated workers, those without a college degree may face more obstacles to finding full-time and stable employment. Although rates of full-time employment are generally lower among young women, patterns by educational attainment are similar to those seen among young men. Overall, having a bachelor's degree seems to diminish racial, ethnic, and immigrant differences with respect to full-time work.

Chapter 3, Settling In, Settling Down: Household and Family Formation, turned to adulthood milestones related to household independence and family formation. Delays in leaving the parental home and establishing an independent household have drawn considerable media and public attention. The growing shares of young adults who "boomerang" back to or "fail to launch" from the parental home stand in stark contrast to norms of residential independence that are culturally enshrined in American ideals of adulthood. Despite the overall increase in the share of young adults who live with their parents, we find significant variation by subgroups in the shares of young people who have established independent households. Once again, educational attainment is positively associated with residential independence. Anywhere from half to three-fourths of young men and women with bachelor's or higher degrees have established their own households compared to less than one-third to about two-thirds of young men and women with no college experience. However, the wide range in rates of residential independence even among similarly educated young people suggests that moving out of the parental home is a milestone that is dependent on factors beyond educational attainment.

Marriage is another adulthood milestone that appears to be increasingly delayed among young people. The majority of the young people in our sample, ages twenty-five to thirty-four, are not currently married. However, we find that those with bachelor's or higher degrees are generally more likely than those with no college experience to be married within this age range. The positive relationship between college education and marriage is consistent with other research showing the increased relevance of men and women's economic standing for their marital prospects.[3] However, there are exceptions to this pattern. Hispanic and Asian immigrant young men and women with no college experience are as or even more likely than their college-educated counterparts to be married. This finding suggests the importance of understanding how young people consider marriage. Young people may not be motivated to marry solely by economic considerations, and there may be racial, ethnic, and immigrant differences in the cultural meanings attached to marriage. It is possible that for some groups of young people, marriage is seen as a more attainable or important signifier of adulthood than a college education or full-time career.

The final milestone of adulthood covered in chapter 3 is parenthood. Due to data limitations, we focused our examination of this milestone on motherhood. For married and unmarried women, we are again reminded of the importance of educational attainment in affecting motherhood. Unmarried motherhood is more common among young women with less education and less common among women with more education. Motherhood is also more common among married women with no college experience than it is among married women with at least a bachelor's degree. In short, college-educated women seem more likely to delay, or perhaps even forgo, motherhood than women with no college experience. The earlier experiences with motherhood among women without a college education suggest that they may experience more economic instability. These differences also affect their children's well-being as differing levels of parental education are associated with corresponding levels of resources for children.[4]

In chapter 4, Mapping Pathways to Adulthood: Connecting Milestones, we bring all the milestones together and characterize some of the most common profiles of adulthood seen among young people today. Since the level of education young people attain affects the likelihood of reaching other adulthood milestones, we sought patterns of milestone attainment that could capture the experiences of young people at both ends of educational attainment, from young people with no college experience to those with bachelor's or higher degrees. We identify three profiles shared among young men and women, including All Milestones, No Milestones, and Working Childless Single profiles. For young men, we also find that a Working Childless Husband profile is relatively common. On the other hand, for young women parenthood is a much more prominent feature, and we identify a Single Mom profile as well as a Married Stay-at-Home Mom profile for women. Collectively, the handful of profiles we identify for young men and women capture the vast majority of patterns of milestones attainment for young people today.

By now, it should come as no surprise that the particular adulthood profiles of young people are strongly related to their educational attainment. For both young men and women with bachelor's or higher degrees, the most common profile of adulthood by far is the Working Childless Single profile. This is defined by full-time employment, being unmarried, and having no children. The All Milestones profile—distinguished from the Working Childless Single profile by the attainment of marriage and parenthood milestones—is also more common among young people with bachelor's or higher degrees. More than half to over two-thirds of college-educated young adults across race, ethnicity, nativity, and gender fit one of these two profiles. Some might delay or forgo family formation in favor of advancing in their careers while others have secured all the traditional markers of adulthood. In contrast, among young people with no college experience, there is no single profile that is prevalent across all groups. That is, unlike their college-educated peers who fall into common patterns of milestone attainment, young people with no college experience have much more varied patterns of milestone attainment. In addition, much larger shares of these young people have not completed any of these milestones. These twenty-five-to-thirty-four-year-olds have not obtained a bachelor's degree, do not work full-time, do not live independently, are not married, and do not live with a child of their own. Compared to their peers with more education and to commonly accepted expectations of adulthood, such young people experience a very challenging transition to adulthood, one that is likely headed toward socioeconomic precarity.

THE CONTINUED RELEVANCE OF RACE, ETHNICITY, AND NATIVITY

So far, we have primarily stressed the relevance of educational attainment for shaping the transition to adulthood. As stated earlier, racial, ethnic, and immigrant differences are more modest among young people with bachelor's degrees than among those with less education. Yet we should keep in mind that educational opportunities are not distributed equally in the United States. Recall that a much greater share of Asian and White young people have attained bachelor's or higher degrees compared to Black and Hispanic young people—a pattern of racial and ethnic inequalities that holds across nativity and gender (chapter 2). This means that even though the transition to adulthood tends to be a rockier experience for young people with no college education, smaller shares of White and Asian young people are affected by such challenges compared to their Black and Hispanic peers. Here, we highlight particular examples where the intersection of race, ethnicity, and nativity in the attainment of adulthood milestones prove illustrative for understanding variation in the futures of young people.

One of the reasons for focusing on race, ethnicity, and nativity in the transition to adulthood is that this transition has implications for the structure of racial and ethnic socioeconomic inequalities in the future. As we mentioned earlier, Hispanic immigrant young men with no college experience stand out from their similarly educated peers in their higher rates of full-time employment (more than three-fourths work full-time). In fact, among young men with no college experience, Hispanic immigrant young men have the highest prevalence of working full-time. On the one hand, this gives such young men a visible marker of adulthood. However, stereotypes that associate Hispanic groups with manual labor might serve to funnel Hispanic immigrant young people into the labor market instead of toward higher education.[5] Research also shows that immigrants are more likely than the native-born to be employed in dangerous occupations, where workplace injuries and fatalities are more common, in part because of their lower levels of educational attainment.[6] Immigrant Hispanic young men with no college experience may have an advantage over their peers in terms of working full-time, but without a college education, they may be headed towards less lucrative and more dangerous jobs.

Attaining residential independence is another adulthood milestone where we observe differences by our subgroups of interest. Hispanic and Asian immigrant young people are typically more likely to have established their own households relative to their native-born peers. At first, this may seem to run counter to notions of collectivism and familism that many believe are innate to Hispanic and Asian cultures. That is, if Hispanic and Asian groups are culturally predisposed to maintaining strong family bonds, why are immigrant Hispanic and Asian young people more likely to have established their own households? One explanation is that immigrant Asian and Hispanic young people are also much more likely to be married than their native-born counterparts and, among women, more likely to be mothers. Having formed their own families may make such young people more likely to establish their own households. Although we cannot test this explanation with our data, it is also possible that immigrant Asian and Hispanic young people at the lower end of educational attainment come from families where their parents are simply unable to support them for extended periods of time. Thus, these young people may have to find their own way at an earlier age than their native-born peers. Another possibility is that these young people actually take responsibility as the head of households that include their parents or other relatives, such as younger siblings. Prior research suggests that this sharing of financial responsibilities is sometimes expected in immigrant-origin households.[7] Patterns of adulthood milestone attainment that offer multiple explanations push us to rethink the connections between *structure* and *culture* (see chapter 1) in accounting for racial, ethnic, and immigrant differences in attitudes and behaviors.

As our final example of how race, ethnicity, and nativity intersect in ways that profoundly shape how young people experience the transition to adulthood, we turn to the share of immigrant Hispanic and Asian young people without college degrees who fit more "traditional" profiles of adulthood. By traditional, we mean their patterns of milestones attainment are less typical of more recent trends, such as an increasing amount of time spent in education and a delay in family formation. Rather, these young people take on adult roles as workers (for young men) and as spouses and parents (for young men and women) at an earlier age than most of their peers. This is evident in the greater share of immigrant Hispanic and Asian young men who fit the All Milestones profile and the greater share of immigrant Hispanic and Asian young women who fit the Stay-at-Home Mom profile compared to their native-born co-ethnics.

Remember that the immigrant young people in our sample arrived in the United States by age thirteen or younger, meaning they would have largely been socialized in the United States. Yet, their paths to adulthood are not identical to those of their native-born co-ethnics. This brings to mind questions around the meaning and desirability of particular milestones for different groups of young people and the origins of such attitudes. Are immigrant-origin young people receiving different cultural messages about adulthood from their families and peers? In constructing their ideals of adulthood, do they compare themselves to their native-born peers or to young people from their countries of origin? We are also reminded that assimilation is not a one-way street—even as immigrants come to adopt some American customs and norms, so too do their unique experiences contribute to the makeup of the American mainstream.[8] New cultural meanings of adulthood seem likely to emerge, especially as native-born and immigrant individuals intermarry across racial, ethnic, and immigrant generational lines in increasing numbers.[9]

We also examine other types of diversity closely related to race, ethnicity, nativity, and gender. Chapter 5, Exploring a Mosaic of Experiences: Ethnicity, Immigrant Status, and Sexual Orientation, focuses on the relevance of ethnicity, undocumented immigrant status, and sexual orientation for understanding the transition to adulthood. These forms of diversity challenge many of our traditional conceptions of young adults' experiences. Most previous work has overlooked racial differences and rarely considers the possibility of ethnic variation within racial groups. In chapter 5, we reveal significant ethnic variation in the attainment of adulthood milestones. This can be seen in the widely varying rates of educational attainment across Hispanic and Asian ethnic groups. For example, only about one in ten Mexican Americans have attained at least a bachelor's degree compared to about three in ten Cuban Americans. Likewise, nearly eight in ten Chinese Americans have attained at least a bachelor's degree compared to about four in ten Filipino Americans. In other words,

Hispanic groups are not universally disadvantaged nor are Asian groups universally advantaged. We also show that in ethnic subgroup comparisons, the association between educational attainment and other adulthood milestones remains consistent with the broader patterns seen in previous chapters. Hispanic and Asian subgroups that have higher rates of bachelor's degree attainment tend to be the most likely to work full-time and are also more likely to delay or forgo marriage and parenthood.

We also highlight the relevance of public policies for the transition to adulthood through the experiences of undocumented immigrant and sexual minority young people. The lack of legal status for undocumented youth is often an insurmountable barrier to college completion, stable employment, and even serious romantic relationships. For LGBTQ young people, only relatively recently have changes to US law allowed them to marry. In addition, there remain considerable legal and social barriers that prevent sexual minority young adults from easily becoming parents. Yet the experiences of undocumented and sexual minority young people also tell us about resilience in the face of adversity and how some individuals may form alternative definitions of what it means to be an adult. These young people force us as researchers to revisit long-established theories and measures of adulthood.

WHAT WILL ADULTHOOD LOOK LIKE IN THE FUTURE?

It is difficult to predict what the transition to adulthood will look like in the near future. We do know that individual behavior is dependent on both evolving norms and structural factors. Factors that are likely to play an important role in shaping the transition to adulthood are often beyond the control of individual young people. These include policies that provide equitable and affordable education and training as well as the availability of jobs and wages that allow young people to live independently and to start families if they wish to do so. In these concluding remarks, we offer our expectations about the transition to adulthood in the coming years.

First, we believe that a sense of *precarity* will touch the lives of most young people, especially though not exclusively the lives of those who have not attained college degrees. Many of the issues that affect the life chances of young people are broader issues that affect all Americans. These include the shrinking middle class, contingent employment and underemployment, and rising income inequality. As the editors of a recent special report on Millennials and inequalities point out, these "stock forces of history" affected prior generations as well—it is just that Millennials are experiencing these major social trends in an "extreme form."[10] Cultural commentators on opposite ends of the political spectrum also seem to agree that Millennials are facing precariousness. For example, in one recent podcast on the legacy of the Boomer generation, two featured guests—one a "conservative writer" and the other a "liberal journalist"—agreed that higher education is a much more important factor for today's young people than it was for the Boomer generation, though they disagreed on whether more college-educated workers is necessarily a good thing for the economy and society. They also concurred that a lack of economic opportunities and security has contributed to lower rates of marriage and fewer births in the United States, though they disagreed on the best policies to address these issues.[11] Anxieties—whether around being able to secure a middle-class lifestyle for their children or being able to feed and house their children— are pervasive among American families.[12] Politicians, pundits, and the public are sympathetic when these issues center around the "typical" American family but are oftentimes less understanding when it comes to the plight of young people, particularly those from disadvantaged backgrounds. The much-maligned Millennial generation—sometimes caricatured as coddled, entitled, and lazy—is a generation of young people that is entering adulthood under very uncertain circumstances.

The precarity of young people's situation has been brought into sharper focus during the COVID-19 pandemic. As of January 2022, the virus has taken more than 5.6 million lives worldwide and more than 880,000 lives in the United States.[13] Colleges and universities moved at least partly if not fully online during the pandemic, and a nontrivial number of young people have deferred their college start dates or taken an involuntary break from their studies. According to the National Conference of State Legislatures, freshmen enrollment in Fall 2020 fell by an "unprecedented" 13 percent. This decline was even worse for community colleges, with public two-year schools reporting a 21 percent decrease in first-time student enrollments.[14] For some students, their families' financial situations suffered so dramatically due to the pandemic that they had to take a break from their educational careers, while for other students and families, online schooling did not seem like a worthwhile investment. The share of young people living with their parents had already been on the rise over the past several decades, but reached 52 percent among young people ages eighteen to twenty-nine in July 2020, a level not seen in the United States since the Great Depression.[15] Businesses have been disrupted and schools shuttered. Some of the jobs lost during the pandemic may never return.

As we are still in the midst of the pandemic, it difficult to even speculate about what the post-pandemic period will look like for the transition to adulthood. Our findings clearly demonstrate that obtaining a college education affects all other markers of adulthood. Earning a college degree leads to full-time work and independent living, but the delays and disruptions in college attendance due to COVID-19 will only depress bachelor's degree completion, especially for the most disadvantaged populations. The disproportionate health and economic impacts that COVID-19 has had on racial and ethnic minority groups will likely hamper their chances of completing college and attaining other adulthood milestones. For those who have already graduated from college, what happens if the job market continues to be uncertain?

The precarity of young people's lives also manifests in their mental and physical health. A recent report from Blue Cross Blue Shield finds that Millennials are less likely to rate their mental health as "good" compared to older generations. They are also more likely to believe that their mental health impacts their physical health.[16] Alarmingly, there is some evidence that a recent increase in "deaths of despair"—deaths involving alcohol, drugs, or suicide—in the United States has been disproportionately experienced by young adults.[17] Moreover, many health researchers and social scientists are concerned about the impact an extended period of social isolation and online learning due to COVID-19 has had on the mental health and learning of young people.

Young people are grappling with serious challenges that make the transition to adulthood more difficult today than in the past. However, in the face of such precarity, we also believe young people will continue to show remarkable *resiliency* as they transition to adulthood. Even the most disadvantaged of young people find passion projects that help them sustain their educational and occupational goals.[18] In the midst of a global pandemic and economic downturn, young people are still finding silver linings and ways to stay engaged with their dreams. When Kimberly-Viola, a twenty-one-year-old college student at the University of Namibia found online learning during the COVID-19 to be an unaffordable luxury, she connected nearly one hundred fellow political science students on a group messaging chain that became a source of motivation and support. As Kimberly-Viola describes, "2020 has forced us to innovate, collaborate and discover resilience we didn't know we had."[19]

The resiliency of young people is also on display in their active participation and leadership in social justice movements. The Black Lives Matter movement, begun by Black Millennials, has galvanized calls for racial justice in the United States and around the world.[20] As we described in chapter 5, young people are also at the forefront of evolving gender and sexual identities. Malala Yousafzai was only seventeen when she was awarded the 2014 Nobel Peace Prize for her advocacy of girls' educational opportunities.[21] The climate activist Greta Thunberg was only sixteen when she was named *Time* magazine's Person of the Year in 2019, and the accompanying article makes note of other young activists across issues, from climate change to gun violence. In the article, former Vice President Al Gore acknowledges the power of young people, remarking, "Throughout history, many great morally based movements have gained traction at the very moment when young people decided to make that movement their cause."[22] The prominent place of young people in leading such movements is incontrovertible. In the United States, sociologist Ruth Milkman points to a series of major contemporary social movements led by college-educated young people—including support for undocumented immigrant rights (the "Dreamers"), Occupy Wall Street, college protests against sexual violence, and Black Lives Matter—as evidence of a "new political generation." Milkman argues that the high levels of education but dim employment prospects of contemporary young adults have spurred activism in ways that differ from young activists in the past, especially in their inclusion of "outsiders" such as racial, ethnic, and sexual minorities.[23] Other research documents protests and social movements throughout Europe, Asia, the Middle East, and Africa, where young people have taken to the streets in response to high rates of unemployment and economic precarity.[24]

Nevertheless, the resiliency of young people may not be enough as they face broader social and economic inequalities during the transition to adulthood. Resiliency is a strategy to survive, not a strategy to thrive. Coming of age in a period of shrinking opportunities, today's young people risk experiencing reinforced inequities by race, ethnicity, and gender. Beyond the measures we have focused on in this book (i.e., educational attainment, full-time employment, residential independence, marriage, and parenthood), young people also seem to be divided in their social attitudes. While Millennials are more likely than past generations to hold strongly egalitarian views on gender and race, many still have ambivalent or traditional views. Thus, the overall trend in the attitudes of Millennials compared to the two preceding generations has shifted very modestly.[25] A survey of about two thousand college-aged Millennials conducted in 2012 found that only a minority of Black and Hispanic Millennials believe the government has paid too much attention to the problems of racial minorities compared to more than half of White Millennials. Similarly, more than half of Black and Hispanic Millennials *disagree* but more than half of White Millennials *agree* that discrimination against Whites is now as big a problem as discrimination against racial minorities.[26] Clearly, Millennials are not uniform in their attitudes about longstanding social inequalities.

Diversity is an important feature of the transition to adulthood. By this we are referring both to the demographic makeup of the child and youth population and also to how young people are defining adulthood for themselves. The future of adulthood is going to be more diverse not only because young people themselves are more diverse in their identities, but also because these young people think about and experience adulthood differently. As they come of age in an era of increasing inequality and also during a period of time that has seen significant changes in cultural norms, young people are more open than previous generations to different interpretations of adulthood. Most young people will probably still want to meet most, if not all, of the traditional milestones, but whether they will be able to and how their opportunities shape their views of the world around them remain pressing issues for researchers and policymakers.

As we bring this book to a close, we reiterate again that our goal is not to prescribe particular paths to adulthood for all young people to follow. Young people should and do have agency in defining adulthood for themselves. Returning to *Real Women Have Curves, Dope,* and *The Half of It,* we are struck by the remarkable similarity in their closing scenes: Ana striding confidently through the streets of New York toward the audience, Malcolm gazing unflinchingly at the audience and challenging us to question our preconceptions about his identity, and Ellie turning away from her backward glance at her town to face the audience as a train carries her away. Though we do not know what the future holds for Ana, Malcom, or Ellie, it is clear that they are all pushing forward into their next stage of life. We trust that the vast majority of young people will also continue to find their own successful and meaningful paths to adulthood. Our hope is that society provides them with ample opportunities to do so.

Appendix

Distribution of Milestone Attainment Patterns among Young Men (ages 25–34), by Educational Attainment

FOR THE MILESTONE ATTAINMENTS REPRESENTED BY EACH NUMBERED PATTERN, SEE TABLE 4.

High School or Less

	WHITE		BLACK		HISPANIC		ASIAN	
	Native-born	*Immigrant*	*Native-born*	*Immigrant*	*Native-born*	*Immigrant*	*Native-born*	*Immigrant*
Pattern 1	0.19	0.19	0.06	0.08	0.15	0.22	0.08	0.13
Pattern 2	0.05	0.06	0.02	0.03	0.03	0.04	0.03	0.05
Pattern 3	0.07	0.04	0.06	0.04	0.08	0.08	0.03	0.04
Pattern 4	0.12	0.10	0.08	0.10	0.08	0.07	0.07	0.07
Pattern 5	0.01	0.01	0.00	0.01	0.02	0.04	0.02	0.04
Pattern 6	0.01	0.03	0.01	0.02	0.03	0.04	0.04	0.05
Pattern 7	0.01	0.01	0.01	0.01	0.02	0.02	0.01	0.02
Pattern 8	0.17	0.21	0.16	0.24	0.22	0.25	0.29	0.24
Pattern 9	0.03	0.03	0.03	0.02	0.03	0.04	0.02	0.03
Pattern 10	0.01	0.01	0.01	0.01	0.01	0.01	0.01	0.01
Pattern 11	0.02	0.01	0.04	0.02	0.03	0.02	0.02	0.01
Pattern 12	0.04	0.03	0.05	0.04	0.03	0.01	0.03	0.02
Pattern 13	0.01	0.01	0.00	0.01	0.01	0.01	0.01	0.01
Pattern 14	0.01	0.02	0.02	0.03	0.02	0.02	0.01	0.02
Pattern 15	0.01	0.01	0.02	0.03	0.01	0.01	0.01	0.01
Pattern 16	0.22	0.22	0.42	0.32	0.24	0.13	0.31	0.23

Some College

	WHITE		BLACK		HISPANIC		ASIAN	
	Native-born	*Immigrant*	*Native-born*	*Immigrant*	*Native-born*	*Immigrant*	*Native-born*	*Immigrant*
Pattern 1	0.25	0.20	0.13	0.13	0.19	0.23	0.09	0.15
Pattern 2	0.10	0.11	0.04	0.07	0.06	0.08	0.06	0.08
Pattern 3	0.06	0.04	0.08	0.08	0.07	0.07	0.03	0.03
Pattern 4	0.20	0.19	0.17	0.15	0.15	0.12	0.14	0.13
Pattern 5	0.01	0.01	0.01	0.00	0.02	0.03	0.02	0.03
Pattern 6	0.01	0.01	0.01	0.02	0.02	0.04	0.03	0.05

Pattern 7	0.01	0.01	0.01	0.01	0.01	0.01	0.01	0.01
Pattern 8	0.16	0.19	0.21	0.25	0.23	0.24	0.33	0.28
Pattern 9	0.02	0.03	0.02	0.01	0.03	0.02	0.01	0.02
Pattern 10	0.01	0.01	0.01	0.01	0.01	0.01	0.01	0.01
Pattern 11	0.01	0.00	0.03	0.01	0.02	0.01	0.01	0.01
Pattern 12	0.04	0.04	0.05	0.05	0.03	0.02	0.03	0.04
Pattern 13	0.00	0.01	0.00	0.00	0.00	0.00	0.00	0.00
Pattern 14	0.01	0.01	0.01	0.02	0.01	0.01	0.01	0.01
Pattern 15	0.00	0.01	0.01	0.01	0.01	0.01	0.01	0.00
Pattern 16	0.11	0.12	0.21	0.19	0.14	0.10	0.21	0.16

Bachelor's or Higher Degree

	WHITE		BLACK		HISPANIC		ASIAN	
	Native-born	Immigrant	Native-born	Immigrant	Native-born	Immigrant	Native-born	Immigrant
Pattern 1	0.24	0.20	0.17	0.18	0.18	0.17	0.09	0.12
Pattern 2	0.18	0.17	0.09	0.08	0.13	0.10	0.13	0.14
Pattern 3	0.02	0.01	0.05	0.04	0.03	0.03	0.01	0.01
Pattern 4	0.28	0.26	0.28	0.29	0.25	0.22	0.27	0.24
Pattern 5	0.00	0.00	0.01	0.01	0.01	0.02	0.01	0.02
Pattern 6	0.01	0.02	0.01	0.02	0.02	0.03	0.02	0.04
Pattern 7	0.00	0.00	0.01	0.00	0.00	0.01	0.00	0.00
Pattern 8	0.16	0.19	0.24	0.25	0.24	0.26	0.33	0.29
Pattern 9	0.01	0.01	0.01	0.01	0.01	0.01	0.01	0.01
Pattern 10	0.01	0.02	0.01	0.01	0.01	0.01	0.01	0.01
Pattern 11	0.00	0.00	0.01	0.00	0.00	0.00	0.00	0.00
Pattern 12	0.03	0.03	0.03	0.02	0.03	0.02	0.03	0.02
Pattern 13	0.00	0.00	0.00	0.00	0.00	0.01	0.00	0.00
Pattern 14	0.00	0.00	0.00	0.00	0.01	0.01	0.01	0.01
Pattern 15	0.00	0.00	0.00	0.00	0.00	0.00	0.00	0.00
Pattern 16	0.05	0.07	0.10	0.10	0.08	0.09	0.09	0.09

SOURCE: US Census Bureau 2017, Five-Year Estimates; Ruggles et al. 2021.

Appendix Table 2   Distribution of Milestone Attainment Patterns among Young Women (ages 25–34), by Educational Attainment

FOR THE MILESTONE ATTAINMENTS REPRESENTED BY EACH
NUMBERED PATTERN, SEE TABLE 4.

High School or Less

	WHITE		BLACK		HISPANIC		ASIAN	
	Native-born	Immigrant	Native-born	Immigrant	Native-born	Immigrant	Native-born	Immigrant
Pattern 1	0.10	0.10	0.04	0.06	0.09	0.11	0.08	0.11
Pattern 2	0.03	0.04	0.01	0.01	0.02	0.02	0.04	0.03
Pattern 3	0.08	0.06	0.16	0.07	0.11	0.10	0.07	0.06
Pattern 4	0.06	0.04	0.06	0.03	0.04	0.02	0.07	0.04
Pattern 5	0.01	0.01	0.01	0.01	0.02	0.02	0.02	0.02
Pattern 6	0.01	0.01	0.01	0.02	0.02	0.02	0.03	0.03
Pattern 7	0.03	0.04	0.05	0.06	0.05	0.05	0.04	0.03
Pattern 8	0.07	0.09	0.08	0.10	0.10	0.07	0.17	0.11
Pattern 9	0.20	0.25	0.05	0.13	0.15	0.24	0.11	0.17
Pattern 10	0.03	0.03	0.01	0.01	0.02	0.02	0.03	0.03
Pattern 11	0.11	0.07	0.21	0.12	0.13	0.12	0.06	0.06
Pattern 12	0.04	0.04	0.06	0.04	0.03	0.02	0.03	0.02
Pattern 13	0.02	0.01	0.01	0.01	0.02	0.03	0.02	0.03
Pattern 14	0.02	0.02	0.01	0.03	0.02	0.03	0.03	0.03
Pattern 15	0.05	0.03	0.08	0.08	0.07	0.05	0.03	0.04
Pattern 16	0.15	0.15	0.16	0.22	0.13	0.08	0.19	0.17

Some College

	WHITE		BLACK		HISPANIC		ASIAN	
	Native-born	Immigrant	Native-born	Immigrant	Native-born	Immigrant	Native-born	Immigrant
Pattern 1	0.17	0.14	0.08	0.09	0.14	0.16	0.11	0.14
Pattern 2	0.07	0.07	0.02	0.03	0.04	0.04	0.06	0.07
Pattern 3	0.10	0.07	0.23	0.17	0.13	0.12	0.08	0.07
Pattern 4	0.11	0.11	0.10	0.10	0.08	0.06	0.12	0.12
Pattern 5	0.01	0.01	0.01	0.01	0.01	0.02	0.02	0.02
Pattern 6	0.01	0.01	0.01	0.02	0.02	0.02	0.03	0.04

Pattern 7	0.02	0.02	0.05	0.06	0.05	0.05	0.03	0.02
Pattern 8	0.08	0.11	0.10	0.15	0.11	0.11	0.18	0.14
Pattern 9	0.21	0.22	0.05	0.09	0.14	0.18	0.10	0.15
Pattern 10	0.03	0.03	0.01	0.01	0.02	0.02	0.03	0.03
Pattern 11	0.07	0.05	0.15	0.08	0.08	0.07	0.04	0.02
Pattern 12	0.03	0.04	0.04	0.03	0.03	0.02	0.03	0.03
Pattern 13	0.01	0.01	0.00	0.00	0.02	0.02	0.02	0.02
Pattern 14	0.01	0.01	0.01	0.02	0.01	0.02	0.01	0.02
Pattern 15	0.02	0.02	0.05	0.04	0.03	0.03	0.02	0.01
Pattern 16	0.06	0.08	0.09	0.11	0.08	0.07	0.12	0.10

Bachelor's or Higher Degree

	WHITE		BLACK		HISPANIC		ASIAN	
	Native-born	*Immigrant*	*Native-born*	*Immigrant*	*Native-born*	*Immigrant*	*Native-born*	*Immigrant*
Pattern 1	0.20	0.15	0.13	0.14	0.16	0.16	0.10	0.14
Pattern 2	0.18	0.17	0.07	0.07	0.12	0.11	0.14	0.15
Pattern 3	0.03	0.02	0.13	0.08	0.06	0.07	0.01	0.02
Pattern 4	0.23	0.22	0.24	0.20	0.20	0.16	0.25	0.21
Pattern 5	0.00	0.01	0.01	0.01	0.01	0.02	0.01	0.01
Pattern 6	0.01	0.02	0.01	0.02	0.02	0.03	0.02	0.03
Pattern 7	0.01	0.01	0.04	0.04	0.02	0.03	0.01	0.01
Pattern 8	0.12	0.14	0.19	0.22	0.18	0.19	0.26	0.20
Pattern 9	0.13	0.13	0.04	0.04	0.09	0.09	0.05	0.09
Pattern 10	0.03	0.03	0.01	0.01	0.02	0.02	0.02	0.03
Pattern 11	0.01	0.01	0.03	0.02	0.02	0.02	0.00	0.00
Pattern 12	0.02	0.03	0.03	0.04	0.02	0.02	0.03	0.03
Pattern 13	0.00	0.01	0.00	0.00	0.01	0.00	0.00	0.01
Pattern 14	0.00	0.01	0.00	0.01	0.01	0.02	0.01	0.01
Pattern 15	0.00	0.00	0.01	0.02	0.01	0.01	0.00	0.00
Pattern 16	0.03	0.05	0.06	0.07	0.06	0.06	0.07	0.07

SOURCE: US Census 2017, Five-Year Estimates; Ruggles et al. 2021.

Notes

NOTES TO INTRODUCTION

1. Oxford Languages n.d.b, n.d.a.
2. Donvito 2019.
3. Fussell and Furstenberg 2005, 35–36.
4. Fry and Parker 2018.
5. Budiman 2020.
6. Budiman et al. 2020, Tamir and Anderson 2022.
7. Rumbaut and Komaie 2010.
8. Settersten and Ray 2010b.
9. Rumbaut and Komaie 2010.
10. Fass 2016; Zelizer 1981.
11. Hogan and Astone 1986; Cepa and Furstenberg 2021; Vespa 2017.
12. Furstenberg et al. 2004; Furstenberg and Kennedy 2016.
13. Furstenberg and Kennedy 2016, emphasis in original.
14. Arnett 2015.
15. Arnett 2000, 2001.
16. Arnett 1997.
17. Arnett 2003.
18. Arnett 2015.
19. Cepa and Furstenberg 2021.
20. Benson and Furstenberg 2006; Shanahan et al. 2005.

21. Breen and Buchmann 2002; Juárez and Gayet 2014; Cook and Furstenberg 2002; Park and Sandefur 2005.

22. Silva 2013.

23. Arnett 2015.

24. Furstenberg and Kennedy 2016.

25. Saez 2017; Piketty and Saez 2014.

26. Autor 2014.

27. Howell and Kalleberg 2019.

28. Hout 2012.

29. Armstrong and Hamilton 2013; Bound, Lovenheim, and Turner 2012; Shapiro et al. 2016.

30. Posselt and Grodsky 2017.

31. Gallup 2016.

32. Gould and Kassa 2020.

33. Nguyen 2020.

34. Fry 2017.

35. Schweizer 2020; Payne 2021.

36. Shanahan 2000.

37. Livingston 2018.

38. Fry, Passel, and Cohn 2020.

39. Nguyen 2020.

40. Shanahan 2000.

41. Kochhar, Fry, and Taylor 2011.

42. Gould and Kassa 2020.

43. Iceland 2017; Ho and Kao 2018; Goyette 2017; Killewald and Bryan 2018.

44. Rumbaut and Komaie 2010; Feliciano 2020; Waters and Pineau 2015.

45. Kao, Vaquera, and Goyette 2013; Zhou and Bankston 2016.

46. Portes and Rumbaut 2001; Kasinitz et al. 2008; Waters et al. 2011.

47. Kasinitz et al. 2008.

48. Cherlin 2013; Sweeney 2002.

49. McLanahan 2004.

50. Emmons and Noeth 2015.

51. Barroso, Parker, and Bennett 2020; Fry, Passel, and Cohn 2020.

NOTES TO CHAPTER 1

1. Goyette 2017; Hummer and Hamilton 2019; Iceland 2017.

2. Kao, Vaquera, and Goyette 2013; Ngai 2004; Pew Research Center 2015.

3. LBJ Presidential Library n.d.

4. Chishti, Hipsman, and Ball 2015.

5. Frey 2021.

6. Frey 2020.

7. Vespa, Medina, and Armstrong 2020.

8. Frey 2020.

9. Johnson 2020.

10. Schaeffer 2019.

11. Hussar et al. 2020.

12. Budiman 2020.

13. Budiman et al. 2020; Zhou and Gonzales 2019.

14. Budiman et al. 2020.

15. Budiman 2020.

16. Iceland 2017.

17. Budiman 2020.

18. Urban Institute 2019.

19. Pattillo-McCoy 2000.

20. Goyette 2017.

21. Kao 2000.

22. Fordham and Ogbu 1986; Ogbu 1987.

23. Ogbu and Simons 1998.

24. Goyette 2017; Ainsworth-Darnell and Downey 1998; Johnson, Crosnoe, and Elder 2001; MacLeod 2009; Tyson 2002; Mickelson 1990.

25. Harding 2011.

26. Lee and Zhou 2015.

27. Chin 2020; Louie 2004; Sue and Okazaki 1990.

28. Edin and Kefalas 2005.

29. Kao, Vaquera, and Goyette 2013; Omi and Winant 2014; Zhou and Gonzales 2019.

30. Alba and Nee 2003; Gans 2007; Gordon 1964; Portes and Rumbaut 2001; Portes and Zhou 1993.

31. Waters and Pineau 2015.

32. Waters and Pineau 2015.

33. Portes and Zhou 1993; Portes, Fernández-Kelly, and Haller 2009.

34. Baum and Flores 2011.

35. Zhou and Bankston 1994; Portes and Rumbaut 2006.

36. Lee and Zhou 2015.

37. Coll and Marks 2012.

38. Louie 2004; Smith-Morris et al. 2013.

39. Caplan, Choy, and Whitmore 1991; Schneider and Lee 1990; Zhou and Bankston 1994.

40. Louie 2004, 2012; Smith 2006.

41. Foner and Dreby 2011; Valenzuela 1999.

42. Cepa and Kao 2019.

43. Fuligni 2007.
44. Ogbu 1991.
45. Kao and Tienda 1995.
46. Ruggles et al. 2021.
47. US Census Bureau 2017, n.d.a.
48. Fry 2020.
49. Rumbaut 2004; Oropesa and Landale 1997.
50. Oropesa and Landale 1997.

NOTES TO CHAPTER 2

1. Danziger and Ratner 2010; Hout 2012; Panel on Youth of the President's Science Advisory Committee 1973; Posselt and Grodsky 2017; Goyette 2017.
2. Furstenberg et al. 2004; Smith 2004; Vespa 2017.
3. Underwood 2018.
4. Goyette 2017.
5. Barrett and Zapotosky 2019; US Attorney's Office, District of Massachusetts n.d.
6. DeLuca, Clampet-Lundquist, and Edin 2016; Waters et al. 2011.
7. Lubrano 2012.
8. Danziger and Ratner 2010; Hout 2012; Autor 2014.
9. Goyette 2008.
10. Snyder, de Brey, and Dillow 2019.
11. Lareau 2011; Friedman 2013; Bennett, Lutz, and Jayaram 2012; Cooper 2014.
12. Ho, Park, and Kao 2019; Park et al. 2016; Buchmann, Condron, and Roscigno 2010.
13. Hussar et al. 2020; Wirt et al. 2000.
14. Snyder, de Brey, and Dillow 2019.
15. De Brey et al. 2021.
16. Long and Kurlaender 2009.
17. Bound, Lovenheim, and Turner 2012.
18. Snyder, de Brey, and Dillow 2019.
19. Woo et al. 2017.
20. Staklis 2016; Velez et al. 2019.
21. De Brey et al. 2021.
22. Iceland 2017; Goyette 2017.
23. Gamoran 2001; Ho and Kao 2018; Kao, Vaquera, and Goyette 2013; Entwisle and Alexander 1993.
24. Iceland 2017.
25. Waters and Pineau 2015; Kao, Vaquera, and Goyette 2013.

26. Kao, Vaquera, and Goyette 2013.

27. Kao and Thompson 2003; Ho and Kao 2018; Waters and Pineau 2015; Portes and Rumbaut 2001; Telles and Ortiz 2008.

28. DiPrete and Buchmann 2013.

29. Smith 2004.

30. Choy and Premo 1995; Bean and Metzner 1985.

31. Posselt and Grodsky 2017.

32. Bozick and DeLuca 2005.

33. Baum et al. 2019.

34. Woo et al. 2017; Baum et al. 2019.

35. Armstrong and Hamilton 2013.

36. Kao and Thompson 2003; Ho and Kao 2018; Waters et al. 2011.

37. DeLuca, Clampet-Lundquist, and Edin 2016; Cottom 2017.

38. Settersten and Ray 2010a, 20–21.

39. Baum 2018.

40. Settersten and Ray 2010a.

41. Hout 2012.

42. Attewell et al. 2007; Currie and Moretti 2003.

43. DiPrete and Buchmann 2013; Bennett and Xie 2003; Kao and Thompson 2003; Downey and Condron 2016.

44. Frye 2012.

45. Goyette 2017.

46. Ho and Kao 2018.

47. Charles et al. 2009.

48. Goldrick-Rab 2006.

49. Hussar et al. 2020.

50. Clark 1960.

51. Monaghan and Attewell 2015.

52. De Brey et al. 2021.

53. Cottom 2017.

54. Steele 1997; Massey et al. 2003.

55. Yosso et al. 2009; Hurtado et al. 1998.

56. Jack 2016, 10.

57. Feliciano 2005b; Portes and Zhou 1993; Kao and Tienda 1995.

58. Ho and Kao 2018.

59. Ochoa 2013.

60. Cherng 2015.

61. Patler 2018.

62. Gibbs et al. 2016.

63. Sakamoto and Wang 2021.

64. Hsin and Xie 2014.

65. Lee and Zhou 2015.

66. Snyder, de Brey, and Dillow 2019.

67. Goldin, Katz, and Kuziemko 2006; Buchmann and DiPrete 2006; Armstrong and Hamilton 2015.

68. Buchmann, DiPrete, and McDaniel 2008.

69. Furstenberg et al. 2004; Vespa 2017; Smith 2004.

70. Autor, Katz, and Kearney 2006.

71. Massey and Hirst 1998; Koval 2008.

72. Kalleberg 2011.

73. Taylor et al. 2012.

74. Hipple 2010.

75. Torpey and Hogan 2016.

76. Nahrgang et al. 2020.

77. Bennett 2021.

78. Fee, Wardrip, and Nelson 2019.

79. Rolen 2019.

80. Taylor et al. 2012.

81. Ma, Pender, and Welch 2016.

82. Torpey 2019.

83. Torpey 2018b, 2018a.

84. Alexander, Entwisle, and Olson 2014.

85. Pager 2007.

86. Gaddis 2015.

87. Kenney and Wissoker 1994.

88. Chin 2016; Zhou and Lee 2017; C. Kim and Sakamoto 2010.

89. Kasinitz et al. 2008.

90. Gerber and Cheung 2008.

91. Xie, Fang, and Shauman 2015.

92. Stephens, Warren, and Harner 2015.

93. OECD 2021.

94. OECD 2016a.

95. Bell and Blanchflower 2011; Mont'Alvao and Johnson 2016.

96. Kalleberg and von Wachter 2017.

97. Bell and Blanchflower 2011; Hout 2012.

98. Kalleberg and Wachter 2017; Bell and Blanchflower 2011. .

99. Desilver 2021.

NOTES TO CHAPTER 3

1. McConville 2020; Okimoto and Stegall 1987.

2. Davidson 2014; Carson 2019; Dickler 2018; Newman 2019.

3. White 1994.

4. White 1994.

5. Barroso, Parker, and Bennett 2020.

6. Leonhardt 2019.

7. Henderson 2016.

8. Martin et al. 2019.

9. Livingston 2018.

10. Wildsmith, Manlove, and Cook 2018.

11. McLanahan 2004.

12. Fry 2013; Furstenberg et al. 2004; Vespa 2017.

13. Fry, Passel, and Cohn 2020.

14. Britton 2013; Fry 2016; Ho and Park 2019; Lei and South 2016.

15. Britton 2013; Rumbaut and Komaie 2010; Kasinitz et al. 2008; Treas and Batalova 2011.

16. Goldscheider and DaVanzo 1985; South and Lei 2015; Ho and Park 2019; Lei and South 2016.

17. Louie 2012; Fuligni 2007.

18. Kasinitz et al. 2008; Holdaway 2011.

19. Holdaway 2011.

20. Britton 2013.

21. Ho and Park 2019.

22. Cepa and Kao 2019.

23. Goldscheider and DaVanzo 1985; South and Lei 2015.

24. Holdaway 2011.

25. Rumbaut and Komaie 2010.

26. Ho and Park 2019; Treas and Batalova 2011.

27. White 1994.

28. US Census Bureau. n.d.c.

29. Schweizer 2020.

30. Parker and Stepler 2017.

31. Burstein 2007; Ellwood and Jencks 2004; Kalmijn 2011; Park and Lee 2017.

32. Goldstein and Kenney 2001.

33. Schweizer 2020.

34. Sweeney 2002.

35. Smock and Schwartz 2020; Stykes, Payne, and Gibbs 2014; Raley, Sweeney, and Wondra 2015.

36. Raley, Sweeney, and Wondra 2015.

37. Rumbaut and Komaie 2010.

38. US Census Bureau. n.d.b.

39. Krieder and Vespa 2015; Yeung and Cheung 2015.

40. Refinery29 2018.

41. Gurrentz 2018.

42. Smock 2000.

43. Smock and Schwartz 2020.

44. Sassler and Miller 2017.

45. Manning, Brown, and Payne 2021.

46. Cherlin 2004.

47. Kennedy and Fitch 2012.

48. Schneider, Harknett, and Stimpson 2018.

49. Smock and Schwartz 2020; Schneider, Harknett, and Stimpson 2018; Cherlin 2004; Kasinitz et al. 2008; Waters et al. 2011; Edin and Kefalas 2005.

50. Raley, Sweeney, and Wondra 2015.

51. Kao, Balistreri, and Joyner 2018.

52. Schneider, Harknett, and Stimpson 2018.

53. Wilson and Neckerman 1987.

54. Massey et al. 2003.

55. Balistreri, Joyner, and Kao 2015.

56. Livingston and Brown 2017; Qian and Lichter 2007.

57. Balistreri, Joyner, and Kao 2015; Kao, Joyner, and Balistreri 2019.

58. Brown 2018.

59. Rumbaut and Komaie 2010.

60. Qian 2014.

61. Borgen and Rumbaut 2011.

62. Nesteruk and Gramescu 2012.

63. Min and Kim 2009; Lichter, Qian, and Tumin 2015; Qian, Glick, and Batson 2012; Glick 2010; Clark, Glick, and Bures 2009.

64. Foner and Dreby 2011; Foner 1997.

65. Gurrentz and Valerio 2019.

66. Livingston 2018.

67. McLanahan 2004.

68. Livingston 2018.

69. Livingston 2015; Mathews and Hamilton 2019.

70. Hymowitz et al. 2013.

71. McLanahan 2004.

72. McLanahan 2004; McLanahan and Booth 1989.

73. Livingston 2018.

74. Livingston 2018.

75. Livingston 2015.

76. Mills et al. 2011.

77. Fussell and Furstenberg 2005.

78. Edin and Kefalas 2005; Cherlin et al. 2008.

79. Edin and Kefalas 2005.

80. Mills et al. 2011.
81. Cherlin et al. 2008.
82. Rumbaut and Komaie 2010.
83. Adserà and Ferrer 2015.
84. Kasinitz et al. 2008.
85. Rumbaut and Komaie 2010.
86. Hasegawa 2019; Park 2015.
87. Newman 2008.
88. OECD 2016b.
89. Eickmeyer et al. 2017.
90. OECD 2018.
91. UN Department of Economic and Social Affairs 2017.
92. BBC News 2020; Grose 2020; Mills et al. 2011.

NOTES TO CHAPTER 4

1. Macmillan and Eliason 2003, 530.
2. Birkeland et al. 2014; Osgood et al. 2005.
3. Sandefur, Eggerling-Boeck, and Park 2005; Osgood et al. 2005; Alexander, Entwisle, and Olson 2014.
4. Waters et al. 2011.
5. Sandefur, Eggerling-Boeck, and Park 2005.
6. Osgood et al. 2005.
7. Alexander, Entwisle, and Olson 2014.
8. Brown 2017; Goyette 2017; Ho and Park 2019.
9. Sandefur, Eggerling-Boeck, and Park 2005.
10. Osgood et al. 2005.
11. Alexander, Entwisle, and Olson 2014.
12. Waters et al. 2011; Settersten, Furstenberg, and Rumbaut 2005.
13. Rumbaut and Komaie 2010.
14. Macmillan and Copher 2005; Amato et al. 2008; Oesterle et al. 2010.
15. Macmillan and Eliason 2003.
16. Smith 2004.
17. Alexander, Entwisle, and Olson 2014; Fussell and Furstenberg 2005.
18. Hout 2012.
19. Preston 2019; Autor 2014; Hout 2012.
20. DeLuca, Clampet-Lundquist, and Edin 2016, 135–136.
21. Alexander, Entwisle, and Olson 2014, 88.
22. Rindfuss 1991.
23. Settersten, Furstenberg, and Rumbaut 2005, 5.
24. Waters et al. 2011.

NOTES TO CHAPTER 5

1. Iceland 2017, 14, emphasis in original.
2. Feliciano 2005a.
3. Portes and Rumbaut 2001.
4. Kao, Vaquera, and Goyette 2013; Rumbaut and Komaie 2010.
5. Rumbaut and Komaie 2010.
6. Rumbaut and Komaie 2010; Fuligni 2007.
7. Ho and Park 2019.
8. Bonilla-Silva 2004.
9. Teranishi 2002.
10. Baker 2015.
11. Gonzales 2011.
12. Gonzales 2011, 610.
13. Bjorklund 2018.
14. Bjorklund 2018.
15. Flores 2010.
16. Flores and Horn 2009.
17. Hsin and Reed 2020.
18. Gonzales 2011; Abrego 2006; Enriquez 2017a; Bjorklund 2018.
19. Terriquez 2015a.
20. Silver 2012, 511.
21. Abrego 2006; Gonzales 2011.
22. Gonzales 2011, 614.
23. Hall, Musick, and Yi 2019.
24. Vargas 2011.
25. Pila 2016; Cebulko 2016; Enriquez 2017b.
26. Enriquez 2017b, 1159.
27. Pila 2016; Enriquez 2017b.
28. Pila 2016; Enriquez 2017b.
29. Pila 2016.
30. Dao 2017; Kim and Yellow Horse 2018.
31. Cho 2017.
32. Duong 2014.
33. Rusin 2015.
34. Huang 2014; Rusin 2015.
35. Enriquez, Vazquez Vera, and Ramakrishnan 2019.
36. Terriquez 2015b; Gentile and Salerno 2019; Cisneros and Bracho 2019.
37. Terriquez 2015b.
38. Dao 2017.
39. Biden 2021.
40. Shear and Davis 2017.

41. Jordan 2020.

42. Gurrentz and Valerio 2019.

43. Conron, Goldberg, and Halpern 2018.

44. Mehus et al. 2017; Roe 2017; Hatchel, Merrin, and Espelage 2019; Olson et al. 2016; Katz-Wise, Rosario, and Tsappis 2016.

45. Corliss et al. 2011.

46. Meier and Allen 2008; Torkelson 2012; Tillman, Brewster, and Holway 2019; Macapagal et al. 2015.

47. Tillman, Brewster, and Holway 2019, 144.

48. Georgetown Law Library n.d.

49. Biblarz and Savci 2010.

50. Easterbrook 2009; Torkelson 2012.

51. Macapagal et al. 2015.

52. Gurrentz and Valerio 2019.

53. Moore and Stambolis-Ruhstorfer 2013.

54. Family Equality 2019.

55. Compton 2019.

56. Kao, Joyner, and Balistreri 2019.

57. Torres, Hopper, and Chang 2019.

58. Terriquez 2015b.

59. Wagaman, Keller, and Cavaliere 2016.

60. Levin 2019.

NOTES TO CHAPTER 6

1. Fussell and Furstenberg 2005.

2. Torche 2011; Hout 1988.

3. Park and Lee 2017; Sweeney 2002.

4. Altintas 2016; McLanahan 2004.

5. Kao 2000; Lee and Zhou 2015; Ochoa 2013.

6. Orrenius and Zavodny 2009.

7. Lee and Zhou 2015; Fuligni 2007.

8. Alba and Nee 2003.

9. Lee, Bean, and Sloane 2003; Qian, Glick, and Batson 2012; Min and Kim 2009.

10. Grusky et al. 2019.

11. Klein 2021.

12. Cooper 2014.

13. Johns Hopkins University Coronavirus Resource Center n.d.

14. Smalley 2020.

15. Fry, Passel, and Cohn 2020.

16. Blue Cross Blue Shield Association 2020.

17. "Alcohol and Drug Misuse and Suicide and the Millennial Generation—A Devastating Impact" 2019.

18. DeLuca, Clampet-Lundquist, and Edin 2016.

19. Peyton 2021.

20. Cullors 2020; Nummi, Jennings, and Feagin 2019.

21. "Malala Yousafzai—Biographical" n.d.

22. Alter, Hayes, and Worland 2019.

23. Milkman 2017.

24. Hooghe 2012; Lima and Artiles 2013; Honwana 2014; Ansani and Daniele 2012; Joo 2018.

25. Johfre and Saperstein 2019.

26. Jones, Cox, and Banchoff 2012.

References

Abrego, Leisy Janet. 2006. "'I Can't Go to College Because I Don't Have Papers':
Incorporation Patterns Of Latino Undocumented Youth." *Latino Studies*
4 (3): 212–31. https://doi.org/10.1057/palgrave.lst.8600200.

Adserà, Alícia, and Ana Ferrer. 2015. "Immigrants and Demography: Marriage,
Divorce, and Fertility." In *Handbook of the Economics of International
Migration*, edited by Barry R. Chiswick and Paul W. Miller, 1:315–74.
Amsterdam: Elsevier and North-Holland.

Ainsworth-Darnell, James W., and Douglas B. Downey. 1998. "Assessing the
Oppositional Culture Explanation for Racial/Ethnic Differences in School
Performance." *American Sociological Review* 63 (4): 536–53. https://doi.org
/10.2307/2657266.

Alba, Richard D., and Victor Nee. 2003. *Remaking the American Mainstream:
Assimilation and Contemporary Immigration.* Cambridge, MA: Harvard
University Press.

"Alcohol and Drug Misuse and Suicide and the Millennial Generation—A
Devastating Impact." 2019. Trust for America's Health. https://www.tfah.org
/report-details/adsandmillennials/.

Alexander, Karl, Doris Entwisle, and Linda Olson. 2014. *The Long Shadow:
Family Background, Disadvantaged Urban Youth, and the Transition to
Adulthood.* New York: Russell Sage Foundation.

Alter, Charlotte, Suyin Hayes, and Justin Worland. 2019. "Greta Thunberg Is TIME's 2019 Person of the Year." *Time*, 2019. https://time.com/person-of-the-year-2019-greta-thunberg/.

Altintas, Evrim. 2016. "The Widening Education Gap in Developmental Child Care Activities in the United States, 1965–2013." *Journal of Marriage and Family* 78 (1): 26–42. https://doi.org/10.1111/jomf.12254.

Amato, Paul R., Nancy S. Landale, Tara C. Havasevich-Brooks, Alan Booth, David J. Eggebeen, Robert Schoen, and Susan M. McHale. 2008. "Precursors of Young Women's Family Formation Pathways." *Journal of Marriage and Family* 70 (5): 1271–86. https://doi.org/10.1111/j.1741-3737.2008.00565.x.

Ansani, Andrea, and Vittorio Daniele. 2012. "About a Revolution: The Economic Motivations of the Arab Spring." *International Journal of Development and Conflict* 2 (3): 1250013. https://doi.org/10.1142/S2010269012500135.

Armstrong, Elizabeth A., and Laura T. Hamilton. 2013. *Paying for the Party*. Cambridge, MA: Harvard University Press.

Arnett, Jeffrey Jensen. 1997. "Young People's Conceptions of the Transition to Adulthood." *Youth & Society* 29 (1): 3–23. https://doi.org/10.1177/0044118X97029001001.

———. 2000. "Emerging Adulthood: A Theory of Development from the Late Teens through the Twenties." *American Psychologist* 55 (5): 469–80. https://doi.org/10.1037/0003-066X.55.5.469.

———. 2001. "Conceptions of the Transition to Adulthood: Perspectives from Adolescence through Midlife." *Journal of Adult Development* 8 (2): 133–43. https://doi.org/10.1023/A:1026450103225.

———. 2003. "Conceptions of the Transition to Adulthood among Emerging Adults in American Ethnic Groups." *New Directions for Child and Adolescent Development* 2003 (100): 63–76. https://doi.org/10.1002/cd.75.

———. 2015. *Emerging Adulthood: The Winding Road from the Late Teens through the Twenties*. 2nd ed. New York: Oxford University Press.

Attewell, Paul, David Lavin, Thurston Domina, and Tania Levey. 2007. *Passing the Torch: Does Higher Education for the Disadvantaged Pay Off across the Generations?* New York: Russell Sage Foundation.

Autor, David H. 2014. "Skills, Education, and the Rise of Earnings Inequality among the 'Other 99 Percent.'" *Science* 344 (6186): 843–51. https://doi.org/10.1126/science.1251868.

Autor, David H., Lawrence F. Katz, and Melissa S. Kearney. 2006. "The Polarization of the U.S. Labor Market." *The American Economic Review* 96 (2): 189–94. https://doi.org/DOI: 10.1257/000282806777212620.

Baker, Bryan. 2015. "Estimates of the Illegal Alien Population Residing in the United States: January 2015." Department of Homeland Security Office of Immigration Statistics. https://www.dhs.gov/sites/default/files/publications/18_1214_PLCY_pops-est-report.pdf.

Balistreri, Kelly Stamper, Kara Joyner, and Grace Kao. 2015. "Relationship Involvement among Young Adults: Are Asian American Men an Exceptional Case?" *Population Research and Policy Review* 34 (5): 709–32. https://doi.org/10.1007/s11113-015-9361-1.

Barrett, Devlin, and Matt Zapotosky. 2019. "FBI Accuses Wealthy Parents, Including Celebrities, in College-Entrance Bribery Scheme." *Washington Post*, March 12, 2019. https://www.washingtonpost.com/world/national-security/fbi-accuses-wealthy-parents-including-celebrities-in-college-entrance-bribery-scheme/2019/03/12/d91c9942-44d1-11e9-8aab-95b8d80a1e4f_story.html.

Barroso, Amanda, Kim Parker, and Jesse Bennett. 2020. "As Millennials Near 40, They're Approaching Family Life Differently Than Previous Generations." Pew Research Center, May 27, 2020. https://www.pewsocialtrends.org/2020/05/27/as-millennials-near-40-theyre-approaching-family-life-differently-than-previous-generations/.

Baum, Sandy. 2018. "How Well Does Graduate School Pay Off?" Urban Institute, April 23, 2018. https://www.urban.org/urban-wire/how-well-does-graduate-school-pay.

Baum, Sandy, and Stella M. Flores. 2011. "Higher Education and Children in Immigrant Families." *The Future of Children* 21 (1): 171–93. https://doi.org/10.1353/foc.2011.0000.

Baum, Sandy, Jennifer Ma, Matea Pender, and C. J. Libassi. 2019. "Trends in Student Aid 2019." Trends in Higher Education. New York: College Board. https://research.collegeboard.org/pdf/trends-student-aid-2019-full-report.pdf.

BBC News. 2020. "How Do Countries Fight Falling Birth Rates?" *BBC News*, January 15, 2020. https://www.bbc.com/news/world-europe-51118616.

Bean, John P., and Barbara S. Metzner. 1985. "A Conceptual Model of Nontraditional Undergraduate Student Attrition." *Review of Educational Research* 55 (4): 485–540. https://doi.org/10.3102/00346543055004485.

Bell, David N. F., and David G. Blanchflower. 2011. "Young People and the Great Recession." *Oxford Review of Economic Policy* 27 (2): 241–67. https://doi.org/10.1093/oxrep/grr011.

Bennett, Jessica. 2021. "The Working Woman's Anthem '9 to 5' Needed an Update. But This?" *New York Times*, February 7, 2021. https://www.nytimes.com/2021/02/07/business/dolly-parton-5-to-9-super-bowl.html.

Bennett, Pamela R., Amy C. Lutz, and Lakshmi Jayaram. 2012. "Beyond the Schoolyard: The Role of Parenting Logics, Financial Resources, and Social Institutions in the Social Class Gap in Structured Activity Participation." *Sociology of Education* 85 (2): 131–57. https://doi.org/10.1177/0038040711431585.

Bennett, Pamela R., and Yu Xie. 2003. "Revisiting Racial Differences in College Attendance: The Role of Historically Black Colleges and Universities." *American Sociological Review* 68 (4): 567–80. https://doi.org/10.2307/1519739.

Benson, Janel E., and Frank F. Furstenberg. 2006. "Entry into Adulthood: Are Adult Role Transitions Meaningful Markers of Adult Identity?" in "Constructing Adulthood: Agency and Subjectivity in Adolescence and Adulthood," ed. Ross Macmillan, special issue, *Advances in Life Course Research* 11 (January): 199–224. https://doi.org/10.1016/S1040-2608(06)11008-4.

Biblarz, Timothy J., and Evren Savci. 2010. "Lesbian, Gay, Bisexual, and Transgender Families." *Journal of Marriage and Family* 72 (3): 480–97. https://doi.org/10.1111/j.1741-3737.2010.00714.x.

Biden, Joseph R. 2021. "Preserving and Fortifying Deferred Action for Childhood Arrivals (DACA)." The White House. January 21, 2021. https://www .whitehouse.gov/briefing-room/presidential-actions/2021/01/20/preserving-and-fortifying-deferred-action-for-childhood-arrivals-daca/.

Birkeland, Marianne Skogbrott, Ingrid Leversen, Torbjørn Torsheim, and Bente Wold. 2014. "Pathways to Adulthood and Their Precursors and Outcomes." *Scandinavian Journal of Psychology* 55 (1): 26–32. https://doi.org/10.1111 /sjop.12087.

Bjorklund, Peter. 2018. "Undocumented Students in Higher Education: A Review of the Literature, 2001 to 2016." *Review of Educational Research* 88 (5): 631–70. https://doi.org/10.3102/0034654318783018.

Blue Cross Blue Shield Association. 2020. "Millennial Health: Trends in Behavioral Health Conditions." Blue Cross Blue Shield Association, October 15, 2020. https://www.bcbs.com/the-health-of-america/reports/millennial-health-trends-behavioral-health-conditions.

Bonilla-Silva, Eduardo. 2004. "From Bi-Racial to Tri-Racial: Towards a New System of Racial Stratification in the USA." *Ethnic and Racial Studies* 27 (6): 931–50. https://doi.org/10.1080/0141987042000268530.

Borgen, Linda, and Rubén G. Rumbaut. 2011. "Coming of Age in 'America's Finest City': Transitions to Adulthood among Children of Immigrants in San Diego." In *Coming of Age in America: The Transition to Adulthood in the Twenty-First Century,* edited by Mary C. Waters, Patrick J. Carr, Maria J. Kefalas, and Jennifer Holdaway, 133–68. Berkeley: University of California Press.

Bound, John, Michael F. Lovenheim, and Sarah Turner. 2012. "Increasing Time to Baccalaureate Degree in the United States." *Education Finance and Policy* 7 (4): 375–424. https://doi.org/10.1162/EDFP_a_00074.

Bozick, Robert, and Stefanie DeLuca. 2005. "Better Late Than Never? Delayed Enrollment in the High School to College Transition." *Social Forces* 84 (1): 531–54. https://doi.org/10.1353/sof.2005.0089.

Breen, Richard, and Marlis Buchmann. 2002. "Institutional Variation and the Position of Young People: A Comparative Perspective." *Annals of the American Academy of Political and Social Science* 580: 288–305. https://www .jstor.org/stable/1049911.

Britton, Marcus L. 2013. "Race/Ethnicity, Attitudes, and Living With Parents during Young Adulthood." *Journal of Marriage and Family* 75 (4): 995–1013. https://doi.org/10.1111/jomf.12042.

Brown, Ashley. 2018. "'Least Desirable'? How Racial Discrimination Plays Out in Online Dating." 2018. *NPR Morning Edition*, January 9, 2018. https://www.npr.org/2018/01/09/575352051/least-desirable-how-racial-discrimination-plays-out-in-online-dating.

Brown, Susan L. 2017. *Families in America*. Oakland: University of California Press.

Buchmann, Claudia, Dennis J. Condron, and Vincent J. Roscigno. 2010. "Shadow Education, American Style: Test Preparation, the SAT and College Enrollment." *Social Forces* 89 (2): 435–61. https://doi.org/10.1353/sof.2010.0105.

Buchmann, Claudia, and Thomas A. DiPrete. 2006. "The Growing Female Advantage in College Completion: The Role of Family Background and Academic Achievement." *American Sociological Review* 71 (4): 515–41.

Buchmann, Claudia, Thomas A. DiPrete, and Anne McDaniel. 2008. "Gender Inequalities in Education." *Annual Review of Sociology* 34 (1): 319–37. https://doi.org/10.1146/annurev.soc.34.040507.134719.

Budiman, Abby. 2020. "Key Findings about U.S. Immigrants." *Pew Research Center Fact Tank*, August 20, 2020. https://www.pewresearch.org/fact-tank/2020/08/20/key-findings-about-u-s-immigrants/.

Budiman, Abby, Christine Tamir, Lauren Mora, and Luis Noe-Bustamante. 2020. "Facts on U.S. Immigrants, 2018: Statistical Portrait of the Foreign-Born Population in the United States." Pew Research Center, August 20, 2020. https://www.pewresearch.org/hispanic/2020/08/20/facts-on-u-s-immigrants/.

Burstein, Nancy R. 2007. "Economic Influences on Marriage and Divorce." *Journal of Policy Analysis and Management* 26 (2): 387–429. https://doi.org/10.1002/pam.20257.

Caplan, Nathan S., Marcella H. Choy, and John K. Whitmore. 1991. *Children of the Boat People: A Study of Educational Success*. Ann Arbor: University of Michigan Press.

Carson, Ron. 2019. "Five Ways to Keep Boomerang Kids from Ruining Your Retirement." *Forbes*, August 11, 2019. https://www.forbes.com/sites/rcarson/2019/08/11/five-ways-to-keep-boomerang-kids-from-ruining-your-retirement/.

Cebulko, Kara. 2016. "Marrying for Papers? From Economically Strategic to Normative and Relational Dimensions of the Transition to Adulthood for Unauthorized 1.5-Generation Brazilians." *Sociological Perspectives* 59 (4): 760–75. https://doi.org/10.1177/0731121415611684.

Cepa, Kennan, and Frank F. Furstenberg. 2021. "Reaching Adulthood: Persistent Beliefs about the Importance and Timing of Adult Milestones."

Journal of Family Issues 42 (1): 27–57. https://doi.org/10.1177/0192513X20918612.

Cepa, Kennan, and Grace Kao. 2019. "Cultural Preferences or Financial Constraints? Understanding Racial and Ethnic Differences in Family Attitudes and Parental Coresidence in Young Adulthood." *Journal of Family Issues* 40 (12): 1705–28. https://doi.org/10.1177/0192513X19842224.

Charles, Camille Z., Mary J. Fischer, Margarita A. Mooney, Douglas S. Massey, Gniesha Dinwiddle, and Brooke Cunningham. 2009. *Taming the River: Negotiating the Academic, Financial, and Social Currents in Selective Colleges and Universities.* Princeton, NJ: Princeton University Press.

Cherlin, Andrew J. 2004. "The Deinstitutionalization of American Marriage." *Journal of Marriage and Family* 66 (4): 848–61. https://doi.org/10.1111/j.0022-2445.2004.00058.x.

———. 2013. "In the Season of Marriage, a Question. Why Bother?" *New York Times,* April 27, 2013. https://www.nytimes.com/2013/04/28/opinion/sunday/why-do-people-still-bother-to-marry.html.

Cherlin, Andrew J., Caitlin Cross-Barnet, Linda M. Burton, and Raymond Garrett-Peters. 2008. "Promises They Can Keep: Low-Income Women's Attitudes toward Motherhood, Marriage, and Divorce." *Journal of Marriage and Family* 70 (4): 919–33. https://doi.org/10.1111/j.1741-3737.2008.00536.x.

Cherng, Hua-Yu Sebastian. 2015. "Social Isolation among Racial/Ethnic Minority Immigrant Youth." *Sociology Compass* 9 (6): 509–18. http://dx.doi.org/10.1111/soc4.12276.

Chin, Margaret M. 2016. "Asian Americans, Bamboo Ceilings, and Affirmative Action." *Contexts* 15 (1): 70–73. https://doi.org/10.1177/1536504216628845.

———. 2020. *Stuck: Why Asian Americans Don't Reach the Top of the Corporate Ladder.* New York: New York University Press.

Chishti, Muzaffar, Faye Hipsman, and Isabel Ball. 2015. "Fifty Years On, the 1965 Immigration and Nationality Act Continues to Reshape the United States." *Migration Information Source,* October 15, 2015. https://www.migrationpolicy.org/article/fifty-years-1965-immigration-and-nationality-act-continues-reshape-united-states.

Cho, Esther Yoona. 2017. "Revisiting Ethnic Niches: A Comparative Analysis of the Labor Market Experiences of Asian and Latino Undocumented Young Adults." *RSF: The Russell Sage Foundation Journal of the Social Sciences* 3 (4): 97–115. https://doi.org/10.7758/RSF.2017.3.4.06.

Choy, Susan P., and Mark D. Premo. 1995. "Profile of Older Undergraduates: 1989–90." NCES 95167. Washington, DC: National Center for Education Statistics. https://nces.ed.gov/pubsearch/pubsinfo.asp?pubid=95167.

Cisneros, Jesus, and Christian Bracho. 2019. "Coming Out of the Shadows and the Closet: Visibility Schemas among Undocuqueer Immigrants."

Journal of Homosexuality 66 (6): 715–34. https://doi.org/10.1080/00918369 .2017.1423221.

Clark, Burton R. 1960. "The 'Cooling-Out' Function in Higher Education." *American Journal of Sociology* 65 (6): 569–76. https://doi.org/10.1086/222787.

Clark, Rebecca L., Jennifer E. Glick, and Regina M. Bures. 2009. "Immigrant Families over the Life Course: Research Directions and Needs." *Journal of Family Issues* 30 (6): 852–72. https://doi.org/10.1177/0192513X09332162.

Coll, Cynthia García, and Amy Kerivan Marks, eds. 2012. *The Immigrant Paradox in Children and Adolescents: Is Becoming American a Developmental Risk?* Washington, DC: American Psychological Association.

Compton, Julie. 2019. "More LGBTQ Millennials Plan to Have Kids Regardless of Income, Survey Finds." *NBC News,* December 27, 2019. https://www .nbcnews.com/feature/nbc-out/more-lgbtq-millennials-plan-have-kids-regardless-income-survey-finds-n1107461.

Conron, Kerith J., Shoshana K. Goldberg, and Carolyn T. Halpern. 2018. "Sexual Orientation and Sex Differences in Socioeconomic Status: A Population-Based Investigation in the National Longitudinal Study of Adolescent to Adult Health." *Journal of Epidemiology and Community Health* 72 (11): 1016–26. https://doi.org/10.1136/jech-2017-209860.

Cook, Thomas D., and Frank F. Furstenberg. 2002. "Explaining Aspects of the Transition to Adulthood in Italy, Sweden, Germany, and the United States: A Cross-Disciplinary, Case Synthesis Approach." *ANNALS of the American Academy of Political and Social Science* 580 (1): 257–87. https://doi.org/10.1177 /000271620258000111.

Cooper, Marianne. 2014. *Cut Adrift: Families in Insecure Times.* Berkeley: University of California Press.

Corliss, Heather L., Carol S. Goodenow, Lauren Nichols, and S. Bryn Austin. 2011. "High Burden of Homelessness among Sexual-Minority Adolescents: Findings from a Representative Massachusetts High School Sample." *American Journal of Public Health* 101 (9): 1683–89. https://doi.org/10.2105 /AJPH.2011.300155.

Cottom, Tressie McMillan. 2017. *Lower Ed: The Troubling Rise of For-Profit Colleges in the New Economy.* New York: The New Press.

Cullors, Patrisse. 2020. "A Decade of Black Lives Matter Gives Us a New Understanding of Black Liberation." *NBC News,* January 1, 2020. https:// www.nbcnews.com/think/opinion/black-lives-matter-began-after-trayvon-martin-s-death-ferguson-ncna1106651.

Currie, Janet, and Enrico Moretti. 2003. "Mother's Education and the Intergenerational Transmission of Human Capital: Evidence from College Openings." *Quarterly Journal of Economics* 118 (4): 1495–1532. https://doi.org/10.1162 /003355303322552856.

Danziger, Sheldon, and David Ratner. 2010. "Labor Market Outcomes and the Transition to Adulthood." *The Future of Children* 20 (1): 133–58. https://doi.org/10.1353/foc.0.0041.

Dao, Loan Thi. 2017. "Out and Asian: How Undocu/DACAmented Asian Americans and Pacific Islander Youth Navigate Dual Liminality in the Immigrant Rights Movement." *Societies* 7 (3): 17. https://doi.org/10.3390/soc7030017.

Davidson, Adam. 2014. "It's Official: The Boomerang Kids Won't Leave." *New York Times Magazine,* June 20, 2014. https://www.nytimes.com/2014/06/22/magazine/its-official-the-boomerang-kids-wont-leave.html.

de Brey, Cristobal, Thomas D. Snyder, Anlan Zhang, and Sally A. Dillow. 2021. "Digest of Education Statistics 2019." NCES 2021009. Washington, DC: National Center for Education Statistics. https://nces.ed.gov/pubsearch/pubsinfo.asp?pubid=2021009.

DeLuca, Stefanie, Susan Clampet-Lundquist, and Kathryn Edin. 2016. *Coming of Age in the Other America.* New York: Russell Sage Foundation.

Desilver, Drew. 2021. "Many U.S. Workers Are Seeing Bigger Paychecks in Pandemic Era, but Gains Aren't Spread Evenly." Pew Research Center. December 22, 2021. https://www.pewresearch.org/fact-tank/2021/12/22/many-u-s-workers-are-seeing-bigger-paychecks-in-pandemic-era-but-gains-arent-spread-evenly/.

Dickler, Jessica. 2018. "For the Boomerang Generation, There Are Pitfalls to Moving Home." *CNBC,* April 1, 2018. https://www.cnbc.com/2018/03/29/for-the-boomerang-generation-there-are-pitfalls-to-moving-home.html.

DiPrete, Thomas A., and Claudia Buchmann. 2013. *The Rise of Women: The Growing Gender Gap in Education and What It Means for American Schools.* New York: Russell Sage Foundation.

Donvito, Tina. 2019. "Yes, 'Adulting Classes' for Millennials Are on the Rise— Here's What You Need to Know About Them." *Parade,* September 19, 2019. https://parade.com/924439/tinadonvito/adulting-classes-for-millennials/.

Downey, Douglas B., and Dennis J. Condron. 2016. "Fifty Years since the Coleman Report: Rethinking the Relationship between Schools and Inequality." *Sociology of Education* 89 (3): 207–20. https://doi.org/10.1177/0038040716651676.

Duong, Tuyet. 2014. "Asian American and Pacific Islander Enrollment in the Deferred Action for Childhood Arrivals (DACA) Program." *The White House: President Barack Obama,* August 7, 2014. https://obamawhitehouse.archives.gov/blog/2014/08/07/asian-american-and-pacific-islander-enrollment-deferred-action-childhood-arrivals-da.

Easterbrook, Adam. 2009. "Rethinking Families over the Life Course Development Perspective: Including the Lives of Same-Sex Families." *Sociology Compass* 3 (6): 1000–16. https://doi.org/10.1111/j.1751-9020.2009.00254.x.

Edin, Kathryn, and Maria J. Kefalas. 2005. *Promises I Can Keep: Why Poor Women Put Motherhood Before Marriage.* Berkeley: University of California Press.

Eickmeyer, Kasey J., Krista K. Payne, Susan L. Brown, and Wendy D. Manning. 2017. "Crossover in the Median Age at First Marriage and First Birth: Thirty-Five Years of Change." *Family Profile* 17 (22). National Center for Family and Marriage Research. https://www.bgsu.edu/ncfmr/resources/data/family-profiles/eickmeyer-payne-brown-manning-crossover-age-first-marriage-birth-fp-17-22.html.

Ellwood, David T., and Christopher Jencks. 2004. "The Spread of Single-Parent Families in the United States Since 1960." KSG Working Paper, RWP04–008. https://papers.ssrn.com/abstract=517662.

Emmons, William R., and Bryan J. Noeth. 2015. "Why Didn't Higher Education Protect Hispanic and Black Wealth?" *In the Balance: Perspectives on Household Balance Sheets,* August 5, 2015. Federal Reserve Bank of St. Louis. https://www.stlouisfed.org/publications/in-the-balance/2015/why-didnt-higher-education-protect-hispanic-and-black-wealth.

Enriquez, Laura E. 2017a. "A 'Master Status' or the 'Final Straw'? Assessing the Role of Immigration Status in Latino Undocumented Youths' Pathways out of School." *Journal of Ethnic and Migration Studies* 43 (9): 1526–43. https://doi.org/10.1080/1369183X.2016.1235483.

———. 2017b. "Gendering Illegality: Undocumented Young Adults' Negotiation of the Family Formation Process." *American Behavioral Scientist* 61 (10): 1153–71. https://doi.org/10.1177/0002764217732103.

Enriquez, Laura E., Daisy Vazquez Vera, and S. Karthick Ramakrishnan. 2019. "Driver's Licenses for All? Racialized Illegality and the Implementation of Progressive Immigration Policy in California." *Law and Policy* 41 (1): 34–58. https://doi.org/10.1111/lapo.12121.

Entwisle, Doris R., and Karl L. Alexander. 1993. "Entry Into School: The Beginning School Transition and Educational Stratification in the United States." *Annual Review of Sociology* 19 (1): 401–23. https://doi.org/10.1146/annurev.so.19.080193.002153.

Family Equality. 2019. "Building LGBTQ+ Families: The Price of Parenthood." Family Equality. https://www.familyequality.org/resources/building-lgbtq-families-price-parenthood/.

Fass, Paula S. 2016. *The End of American Childhood.* Princeton, NJ: Princeton University Press.

Fee, Kyle, Keith Wardrip, and Lisa Nelson. 2019. "Opportunity Occupation Revisited: Exploring Employment for Sub-Baccalaureate Workers across Metro Areas and over Time." Federal Reserve Bank of Philadelphia, Federal Reserve Bank of Cleveland. https://www.philadelphiafed.org/-/media/frbp/assets/community-development/reports/opportunity-occupations-revisited/0419-opportunity-occupations-revisited-report.pdf.

Feliciano, Cynthia. 2005a. "Educational Selectivity in U.S. Immigration: How Do Immigrants Compare to Those Left Behind?" *Demography* 42 (1): 131–52. https://doi.org/10.1353/dem.2005.0001.

———. 2005b. *Unequal Origins: Immigrant Selection and the Education of the Second Generation*. New York: LFB Scholarly Publishing.

———. 2020. "Immigrant Selectivity Effects on Health, Labor Market, and Educational Outcomes." *Annual Review of Sociology* 46 (1): 315–34. https://doi.org/10.1146/annurev-soc-121919-054639.

Flores, Stella M. 2010. "State Dream Acts: The Effect of In-State Resident Tuition Policies and Undocumented Latino Students." *Review of Higher Education* 33 (2): 239–83. https://doi.org/10.1353/rhe.0.0134.

Flores, Stella M., and Catherine L. Horn. 2009. "College Persistence among Undocumented Students at a Selective Public University: A Quantitative Case Study Analysis." *Journal of College Student Retention: Research, Theory and Practice*, August 11, 2009. https://doi.org/10.2190/CS.11.1.d.

Foner, Nancy. 1997. "The Immigrant Family: Cultural Legacies and Cultural Changes." *International Migration Review* 31 (4): 961–74. https://doi.org/10.2307/2547420.

Foner, Nancy, and Joanna Dreby. 2011. "Relations between the Generations in Immigrant Families." *Annual Review of Sociology* 37 (1): 545–64. https://doi.org/10.1146/annurev-soc-081309-150030.

Fordham, Signithia, and John U. Ogbu. 1986. "Black Students' School Success: Coping with the 'Burden of "Acting White."'" *The Urban Review* 18 (3): 176–206. https://doi.org/10.1007/BF01112192.

Frey, William H. 2020. "The Nation Is Diversifying Even Faster than Predicted, According to New Census Data." *Brookings*, July 1, 2020. https://www.brookings.edu/research/new-census-data-shows-the-nation-is-diversifying-even-faster-than-predicted/.

———. 2021. "New 2020 Census Results Show Increased Diversity Countering Decade-Long Declines in America's White and Youth Populations." *Brookings*, August 13, 2021. https://www.brookings.edu/research/new-2020-census-results-show-increased-diversity-countering-decade-long-declines-in-americas-white-and-youth-populations/.

Friedman, Hilary Levey. 2013. *Playing to Win: Raising Children in a Competitive Culture*. Berkeley: University of California Press.

Fry, Richard. 2013. "A Rising Share of Young Adults Live in Their Parents' Home: A Record 21.6 Million in 2012." Pew Research Center, August 1, 2013. https://www.pewresearch.org/social-trends/2013/08/01/a-rising-share-of-young-adults-live-in-their-parents-home/.

———. 2016. "For First Time in Modern Era, Living With Parents Edges Out Other Living Arrangements for 18- to 34-Year-Olds: Share Living with Spouse or Partner Continues to Fall." Pew Research Center, May 24, 2016.

https://www.pewsocialtrends.org/2016/05/24/for-first-time-in-modern-era-living-with-parents-edges-out-other-living-arrangements-for-18-to-34-year-olds/.

———. 2017. "It's Becoming More Common for Young Adults to Live at Home—and for Longer Stretches." *Pew Research Center Fact Tank*, May 5, 2017. https://www.pewresearch.org/fact-tank/2017/05/05/its-becoming-more-common-for-young-adults-to-live-at-home-and-for-longer-stretches/.

———. 2020. "Millennials Overtake Baby Boomers as America's Largest Generation." *Pew Research Center Fact Tank*, April 28, 2020. https://www.pewresearch.org/fact-tank/2020/04/28/millennials-overtake-baby-boomers-as-americas-largest-generation/.

Fry, Richard, and Kim Parker. 2018. "'Post-Millennial' Generation on Track To Be Most Diverse, Best-Educated." Pew Research Center, November 15, 2018. https://www.pewsocialtrends.org/2018/11/15/early-benchmarks-show-post-millennials-on-track-to-be-most-diverse-best-educated-generation-yet/.

Fry, Richard, Jeffrey S. Passel, and D'Vera Cohn. 2020. "A Majority of Young Adults in the U.S. Live with Their Parents for the First Time Since the Great Depression." *Pew Research Center Fact Tank*, September 4, 2020. https://www.pewresearch.org/fact-tank/2020/09/04/a-majority-of-young-adults-in-the-u-s-live-with-their-parents-for-the-first-time-since-the-great-depression/.

Frye, Margaret. 2012. "Bright Futures in Malawi's New Dawn: Educational Aspirations as Assertions of Identity." *American Journal of Sociology* 117 (6): 1565–1624. https://doi.org/10.1086/664542.

Fuligni, Andrew J. 2007. "Family Obligation, College Enrollment, and Emerging Adulthood in Asian and Latin American Families." *Child Development Perspectives* 1 (2): 96–100. https://doi.org/10.1111/j.1750-8606.2007.00022.x.

Furstenberg, Frank F., and Sheela Kennedy. 2016. "Growing Up Is Harder to Do.2: After the Great Recession." *Contexts*, November 4, 2016. https://contexts.org/blog/growing-up-is-harder-to-do-2-after-the-great-recession/.

Furstenberg, Frank F., Sheela Kennedy, Vonnie C. McLoyd, Rubén G. Rumbaut, and Richard A. Settersten. 2004. "Growing Up Is Harder to Do." *Contexts* 3 (3): 33–41. https://doi.org/10.1525/ctx.2004.3.3.33.

Fussell, Elizabeth, and Frank F. Furstenberg. 2005. "The Transition to Adulthood during the Twentieth Century: Race, Nativity, and Gender." In *On the Frontier of Adulthood: Theory, Research, and Public Policy*, edited by Richard A. Settersten Jr., Frank F. Furstenberg, and Rubén G. Rumbaut, 29–75. Chicago: University of Chicago Press.

Gaddis, S. Michael. 2015. "Discrimination in the Credential Society: An Audit Study of Race and College Selectivity in the Labor Market." *Social Forces* 93 (4): 1451–1479. https://doi.org/10.1093/sf/sou111.

Gallup. 2016. "How Millennials Want to Work and Live." 2016. Washington, DC: Gallup. https://www.gallup.com/workplace/238073/millennials-work-live.aspx.

Gamoran, Adam. 2001. "American Schooling and Educational Inequality: A Forecast for the Twenty-first Century." *Sociology of Education* 74: 135–53. https://doi.org/10.2307/2673258.

Gans, Herbert J. 2007. "Acculturation, Assimilation and Mobility." *Ethnic and Racial Studies* 30 (1): 152–64. https://doi.org/10.1080/01419870601006637.

Gentile, Haley, and Stacy Salerno. 2019. "Communicating Intersectionality through Creative Claims Making: The Queer Undocumented Immigrant Project." *Social Identities* 25 (2): 207–23. https://doi.org/10.1080/13504630.2017.1376279.

Georgetown Law Library. n.d. "Guides: A Brief History of Civil Rights in the United States: A Timeline of the Legalization of Same-Sex Marriage in the U.S." Accessed June 2020. https://guides.ll.georgetown.edu/c.php?g=592919&p=4182201.

Gerber, Theodore P., and Sin Yi Cheung. 2008. "Horizontal Stratification in Postsecondary Education: Forms, Explanations, and Implications." *Annual Review of Sociology* 34 (1): 299–318. https://doi.org/10.1146/annurev.soc.34.040507.134604.

Gibbs, Benjamin G., Priyank G. Shah, Douglas B. Downey, and Jonathan A. Jarvis. 2016. "The Asian American Advantage in Math among Young Children: The Complex Role of Parenting." *Sociological Perspectives* 60 (2): 315–337. https://doi.org/10.1177/0731121416641676.

Glick, Jennifer E. 2010. "Connecting Complex Processes: A Decade of Research on Immigrant Families." *Journal of Marriage and Family* 72 (3): 498–515. https://doi.org/10.1111/j.1741-3737.2010.00715.x.

Goldin, Claudia, Lawrence F. Katz, and Ilyana Kuziemko. 2006. "The Homecoming of American College Women: The Reversal of the College Gender Gap." *Journal of Economic Perspectives* 20 (4): 133–56. https://doi.org/10.1257/jep.20.4.133.

Goldrick-Rab, Sara. 2006. "Following Their Every Move: An Investigation of Social-Class Differences in College Pathways." *Sociology of Education* 79 (1): 61–79. https://doi.org/10.1177/003804070607900104.

Goldscheider, Frances Kobrin, and Julie DaVanzo. 1985. "Living Arrangements and the Transition to Adulthood." *Demography* 22 (4): 545–63. https://doi.org/10.2307/2061587.

Goldstein, Joshua R., and Catherine T. Kenney. 2001. "Marriage Delayed or Marriage Forgone? New Cohort Forecasts of First Marriage for U.S. Women." *American Sociological Review* 66 (4): 506–19. https://doi.org/10.2307/3088920.

Gonzales, Roberto G. 2011. "Learning to Be Illegal: Undocumented Youth and Shifting Legal Contexts in the Transition to Adulthood." *American Sociological Review* 76 (4): 602–19. https://doi.org/10.1177/0003122411411901.

Gordon, Milton M. 1964. *Assimilation in American Life: The Role of Race, Religion and National Origins.* New York: Oxford University Press.

Gould, Elise, and Melat Kassa. 2020. "Young Workers Hit Hard by the COVID-19 Economy." *Economic Policy Institute*, October 14, 2020. https://www.epi.org/publication/young-workers-covid-recession/.

Goyette, Kimberly A. 2008. "College for Some to College for All: Social Background, Occupational Expectations, and Educational Expectations over Time." *Social Science Research* 37 (2): 461–84. https://doi.org/10.1016/j.ssresearch.2008.02.002.

———. 2017. *Education in America*. Oakland: University of California Press.

Grose, Jessica. 2020. "Why Dads Don't Take Parental Leave." *New York Times*, February 19, 2020. https://www.nytimes.com/2020/02/19/parenting/why-dads-dont-take-parental-leave.html.

Grusky, David B., Marybeth Mattingly, Charles Varner, and Stephanie Garlow. 2019. "Millennials in the United States" in "State of the Union: Millennial Dilemma." Special issue, *Pathways: A Magazine on Poverty, Inequality and Social Policy*. Stanford Center on Poverty and Inequality. https://inequality.stanford.edu/publications/pathway/state-union-2019.

Gurrentz, Benjamin. 2018. "For Young Adults, Cohabitation Is Up, Marriage Is Down: Living with an Unmarried Partner Now Common for Young Adults." *America Counts: Stories Behind the Numbers*, November 15, 2018. US Census Bureau. https://www.census.gov/library/stories/2018/11/cohabitation-is-up-marriage-is-down-for-young-adults.html.

Gurrentz, Benjamin, and Tayelor Valerio. 2019. "For First Time, Same-Sex Couples in Current Population Survey Tables: More than 190,000 Children Living with Two Same-Sex Parents in 2019." *America Counts: Stories Behind the Numbers*, November 19, 2019. U.S. Census Bureau. https://www.census.gov/library/stories/2019/11/first-time-same-sex-couples-in-current-population-survey-tables.html.

Hall, Matthew, Kelly Musick, and Youngmin Yi. 2019. "Living Arrangements and Household Complexity among Undocumented Immigrants." *Population and Development Review* 45 (1): 81–101. https://doi.org/10.1111/padr.12227.

Harding, David J. 2011. "Rethinking the Cultural Context of Schooling Decisions in Disadvantaged Neighborhoods: From Deviant Subculture to Cultural Heterogeneity." *Sociology of Education* 84 (4): 322–39. https://doi.org/10.1177/0038040711417008.

Hasegawa, Kyoko. 2019. "'Parasite Singles': Why Young Japanese Aren't Getting Married." *Agence France-Presse*, December 6, 2019. https://www.france24.com/en/20191206-parasite-singles-why-young-japanese-aren-t-getting-married.

Hatchel, Tyler, Gabriel J. Merrin, and and Dorothy Espelage. 2019. "Peer Victimization and Suicidality among LGBTQ Youth: The Roles of School Belonging, Self-Compassion, and Parental Support." *Journal of LGBT Youth* 16 (2): 134–56. https://doi.org/10.1080/19361653.2018.1543036.

Henderson, Tim. 2016. "For Many Millennials, Marriage Can Wait." *Stateline,* December 20, 2016. Pew Charitable Trust. https://www.pewtrusts.org/en /research-and-analysis/blogs/stateline/2016/12/20/for-many-millennials-marriage-can-wait.

Hipple, Steven F. 2010. "Multiple Jobholding during the 2000s." *Monthly Labor Review,* July 2010: 21–32. https://www.bls.gov/opub/mlr/2010/07/art3full .pdf.

Ho, Phoebe, and Grace Kao. 2018. "Educational Achievement and Attainment Differences among Minorities and Immigrants." In *Handbook of the Sociology of Education in the Twenty-first Century,* edited by Barbara Schneider, 109–29. Handbooks of Sociology and Social Research. Cham: Springer International Publishing.

Ho, Phoebe, and Hyunjoon Park. 2019. "Young Adults' Patterns of Leaving the Parental Home: A Focus on Differences among Asian Americans." *Journal of Marriage and Family* 81 (3): 696–712. https://doi.org/10.1111/jomf .12566.

Ho, Phoebe, Hyunjoon Park, and Grace Kao. 2019. "Racial and Ethnic Differences in Student Participation in Private Supplementary Education Activities." *Research in Social Stratification and Mobility* 59 (February): 46–59. https:// doi.org/10.1016/j.rssm.2018.11.004.

Hogan, Dennis P., and Nan Marie Astone. 1986. "The Transition to Adulthood." *Annual Review of Sociology* 12 (1): 109–30. https://doi.org/10.1146/annurev .so.12.080186.000545.

Holdaway, Jennifer. 2011. "If You Can Make It There . . . : The Transition to Adulthood in New York City." In *Coming of Age in America: The Transition to Adulthood in the Twenty-First Century,* edited by Mary C. Waters, Patrick J. Carr, Maria J. Kefalas, and Jennifer Holdaway, 133–68. Berkeley: University of California Press.

Honwana, Alcinda. 2014. "'Waithood': Youth Transitions and Social Change." In *Development and Equity: An Interdisciplinary Exploration by Ten Scholars from Africa, Asia and Latin America,* edited by Dick Foeken, Ton Dietz, Linda Johnson, and Leo de Haan, 28–40. Leiden: Brill.

Hooghe, Marc. 2012. "Taking to the Streets: Economic Crises and Youth Protest in Europe." *Harvard International Review* 34 (2): 34–38.

Hout, Michael. 1988. "More Universalism, Less Structural Mobility: The American Occupational Structure in the 1980s." *American Journal of Sociology* 93 (6): 1358–1400. https://doi.org/10.1086/228904.

———. 2012. "Social and Economic Returns to College Education in the United States." *Annual Review of Sociology* 38 (1): 379–400. https://doi.org/10.1146 /annurev.soc.012809.102503.

Howell, David R., and Arne L. Kalleberg. 2019. "Declining Job Quality in the United States: Explanations and Evidence." *RSF: The Russell Sage Founda-*

tion Journal of the Social Sciences 5 (4): 1–53. https://doi.org/10.7758/RSF
.2019.5.4.01.

Hsin, Amy, and Holly E. Reed. 2020. "The Academic Performance of
Undocumented Students in Higher Education in the United States."
International Migration Review 54 (1): 289–315. https://doi.org/10.1177
/0197918318825478.

Hsin, Amy, and Yu Xie. 2014. "Explaining Asian Americans' Academic Advantage over Whites." *Proceedings of the National Academy of Sciences* 111 (23):
8416–21. https://doi.org/10.1073/pnas.1406402111.

Huang, Josie. 2014. "Low Rates of Asian Immigrant Applicants for DACA Show a
Stigma within the Community over Being Undocumented." *The World,* August
28, 2014. https://theworld.org/stories/2014-08-28/undocumented-asian
-immigrants-shy-away-revealing-their-status.

Hummer, Robert A., and Erin R. Hamilton. 2019. *Population Health in
America.* Oakland: University of California Press.

Hurtado, Sylvia, Alma R. Clayton-Pedersen, Walter Recharde Allen, and Jeffrey
F. Milem. 1998. "Enhancing Campus Climates for Racial/Ethnic Diversity:
Educational Policy and Practice." *The Review of Higher Education* 21 (3):
279–302. https://doi.org/10.1353/rhe.1998.0003.

Hussar, Bill, Jijun Zhang, Sarah Hein, Ke Wang, Ashley Roberts, Jiashan
Cui, Mary Smith, Farrah Bullock Mann, Amy Barmer, and Rita Dilig.
2020. "The Condition of Education 2020." NCES 2020144. National
Center for Education Statistics. https://nces.ed.gov/pubsearch/pubsinfo
.asp?pubid=2020144.

Hymowitz, Kay, Jason S. Carroll, W. Bradford Wilcox, and Kelleen Kaye. 2013.
"Knot Yet: The Benefits and Costs of Delayed Marriage in America." Char-
lottesville, VA: National Marriage Project at the University of Virginia,
National Campaign to Prevent Teen and Unplanned Pregnancy, and the
Relate Institute. http://nationalmarriageproject.org/wordpress/wp-content
/uploads/2013/04/KnotYet-FinalForWeb-041413.pdf.

Iceland, John. 2017. *Race and Ethnicity in America.* Oakland: University of
California Press.

Jack, Anthony Abraham. 2016. "(No) Harm in Asking: Class, Acquired Cultural
Capital, and Academic Engagement at an Elite University." *Sociology of
Education* 89 (1): 1–19. https://doi.org/10.1177/0038040715614913.

Johfre, Sasha Shen, and Aliya Saperstein. 2019. "Racial and Gender Identities."
In State of the Union: Millennial Dilemma. Special issue, *Pathways: A
Magazine on Poverty, Inequality and Social Policy,* 7–10. https://inequality
.stanford.edu/publications/pathway/state-union-2019.

Johns Hopkins University Coronavirus Resource Center. n.d.COVID-19 United
States Cases by County." Accessed May 2021. https://coronavirus.jhu.edu/us-
map.

Johnson, M. K., R. Crosnoe, and G. H. Elder Jr. 2001. "Students' Attachment and Academic Engagement: The Role of Race and Ethnicity." *Sociology of Education* 74 (4): 318–40.

Johnson, Sandra. 2020. "A Changing Nation: Population Projections under Alternative Immigration Scenarios." Current Population Reports, P25-1146. Washington, DC: US Census Bureau. https://www.census.gov/content/dam /Census/library/publications/2020/demo/p25-1146.pdf.

Jones, Robert P., Daniel Cox, and Thomas Banchoff. 2012. "A Generation in Transition: Religion, Values, and Politics among College-Age Millennials." Public Religion Research Institute. https://www.prri.org/research/millennial-values-survey-2012/.

Joo, Yunjeong. 2018. "Same Despair but Different Hope: Youth Activism in East Asia and Contentious Politics." *Development and Society* 47 (3): 401–22.

Jordan, Miriam. 2020. "One Brother Got DACA, One Didn't. It Made All the Difference." *New York Times,* July 3, 2020. https://www.nytimes.com/2020/07 /03/us/immigration-daca-applications.html.

Juárez, Fatima, and Cecilia Gayet. 2014. "Transitions to Adulthood in Developing Countries." *Annual Review of Sociology* 40 (1): 521–38. https://doi.org /10.1146/annurev-soc-052914-085540.

Kalleberg, Arne L. 2011. *Good Jobs, Bad Jobs: The Rise of Polarized and Precarious Employment Systems in the United States, 1970s to 2000s.* New York: Russell Sage Foundation.

Kalleberg, Arne L., and Till M. von Wachter. 2017. "The U.S. Labor Market During and After the Great Recession: Continuities and Transformations." *RSF: The Russell Sage Foundation Journal of the Social Sciences* 3 (3): 1–19. https://doi.org/10.7758/rsf.2017.3.3.01.

Kalmijn, Matthijs. 2011. "The Influence of Men's Income and Employment on Marriage and Cohabitation: Testing Oppenheimer's Theory in Europe." *European Journal of Population / Revue Européenne de Démographie* 27 (3): 269–93. https://doi.org/10.1007/s10680-011-9238-x.

Kao, Grace. 2000. "Group Images and Possible Selves among Adolescents: Linking Stereotypes to Expectations by Race and Ethnicity." *Sociological Forum* 15 (3): 407–30. https://doi.org/10.1023/A:1007572209544.

Kao, Grace, Kelly Stamper Balistreri, and Kara Joyner. 2018. "Asian American Men in Romantic Dating Markets." *Contexts,* December 13, 2018. https://doi.org/10.1177/1536504218812869.

Kao, Grace, Kara Joyner, and Kelly Stamper Balistreri. 2019. *The Company We Keep: Interracial Friendships and Romantic Relationships from Adolescence to Adulthood.* New York: Russell Sage Foundation.

Kao, Grace, and Jennifer S. Thompson. 2003. "Racial and Ethnic Stratification in Educational Achievement and Attainment." *Annual Review of Sociology* 29 (1): 417–42. https://doi.org/10.1146/annurev.soc.29.010202.100019.

Kao, Grace, and Marta Tienda. 1995. "Optimism and Achievement: The Educational Performance of Immigrant Youth." *Social Science Quarterly* 76 (1): 1–19.

Kao, Grace, Elizabeth Vaquera, and Kimberly Goyette. 2013. *Education and Immigration*. Cambridge: Polity Press.

Kasinitz, Philip, John H. Mollenkopf, Mary C. Waters, and Jennifer Holdaway. 2008. *Inheriting the City: The Children of Immigrants Come of Age*. New York: Russell Sage Foundation.

Katz-Wise, Sabra L., Margaret Rosario, and Michael Tsappis. 2016. "LGBT Youth and Family Acceptance." *Pediatric Clinics of North America* 63 (6): 1011–25. https://doi.org/10.1016/j.pcl.2016.07.005.

Kennedy, S., and C. Fitch. 2012. "Measuring Cohabitation and Family Structure in the United States: Assessing the Impact of New Data from the Current Population Survey." *Demography* 49 (4): 1479–98. https://doi.org/10.1007/s13524-012-0126-8.

Kenney, Genevieve M., and Douglas A. Wissoker. 1994. "An Analysis of the Correlates of Discrimination Facing Young Hispanic Job-Seekers." *The American Economic Review* 84 (3): 674–83.

Killewald, Alexandra, and Brielle Bryan. 2018. "Falling Behind: The Role of Inter- and Intragenerational Processes in Widening Racial and Ethnic Wealth Gaps through Early and Middle Adulthood." *Social Forces* 97 (2): 705–40. https://doi.org/10.1093/sf/soy060.

Kim, ChangHwan, and Arthur Sakamoto. 2010. "Have Asian American Men Achieved Labor Market Parity with White Men?" *American Sociological Review* 75 (6): 934–57. https://doi.org/10.1177/0003122410388501.

Kim, Soo Mee, and Aggie J. Yellow Horse. 2018. "Undocumented Asians, Left in theShadows."*Contexts*17(4):70–71.https://doi.org/10.1177/1536504218812875.

Klein, Ezra. 2021. "Did the Boomers Ruin America? A Debate." *The Ezra Klein Show*, April 6, 2021. https://www.nytimes.com/2021/04/06/opinion/ezra-klein-podcast-helen-andrews-jill-filipovic-boomers.html.

Kochhar, Rakesh, Richard Fry, and Paul Taylor. 2011. "Wealth Gaps Rise to Record Highs between Whites, Blacks, Hispanics." Pew Research Center, July 26, 2011. https://www.pewsocialtrends.org/2011/07/26/wealth-gaps-rise-to-record-highs-between-whites-blacks-hispanics/.

Koval, John. 2008. "Hourglass Economy." In *Encyclopedia of Race, Ethnicity, and Society,* edited by Richard T. Schaefer, 655–56. Thousand Oaks, CA: SAGE Publications.

Krieder, Rose M., and Jonathan Vespa. 2015. "Historic Rise of Living Alone and Fall of Boarders in the United States: 1850–2010." SEHSD Working Paper No. 2015-11. Presented at the Population Association of American annual meeting, April 30–May 2, 2015. https://www.census.gov/content/dam/Census/library/working-papers/2015/demo/SEHSD-WP2015-11.pdf.

Lareau, Annette. 2011. *Unequal Childhoods: Class, Race, and Family Life.* 2nd ed. Berkeley: University of California Press.

LBJ Presidential Library. n.d. "Signing of the Immigration and Nationality Act, October 3, 1965." Accessed January 2022. https://www.lbjlibrary.org/object /text/signing-immigration-and-nationality-act-10-03-1965.

Lee, Jennifer, Frank D. Bean, and Kathy Sloane. 2003. "Beyond Black and White: Remaking Race in America." *Contexts* 2 (3): 26–33. https://doi.org /10.1525/ctx.2003.2.3.26.

Lee, Jennifer, and Min Zhou. 2015. *The Asian American Achievement Paradox.* New York: Russell Sage Foundation.

Lei, Lei, and Scott J. South. 2016. "Racial and Ethnic Differences in Leaving and Returning to the Parental Home: The Role of Life Course Transitions, Socioeconomic Resources, and Family Connectivity." *Demographic Research* 34 (4): 109–42. https://doi.org/10.4054/DemRes.2016.34.4.

Leonhardt, Megan. 2019. "What It's Like Trying to Live on Minimum Wage— It's a 'Constant Struggle.'" *CNBC*, July 18, 2019. https://www.cnbc.com/2019 /07/18/what-its-like-to-live-on-minimum-wage-in-the-us.html.

Levin, Dan. 2019. "The Human Experience Is Infinite." *New York Times*, June 28, 2019. https://www.nytimes.com/interactive/2019/06/28/us/pride-identity .html.

Lichter, Daniel T., Zhenchao Qian, and Dmitry Tumin. 2015. "Whom Do Immigrants Marry? Emerging Patterns of Intermarriage and Integration in the United States." *ANNALS of the American Academy of Political and Social Science* 662 (1): 57–78. https://doi.org/10.1177/0002716215594614.

Lima, Maria da Paz Campos, and Antonio Martín Artiles. 2013. "Youth Voice(s) in EU Countries and Social Movements in Southern Europe." *Transfer: European Review of Labour and Research* 19 (3): 345–64. https://doi .org/10.1177/1024258913493732.

Livingston, Gretchen. 2015. "For Most Highly Educated Women, Motherhood Doesn't Start until the 30s." Pew Research Center, January 15, 2015. https:// www.pewresearch.org/fact-tank/2015/01/15/for-most-highly-educated-women-motherhood-doesnt-start-until-the-30s/.

———. 2018. "The Changing Profile of Unmarried Parents." Pew Research Center, April 25, 2018. https://www.pewsocialtrends.org/2018/04/25/the-changing-profile-of-unmarried-parents/.

Livingston, Gretchen, and Anna Brown. 2017. "Intermarriage in the U.S. 50 Years after Loving v. Virginia." Pew Research Center, May 18, 2017. https:// www.pewresearch.org/social-trends/2017/05/18/intermarriage-in-the-u-s-50-years-after-loving-v-virginia/.

Long, Bridget Terry, and Michael Kurlaender. 2009. "Do Community Colleges Provide a Viable Pathway to a Baccalaureate Degree?" *Educational Evaluation and Policy Analysis* 31 (1): 30–53. https://doi .org/10.3102/0162373708327756.

Louie, Vivian. 2004. *Compelled to Excel: Immigration, Education, and Opportunity among Chinese Americans*. Stanford, CA: Stanford University Press.

———. 2012. *Keeping the Immigrant Bargain: The Costs and Rewards of Success in America*. New York: Russell Sage Foundation Publications.

Lubrano, Alfred. 2012. "Diminished Diplomas." *Philadelphia Inquirer*, December 30, 2012. https://www.inquirer.com/philly/business/20121230_Degrees_of_Despair.html.

Ma, Jennifer, Matea Pender, and Meredith Welch. 2016. "Education Pays 2016: The Benefits of Higher Education for Individuals and Society." Trends in Higher Education Series. New York: College Board. https://research.collegeboard.org/pdf/education-pays-2016-full-report.pdf.

Macapagal, Kathryn, George J. Greene, Zenaida Rivera, and Brian Mustanski. 2015. "'The Best Is Always Yet to Come': Relationship Stages and Processes among Young LGBT Couples." *Journal of Family Psychology* 29 (3): 309–20. https://doi.org/10.1037/fam0000094.

MacLeod, Jay. 2009. *Ain't No Makin' it: Aspirations and Attainment in a Low-Income Neighborhood*. 3rd ed. Boulder, CO: Westview Press.

Macmillan, Ross, and Ronda Copher. 2005. "Families in the Life Course: Interdependency of Roles, Role Configurations, and Pathways." *Journal of Marriage and Family* 67 (4): 858–79. https://doi.org/10.1111/j.1741-3737.2005.00180.x.

Macmillan, Ross, and Scott R. Eliason. 2003. "Characterizing the Life Course as Role Configurations and Pathways." In *Handbook of the Life Course*, edited by Jeylan T. Mortimer and Michael J. Shanahan, 529–54. Handbooks of Sociology and Social Research. Boston, MA: Springer US.

"Malala Yousafzai—Biographical." n.d. The Nobel Peace Prize 2014. Accessed October 2021. https://www.nobelprize.org/prizes/peace/2014/yousafzai/biographical/.

Manning, Wendy D., Susan L. Brown, and Krista K. Payne. 2021. "Does Cohabitation Compensate for Marriage Decline?" *Contexts* 20 (2): 68–69. https://doi.org/10.1177/15365042211012076.

Martin, Joyce A., Brady E. Hamilton, Michelle J. K. Osterman, and Anne K. Driscoll. 2019. "Births: Final Data for 2018." *National Vital Statistics Reports* 68 (13).

Massey, Douglas S., Camille Z. Charles, Garvey F. Lundy, and Mary J. Fischer. 2003. *The Source of the River: The Social Origins of Freshmen at America's Selective Colleges and Universities*. Princeton, NJ: Princeton University Press.

Massey, Douglas S., and Deborah S. Hirst. 1998. "From Escalator to Hourglass: Changes in the U.S. Occupational Wage Structure 1949–1989." *Social Science Research* 27 (1): 51–71. https://doi.org/10.1006/ssre.1997.0612.

Mathews, T. J., and Brady E. Hamilton. 2019. "Educational Attainment of Mothers Aged 25 and Over: United States, 2017." *National Center for Health Statistics Data Brief,* no. 332. https://www.cdc.gov/nchs/products/databriefs /db332.htm.

McConville, Mark. 2020. *Failure to Launch: Why Your Twentysomething Hasn't Grown Up . . . and What to Do About It.* New York: G. P. Putnam's Sons.

McLanahan, Sara. 2004. "Diverging Destinies: How Children Are Faring under the Second Demographic Transition." *Demography* 41 (4): 607–27. https:// doi.org/10.1353/dem.2004.0033.

McLanahan, Sara, and Karen Booth. 1989. "Mother-Only Families: Problems, Prospects, and Politics." *Journal of Marriage and Family* 51 (3): 557–80. https://doi.org/10.2307/352157.

Mehus, Christopher J., Ryan J. Watson, Marla E. Eisenberg, Heather L. Corliss, and Carolyn M. Porta. 2017. "Living as an LGBTQ Adolescent and a Parent's Child: Overlapping or Separate Experiences." *Journal of Family Nursing* 23 (2): 175–200. https://doi.org/10.1177/1074840717696924.

Meier, Ann, and Gina Allen. 2008. "Intimate Relationship Development during the Transition to Adulthood: Differences by Social Class." *New Directions for Child and Adolescent Development* 2008 (119): 25–39. https://doi.org/10.1002 /cd.207.

Mickelson, Roslyn Arlin. 1990. "The Attitude-Achievement Paradox among Black Adolescents." *Sociology of Education* 63 (1): 44–61. https://doi.org/10 .2307/2112896.

Milkman, Ruth. 2017. "A New Political Generation: Millennials and the Post-2008 Wave of Protest." *American Sociological Review* 82 (1): 1–31. https://doi .org/10.1177/0003122416681031.

Mills, Melinda, Ronald R. Rindfuss, Peter McDonald, Egbert te Velde, on behalf of the ESHRE Reproduction and Society Task Force. 2011. "Why Do People Postpone Parenthood? Reasons and Social Policy Incentives." *Human Reproduction Update* 17 (6): 848–60. https://doi.org/10.1093/humupd /dmr026.

Min, Pyong Gap, and Chigon Kim. 2009. "Patterns of Intermarriages and Cross-Generational In-Marriages among Native-Born Asian Americans." *The International Migration Review* 43 (3): 447–70. https://doi.org/10.1111 /j.1747-7379.2009.00773.x.

Monaghan, David B., and Paul Attewell. 2015. "The Community College Route to the Bachelor's Degree." *Educational Evaluation and Policy Analysis* 37 (1): 70–91. https://doi.org/10.3102/0162373714521865.

Mont'Alvao, Arnaldo, and Monica K. Johnson. 2016. "The Great Recession and Young Adults' Labor Market Outcomes around the World." *Emerging Trends in the Social and Behavioral Sciences,* November 29, 2016. https://doi.org /10.1002/9781118900772.etrds0404.

Moore, Mignon R., and Michael Stambolis-Ruhstorfer. 2013. "LGBT Sexuality and Families at the Start of the Twenty-First Century." *Annual Review of Sociology* 39 (1): 491–507. https://www.annualreviews.org/doi/10.1146/annurev-soc-071312-145643.

Nahrgang, Jennifer D., Hudson Sessions, Manuel Vaulont, and Amy Bartels. 2020. "Make Your Side Hustle Work." *Harvard Business Review*, March 18, 2020. https://hbr.org/2020/03/make-your-side-hustle-work.

Nesteruk, Olena, and Alexandra Gramescu. 2012. "Dating and Mate Selection among Young Adults from Immigrant Families." *Marriage and Family Review* 48 (1): 40–58. https://doi.org/10.1080/01494929.2011.620732.

Newman, Judith. 2019. "Help! My Adult Kid Has 'Failed to Launch.'" *AARP*, February 27, 2019. http://www.aarp.org/disrupt-aging/stories/info-2019/failure-to-launch.html.

Newman, Katherine S. 2008. "Ties That Bind: Cultural Interpretations of Delayed Adulthood in Western Europe and Japan." *Sociological Forum* 23 (4): 645–69. https://doi.org/10.1111/j.1573-7861.2008.00089.x.

———. 2012. *The Accordion Family: Boomerang Kids, Anxious Parents, and the Private Toll of Global Competition*. Boston: Beacon Press.

Ngai, Mae M. 2004. *Impossible Subjects: Illegal Aliens and the Making of Modern America*. Princeton, NJ: Princeton University Press.

Nguyen, Terry. 2020. "The Class of 2020 Was Full of Hope. Then the Pandemic Hit." *Vox*, December 9, 2020. https://www.vox.com/the-goods/22158622/youth-unemployment-rate.

Nummi, Jozie, Carly Jennings, and Joe Feagin. 2019. "#BlackLivesMatter: Innovative Black Resistance." *Sociological Forum* 34 (S1): 1042–64. https://doi.org/10.1111/socf.12540.

Ochoa, Gilda L. 2013. *Academic Profiling: Latinos, Asian Americans, and the Achievement Gap*. Minneapolis: University of Minnesota Press.

Oesterle, Sabrina, J. David Hawkins, Karl G. Hill, and Jennifer A. Bailey. 2010. "Men's and Women's Pathways to Adulthood and Their Adolescent Precursors." *Journal of Marriage and Family* 72 (5): 1436–53. https://doi.org/10.1111/j.1741-3737.2010.00775.x.

Ogbu, John U. 1987. "Variability in Minority School Performance: A Problem in Search of an Explanation." *Anthropology and Education Quarterly* 18 (4): 312–34. https://doi.org/10.1525/aeq.1987.18.4.04x0022v.

———. 1991. "Immigrant and Involuntary Minorities in Comparative Perspective." In *Minority Status and Schooling: A Comparative Study of Immigrants and Involuntary Minorities*, edited by Margaret A. Gibson and John U. Ogbu, 3–33. New York: Garland Publishing.

Ogbu, John U., and Herbert D. Simons. 1998. "Voluntary and Involuntary Minorities: A Cultural-Ecological Theory of School Performance with Some Implications for Education." *Anthropology and Education Quarterly* 29 (2): 155–88. https://doi.org/10.1525/aeq.1998.29.2.155.

Okimoto, Jean Davies, and Phyllis Jackson Stegall. 1987. *Boomerang Kids: How to Live with Adult Children Who Return Home.* Boston: Little Brown and Company.

Olson, Kristina R., Lily Durwood, Madeleine DeMeules, and Katie A. McLaughlin. 2016. "Mental Health of Transgender Children Who Are Supported in Their Identities." *Pediatrics* 137 (3): e20153223. https://doi.org/10.1542/peds.2015-3223.

Omi, Michael, and Howard Winant. 2014. *Racial Formation in the United States: From the 1960s to the 1990s.* 3rd ed. New York: Routledge.

Organisation for Economic Co-operation and Development (OECD). 2016a. "The NEET Challenge: What Can Be Done for Jobless and Disengaged Youth?" In *Society at a Glance 2016: OECD Social Indicators,* 13–68. Paris: OECD Publishing. https://doi.org/10.1787/9789264261488-en.

———. 2016b. "SF3.3: Cohabitation Rate and Prevalence of Other Forms of Partnership." OECD Family Database. http://www.oecd.org/els/family/SF_3-3-Cohabitation-forms-partnership.pdf.

———. 2018. "SF2.4: Share of Births Outside of Marriage." OECD Family Database. https://www.oecd.org/els/family/SF_2_4_Share_births_outside_marriage.pdf.

———. 2019. *Society at a Glance 2019.* Paris: OECD Publishing. https://www.oecd-ilibrary.org/social-issues-migration-health/society-at-a-glance_19991290.

———. 2021. *Education at a Glance 2021: OECD Indicators.* Paris: OECD Publishing, https://doi.org/10.1787/b35a14e5-en.

Oropesa, R. S., and Nancy S. Landale. 1997. "In Search of the New Second Generation: Alternative Strategies for Identifying Second Generation Children and Understanding Their Acquisition of English." *Sociological Perspectives* 40 (3): 429–55. https://doi.org/10.2307/1389451.

Orrenius, Pia M., and Madeline Zavodny. 2009. "Do Immigrants Work in Riskier Jobs?" *Demography* 46 (3): 535–51. https://doi.org/10.1353/dem.0.0064.

Osgood, D. Wayne, Gretchen Ruth, Jacquelynne S. Eccles, Janis E. Jacobs, and Bonnie L. Barber. 2005. "Six Paths to Adulthood: Fast Starters, Parents without Careers, Educated Partners, Educated Singles, Working Singles, and Slow Starters." In *On the Frontier of Adulthood: Theory, Research, and Public Policy,* edited by Richard A. Settersten Jr., Frank F. Furstenberg Jr., and Rubén G. Rumbaut, 320–55. Chicago: University of Chicago Press.

Oxford Languages. n.d.a. "Word of the Year." *Oxford Languages.* Accessed February 2021. https://languages.oup.com/word-of-the-year/.

———. n.d.b. "Word of the Year 2016: Shortlist." *Oxford Languages.* Accessed February 2021. https://languages.oup.com/word-of-the-year/2016-shortlist/.

Pager, Devah. 2007. "The Use of Field Experiments for Studies of Employment Discrimination: Contributions, Critiques, and Directions for the Future." *ANNALS of the American Academy of Political and Social Science* 609 (1): 104–33. https://doi.org/10.1177/0002716206294796.

Panel on Youth of the President's Science Advisory Committee. 1973. "Youth: Transition to Adulthood." Washington, DC: Office of Science and Technology, Executive Office of the President.

Park, Hyunjoon, Claudia Buchmann, Jaesung Choi, and Joseph J. Merry. 2016. "Learning beyond the School Walls: Trends and Implications." *Annual Review of Sociology* 42 (1): 231–52. https://doi.org/10.1146/annurev-soc-081715-074341.

Park, Hyunjoon, and Jae Kyung Lee. 2017. "Growing Educational Differentials in the Retreat from Marriage among Korean Men." *Social Science Research* 66 (August): 187–200. https://doi.org/10.1016/j.ssresearch.2016.10.003.

Park, Hyunjoon, and Gary D. Sandefur. 2005. "Transition to Adulthood in Japan and Korea: An Overview." In *Sociological Studies of Children and Youth*, edited by Loretta Bass, 10:43–73. Sociological Studies of Children and Youth. Bingley, UK: Emerald Group Publishing.

Park, Jung-Youn. 2015. "Korea's 'Kangaroo Tribe' Gets Larger." *Korea JoongAng Daily*, May 25, 2015. https://koreajoongangdaily.joins.com/2015/05/25/economy/Koreas-kangaroo-tribe-gets-larger/3004594.html.

Parker, Kim, and Renee Stepler. 2017. "As U.S. Marriage Rate Hovers at 50%, Education Gap in Marital Status Widens." *Pew Research Center Fact Tank*, September 14, 2017. https://www.pewresearch.org/fact-tank/2017/09/14/as-u-s-marriage-rate-hovers-at-50-education-gap-in-marital-status-widens/.

Patler, Caitlin. 2018. "Citizen Advantage, Undocumented Disadvantage, or Both? The Comparative Educational Outcomes of Second and 1.5-Generation Latino Young Adults." *International Migration Review*, August 13, 2018. https://doi.org/10.1111/imre.12347.

Pattillo-McCoy, Mary. 2000. "The Limits of Out-Migration for the Black Middle Class." *Journal of Urban Affairs* 22 (3): 225–41. https://doi.org/10.1111/0735-2166.00054.

Payne, Krista K. 2021. "Median Age at First Marriage, 2019." *Family Profile* 21 (12). National Center for Family and Marriage Research. https://www.bgsu.edu/ncfmr/resources/data/family-profiles/payne-median-age-marriage-2020-fp-21-12.html.

Pew Research Center. 2015. "Modern Immigration Wave Brings 59 Million to U.S., Driving Population Growth and Change Through 2065: Views of Immigration's Impact on U.S. Society Mixed." Washington, DC: Pew Research Center. http://www.pewhispanic.org/2015/09/28/modern-immigration-wave-brings-59-million-to-u-s-driving-population-growth-and-change-through-2065/.

Peyton, Nellie. 2021. "Generation COVID: How the Young Are Working Round Pandemic-Hit Job Market." *Reuters,* January 11, 2021. https://www.reuters .com/article/health-coronavirus-youth-employment-idUSL8N2IQ5PA.

Piketty, Thomas, and Emmanuel Saez. 2014. "Inequality in the Long Run." *Science* 344 (6186): 838–43. https://doi.org/10.1126/science.1251936.

Pila, Daniela. 2016. "'I'm Not Good Enough for Anyone': Legal Status and the Dating Lives of Undocumented Young Adults." *Sociological Forum* 31 (1): 138–58. https://doi.org/10.1111/socf.12237.

Portes, Alejandro, Patricia Fernández-Kelly, and William Haller. 2009. "The Adaptation of the Immigrant Second Generation in America: A Theoretical Overview and Recent Evidence." *Journal of Ethnic and Migration Studies* 35 (7): 1077–1104. https://doi.org/10.1080/13691830903006127.

Portes, Alejandro, and Rubén G. Rumbaut. 2001. *Legacies: The Story of the Immigrant Second Generation.* Berkeley: University of California Press.

———. 2006. *Immigrant America: A Portrait.* Berkeley: University of California Press.

Portes, Alejandro, and Min Zhou. 1993. "The New Second Generation: Segmented Assimilation and Its Variants." *ANNALS of the American Academy of Political and Social Science* 530 (1): 74–96. https://doi.org/10.1177/00027 16293530001006.

Posselt, Julie R., and Eric Grodsky. 2017. "Graduate Education and Social Stratification." *Annual Review of Sociology* 43 (1): 353–78. https://doi.org /10.1146/annurev-soc-081715-074324.

Preston, Caroline. 2019. "When a College Degree Is No Longer a Ticket to the Middle Class." *The Hechinger Report,* February 7, 2019. https://hechingerreport .org/when-a-college-degree-is-no-longer-a-ticket-to-the-middle-class/.

Qian, Zhenchao. 2014. "The Divergent Paths of American Families." In *Diversity and Disparities,* edited by John R. Logan, 237–69. America Enters a New Century. New York: Russell Sage Foundation.

Qian, Zhenchao, Jennifer E. Glick, and Christie D. Batson. 2012. "Crossing Boundaries: Nativity, Ethnicity, and Mate Selection." *Demography* 49 (2): 651–75. https://doi.org/10.1007/s13524-012-0090-3.

Qian, Zhenchao, and Daniel T. Lichter. 2007. "Social Boundaries and Marital Assimilation: Interpreting Trends in Racial and Ethnic Intermarriage." *American Sociological Review* 72 (1): 68–94. https://doi.org/10.1177 /000312240707200104.

Raley, R. Kelly, Megan M. Sweeney, and Danielle Wondra. 2015. "The Growing Racial and Ethnic Divide in U.S. Marriage Patterns." *The Future of Children* 25 (2): 89–109. https://doi.org/10.1353/foc.2015.0014.

Refinery29. 2018. "8 Millennial Women on Why They Love Living Alone: And How They Make It Work." *Refinery29,* November 13, 2018. https://www .refinery29.com/en-us/living-alone-pros-benefits-women.

Rindfuss, Ronald R. 1991. "The Young Adult Years: Diversity, Structural Change, and Fertility." *Demography* 28 (4): 493–512. https://doi.org/10.2307/2061419.

Roe, Stuart. 2017. "'Family Support Would Have Been Like Amazing': LGBTQ Youth Experiences with Parental and Family Support." *Family Journal* 25 (1): 55–62. https://doi.org/10.1177/1066480716679651.

Rolen, Emily. 2019. "Occupational Employment Projections through the Perspective of Education and Training." *Spotlight on Statistics*, January 2019. US Bureau of Labor Statistics. https://www.bls.gov/spotlight/2019/education-projections/home.htm.

Ruggles, Steven, Sarah Flood, Sophia Foster, Ronald Goeken, Jose Pacas, Megan Schouweiler, and Matthew Sobek. 2021. *IPUMS USA: Version 11.0 [Dataset]*. Minneapolis: IPUMS. https://doi.org/10.18128/D010.V11.0.

Rumbaut, Rubén G. 2004. "Ages, Life Stages, and Generational Cohorts: Decomposing the Immigrant First and Second Generations in the United States." *International Migration Review* 38 (3): 1160–1205. https://doi.org/10.1111/j.1747-7379.2004.tb00232.x.

Rumbaut, Rubén G., and Golnaz Komaie. 2010. "Immigration and Adult Transitions." *The Future of Children* 20 (1): 43–66. https://doi.org/10.1353/foc.0.0046.

Rusin, Sylvia. 2015. "Origin and Community: Asian and Latin American Unauthorized Youth and U.S. Deportation Relief." *Migration Information Source*, August 13, 2015. https://www.migrationpolicy.org/article/origin-and-community-asian-and-latin-american-unauthorized-youth-and-us-deportation-relief.

Saez, Emmanuel. 2017. "Income and Wealth Inequality: Evidence and Policy Implications." *Contemporary Economic Policy* 35 (1): 7–25. https://doi.org/10.1111/coep.12210.

Sakamoto, Arthur, and Sharron Xuanren Wang. 2021. "Deconstructing Hyper-Selectivity: Are the Socioeconomic Attainments of Second-Generation Asian Americans Only Due to Their Class Background?" *Chinese Journal of Sociology* 7 (1): 3–21. https://doi.org/10.1177/2057150X20973802.

Sandefur, Gary D., Jennifer Eggerling-Boeck, and Hyunjoon Park. 2005. "Off to a Good Start? Postsecondary Education and Early Adult Life." In *On the Frontier of Adulthood: Theory, Research, and Public Policy,* edited by Richard A. Settersten Jr., Frank F. Furstenberg Jr., and Rubén G. Rumbaut, 292–319. Chicago: University of Chicago Press.

Sassler, Sharon, and Amanda Jayne Miller. 2017. *Cohabitation Nation: Gender, Class, and the Remaking of Relationships.* Oakland: University of California Press.

Schaeffer, Katherine. 2019. "The Most Common Age among Whites in U.S. Is 58—More than Double That of Racial and Ethnic Minorities." *Pew Research*

Center Fact Tank, July 30, 2019. https://www.pewresearch.org/fact-tank/2019/07/30/most-common-age-among-us-racial-ethnic-groups/.

Schneider, Barbara, and Yongsook Lee. 1990. "A Model for Academic Success: The School and Home Environment of East Asian Students." *Anthropology and Education Quarterly* 21 (4): 358–77. https://doi.org/10.1525/aeq.1990.21.4.04x0596x.

Schneider, Daniel, Kristen Harknett, and Matthew Stimpson. 2018. "What Explains the Decline in First Marriage in the United States? Evidence from the Panel Study of Income Dynamics, 1969 to 2013." *Journal of Marriage and Family* 80 (4): 791–811. https://doi.org/10.1111/jomf.12481.

Schweizer, Valerie . 2020. "Marriage: More than a Century of Change, 1900–2018." *Family Profile* 20 (21). National Center for Family and Marriage Research. https://www.bgsu.edu/ncfmr/resources/data/family-profiles/schweizer-marriage-century-change-1900-2018-fp-20-21.html.

Settersten Jr., Richard A., Frank F. Furstenberg, and Rubén G. Rumbaut, eds. 2005. *On the Frontier of Adulthood: Theory, Research, and Public Policy.* Chicago: University of Chicago Press.

Settersten, Richard A., and Barbara Ray. 2010a. *Not Quite Adults: Why 20-Somethings Are Choosing a Slower Path to Adulthood, and Why It's Good for Everyone.* New York: Bantam Books.

———. 2010b. "What's Going on with Young People Today? The Long and Twisting Path to Adulthood." *The Future of Children* 20 (1): 19–41. https://doi.org/10.1353/foc.0.0044.

Shanahan, Michael J. 2000. "Pathways to Adulthood in Changing Societies: Variability and Mechanisms in Life Course Perspective." *Annual Review of Sociology* 26 (1): 667–92. https://doi.org/10.1146/annurev.soc.26.1.667.

Shanahan, Michael J., Erik J. Porfeli, Jeylan T. Mortimer, and Lance D. Erikson. 2005. "Subjective Age Identity and the Transition to Adulthood: When Does One Become an Adult?" In *On the Frontier of Adulthood: Theory, Research, and Public Policy,* edited by Richard A. Settersten Jr., Frank F. Furstenberg, and Rubén G. Rumbaut, 225–55. Chicago: University of Chicago Press.

Shapiro, Doug, Afet Dundar, Phoebe Khasiala Wakhungu, Xin Yuan, Angel Nathan, and Youngsik Hwang. 2016. "Time to Degree: A National View of the Time Enrolled and Elapsed for Associate and Bachelor's Degree Earners." *National Student Clearinghouse,* no. 11. https://eric.ed.gov/?id=ED580231.

Shear, Michael D., and Julie Hirschfeld Davis. 2017. "Trump Moves to End DACA and Calls on Congress to Act." *New York Times,* September 5, 2017. https://www.nytimes.com/2017/09/05/us/politics/trump-daca-dreamers-immigration.html.

Silva, Jennifer M. 2013. *Coming Up Short: Working-Class Adulthood in an Age of Uncertainty.* New York: Oxford University Press.

Silver, Alexis. 2012. "Aging into Exclusion and Social Transparency: Undocumented Immigrant Youth and the Transition to Adulthood." *Latino Studies* 10 (4): 499–522. https://doi.org/10.1057/lst.2012.41.

Smalley, Andrew. 2020. "Higher Education Responses to Coronavirus (COVID-19)." *National Conference of State Legislatures,* December 28, 2020. https://www.ncsl.org/research/education/higher-education-responses-to-coronavirus-covid-19.aspx.

Smith, Robert Courtney. 2006. *Mexican New York: Transnational Lives of New Immigrants.* Berkeley: University of California Press.

Smith, Tom W. 2004. "Coming of Age in Twenty-First Century America: Public Attitudes Towards the Importance and Timing of Transitions to Adulthood." *Ageing International* 29 (2): 136–48. https://doi.org/10.1007/s12126-004-1014-3.

Smith-Morris, Carolyn, Daisy Morales-Campos, Edith Alejandra Castañeda Alvarez, and Matthew Turner. 2013. "An Anthropology of Familismo: On Narratives and Description of Mexican/Immigrants." *Hispanic Journal of Behavioral Sciences* 35 (1): 35–60. https://doi.org/10.1177/0739986312459508.

Smock, Pamela J. 2000. "Cohabitation in the United States: An Appraisal of Research Themes, Findings, and Implications." *Annual Review of Sociology* 26 (1): 1–20. https://doi.org/10.1146/annurev.soc.26.1.1.

Smock, Pamela J., and Christine R. Schwartz. 2020. "The Demography of Families: A Review of Patterns and Change." *Journal of Marriage and Family* 82 (1): 9–34. https://doi.org/10.1111/jomf.12612.

Snyder, Thomas D., Cristobal de Brey, and Sally A. Dillow. 2019. "Digest of Education Statistics 2018." NCES 2020009. Washington, DC: National Center for Education Statistics. https://nces.ed.gov/pubsearch/pubsinfo.asp?pubid=2020009.

South, Scott J., and Lei Lei. 2015. "Failures-to-Launch and Boomerang Kids: Contemporary Determinants of Leaving and Returning to the Parental Home." *Social Forces* 94 (2): 863–90. https://doi.org/10.1093/sf/sov064.

Staklis, Sandra. 2016. "Employment and Enrollment Status of Baccalaureate Degree Recipients 1 Year After Graduation: 1994, 2001, and 2009." NCES 2017407. Washington, DC: National Center for Education Statistics. https://nces.ed.gov/pubsearch/pubsinfo.asp?pubid=2017407.

Steele, Claude M. 1997. "A Threat in the Air: How Stereotypes Shape Intellectual Identity and Performance." *American Psychologist* 52 (6): 613–29. https://doi.org/10.1037/0003-066X.52.6.613.

Stephens, Maria, Laura K. Warren, and Ariana L. Harner. 2015. "Comparative Indicators of Education in the United States and Other G-20 Countries: 2015." NCES 2016100. Washington, DC: National Center for Education Statistics. https://nces.ed.gov/pubs2016/2016100/.

Stykes, Bart, Krista K. Payne, and Larry Gibbs. 2014. "First Marriage Rate in the U.S., 2012." *Family Profiles,* FP-14-08. National Center for Family and Marriage Research. https://www.bgsu.edu/content/dam/BGSU/college-of-arts-and-sciences/NCFMR/documents/FP/FP-14-08-marriage-rate-2012.pdf.

Sue, Stanley, and Sumie Okazaki. 1990. "Asian-American Educational Achievements: A Phenomenon in Search of an Explanation." *American Psychologist* 45 (8): 913–20. https://doi.org/10.1037/0003-066X.45.8.913.

Sweeney, Megan M. 2002. "Two Decades of Family Change: The Shifting Economic Foundations of Marriage." *American Sociological Review* 67 (1): 132–47. https://doi.org/10.2307/3088937.

Tamir, Christine, and Monica Anderson. 2022. "One-in-Ten Black People Living in the U.S. Are Immigrants." Pew Research Center, January 20, 2022. https://www.pewresearch.org/race-ethnicity/2022/01/20/one-in-ten-black-people-living-in-the-u-s-are-immigrants/.

Taylor, Paul, Kim Parker, Rakesh Kochhar, Richard Fry, Cary Funk, Eileen Patten, and Seth Motel. 2012. "Young, Underemployed and Optimistic: Coming of Age, Slowly, in a Tough Economy." Pew Research Center, February 9, 2012. https://www.pewsocialtrends.org/2012/02/09/young-underemployed-and-optimistic/.

Telles, Edward M., and Vilma Ortiz. 2008. *Generations of Exclusion: Mexican-Americans, Assimilation, and Race.* New York: Russell Sage Foundation.

Teranishi, Robert T. 2002. "Asian Pacific Americans and Critical Race Theory: An Examination of School Racial Climate." *Equity and Excellence in Education* 35 (2): 144–54. https://doi.org/10.1080/713845281.

Terriquez, Veronica. 2015a. "Dreams Delayed: Barriers to Degree Completion among Undocumented Community College Students." *Journal of Ethnic and Migration Studies* 41 (8): 1302–23. https://doi.org/10.1080/1369183X.2014.968534.

———. 2015b. "Intersectional Mobilization, Social Movement Spillover, and Queer Youth Leadership in the Immigrant Rights Movement." *Social Problems* 62 (3): 343–62. https://doi.org/10.1093/socpro/spv010.

Tillman, Kathryn Harker, Karin L. Brewster, and Giuseppina Valle Holway. 2019. "Sexual and Romantic Relationships in Young Adulthood." *Annual Review of Sociology* 45 (1): 133–53. https://doi.org/10.1146/annurev-soc-073018-022625.

Torche, Florencia. 2011. "Is a College Degree Still the Great Equalizer? Intergenerational Mobility across Levels of Schooling in the United States." *American Journal of Sociology* 117 (3): 763–807. https://doi.org/10.1086/661904.

Torkelson, Jason. 2012. "A Queer Vision of Emerging Adulthood: Seeing Sexuality in the Transition to Adulthood." *Sexuality Research and Social Policy* 9 (2): 132–42. https://doi.org/10.1007/s13178-011-0078-6.

Torpey, Elka. 2018a. "Employment Outlook for Bachelor's-Level Occupations." *Career Outlook*, April 2018. US Bureau of Labor Statistics. https://www.bls.gov/careeroutlook/2018/article/bachelors-degree-outlook.htm.

———. 2018b. "Employment Outlook for High School-Level Occupations." *Career Outlook*, September 2018. US Bureau of Labor Statistics. https://www.bls.gov/careeroutlook/2018/article/high-school-outlook.htm.

———. 2019. "Education Pays." *Career Outlook*, February 2019. US Bureau of Labor Statistics. https://www.bls.gov/careeroutlook/2019/data-on-display/education_pays.htm.

Torpey, Elka, and Andrew Hogan. 2016. "Working in a Gig Economy." *Career Outlook*, May 2016. US Bureau of Labor Statistics. https://www.bls.gov/careeroutlook/2016/article/what-is-the-gig-economy.htm.

Torres, Ignacio, Jessica Hopper, and Juju Chang. 2019. "For Trans Women of Color Facing 'Epidemic' of Violence, Each Day Is a Fight for Survival: 'I'm an Endangered Species . . . but I Cannot Stop Living.'" *ABC News*, November 20, 2019. https://abcnews.go.com/US/trans-women-color-facing-epidemic-violence-day-fight/story?id=66015811.

Treas, Judith, and Jeanne Batalova. 2011. "Residential Independence: Race and Ethnicity on the Road to Adulthood in Two U.S. Immigrant Gateways." *Advances in Life Course Research* 16 (1): 13–24. https://doi.org/10.1016/j.alcr.2011.01.001.

Tyson, Karolyn. 2002. "Weighing In: Elementary-Age Students and the Debate on Attitudes toward School among Black Students." *Social Forces* 80 (4): 1157–89. https://doi.org/10.1353/sof.2002.0035.

UN Department of Economic and Social Affairs, Population Division. 2017. "Government Policies to Raise or Lower the Fertility Level." *Population Facts*, no. 2017/10. https://www.un.org/en/development/desa/population/publications/pdf/popfacts/PopFacts_2017-10.pdf.

Underwood, Lindsey. 2018. "Meet The Edit's New Contributors." *New York Times*, August 28, 2018. https://www.nytimes.com/2018/08/28/smarter-living/the-edit-contributors.html.

Urban Institute. 2019. "Part of Us: A Data-Driven Look at Children of Immigrants." *Urban Institute*, March 14, 2019. https://www.urban.org/features/part-us-data-driven-look-children-immigrants.

US Attorney's Office, District of Massachusetts. n.d. "Investigations of College Admissions and Testing Bribery Scheme." Accessed May 2021. https://www.justice.gov/usao-ma/investigations-college-admissions-and-testing-bribery-scheme.

US Census Bureau. 2017. "American Community Survey: Information Guide." US Census Bureau, October 2017. https://www.census.gov/content/dam/Census/programs-surveys/acs/about/ACS_Information_Guide.pdf.

———. n.d.a. "American Community Survey: Response Rates." Accessed December 2020. https://www.census.gov/acs/www/methodology/sample-size-and-data-quality/response-rates/.

———. n.d.b. "Historical Households Table: Table HH-4. Households by Size: 1960 to Present." US Census Bureau. Accessed 2019. https://www.census .gov/data/tables/time-series/demo/families/households.html.

———. n.d.c. "Table MS-2. Estimated Median Age at First Marriage, by Sex: 1890 to the Present." US Census Bureau. https://www.census.gov/data /tables/time-series/demo/families/marital.html.

US National Park Service. n.d. "The New Colossus." Statue Of Liberty National Monument. Accessed December 2020. https://www.nps.gov/stli/learn /historyculture/colossus.htm.

Valenzuela, Angela. 1999. *Subtractive Schooling: U.S.-Mexican Youth and the Politics of Caring.* Albany: State University of New York Press.

Vargas, Jose Antonio. 2011. "My Life as an Undocumented Immigrant." *New York Times Magazine,* June 26, 2011. https://www.nytimes.com/2011/06/26 /magazine/my-life-as-an-undocumented-immigrant.html.

Velez, Erin Dunlop, Terry Lew, Erin Thomsen, Katie Johnson, Jennifer Wine, and Jennifer Cooney. 2019. "Baccalaureate and Beyond (B&B:16/17): A First Look at the Employment and Educational Experiences of College Graduates, 1 Year Later." NCES 2019241. National Center for Education Statistics. https://nces.ed.gov/pubsearch/pubsinfo.asp?pubid= 2019241.

Vespa, Jonathan. 2017. "The Changing Economics and Demographics of Young Adulthood: 1975–2016." *Current Population Reports,* P20–579. US Census Bureau. https://www.census.gov/content/dam/Census/library/publications /2017/demo/p20-579.pdf.

Vespa, Jonathan, Lauren Medina, and David M Armstrong. 2020. "Demographic Turning Points for the United States: Population Projections for 2020 to 2060." *Current Population Reports,* P25–1144. US Census Bureau. https://www.census.gov/content/dam/Census/library/publications/2020 /demo/p25-1144.pdf.

Wagaman, M. Alex, Melissa Foushee Keller, and Stacey Jay Cavaliere. 2016. "What Does It Mean to Be a Successful Adult? Exploring Perceptions of the Transition into Adulthood among LGBTQ Emerging Adults in a Community-Based Service Context." *Journal of Gay and Lesbian Social Services* 28 (2): 140–58. https://doi.org/10.1080/10538720.2016 .1155519.

Waters, Mary C., Patrick J. Carr, Maria J. Kefalas, and Jennifer Holdaway, eds. 2011. *Coming of Age in America: The Transition to Adulthood in the Twenty-First Century.* Berkeley: University of California Press.

Waters, Mary C., and Marisa Gerstein Pineau, eds. 2015. *The Integration of Immigrants into American Society*. Washington, DC: National Academies Press. https://doi.org/10.17226/21746.

White, Lynn. 1994. "Coresidence and Leaving Home: Young Adults and Their Parents." *Annual Review of Sociology* 20 (1): 81–102. https://doi.org/10.1146/annurev.so.20.080194.000501.

Wildsmith, Elizabeth, Jennifer Manlove, and Elizabeth Cook. 2018. "Dramatic Increase in the Proportion of Births Outside of Marriage in the United States from 1990 to 2016." *Child Trends*, August 8, 2018. https://www.childtrends.org/publications/dramatic-increase-in-percentage-of-births-outside-marriage-among-whites-hispanics-and-women-with-higher-education-levels.

Wilson, William Julius, and Kathryn M. Neckerman. 1987. "Poverty and Family Structure: The Widening Gap between Evidence and Public Policy Issues." In William Julius Wilson, *The Truly Disadvantaged: The Inner City, the Underclass, and Public Policy*, 63–92. Chicago: University of Chicago Press.

Wirt, John, Susan Choy, Allison Gruner, Jennifer Sable, Richard Tobin, Yupin Bae, Jim Sexton, et al. 2000. "The Condition of Education 2000." NCES 2000062. National Center for Education Statistics. https://nces.ed.gov/pubsearch/pubsinfo.asp?pubid=2000062.

Woo, Jennie H., Alexander H. Bentz, Stephen Lew, Erin Dunlop Velez, and Nichole Smith. 2017. "Repayment of Student Loans as of 2015 among 1995–96 and 2003–04 First-Time Beginning Students." NCES 2018–410. National Center for Education Statistics. https://nces.ed.gov/pubsearch/pubsinfo.asp?pubid=2018410.

Xie, Yu, Michael Fang, and Kimberlee Shauman. 2015. "STEM Education." *Annual Review of Sociology* 41 (1): 331–57. https://doi.org/10.1146/annurev-soc-071312-45659.

Yeung, Wei-Jun Jean, and Adam Ka-Lok Cheung. 2015. "Living Alone: One-Person Households in Asia." *Demographic Research* 32: 1099–1112. https://doi.org/10.4054/DemRes.2015.32.40.

Yosso, Tara J., William A. Smith, Miguel Ceja, and Daniel G. Solórzano. 2009. "Critical Race Theory, Racial Microaggressions, and Campus Racial Climate for Latina/o Undergraduates." *Harvard Educational Review* 79 (4): 659–691. https://doi.org/10.17763/haer.79.4.m6867014157m7071.

Zelizer, Viviana A. 1981. "The Price and Value of Children: The Case of Children's Insurance." *American Journal of Sociology* 86 (5): 1036–56. https://doi.org/10.1086/227353.

Zhou, Min, and Carl L. Bankston. 1994. "Social Capital and the Adaptation of the Second Generation: The Case of Vietnamese Youth in New Orleans."

International Migration Review 28 (4): 821–45. https://doi.org/10.2307 /2547159.

———. 2016. *The Rise of the New Second Generation*. Cambridge: Polity Press.

Zhou, Min, and Roberto G. Gonzales. 2019. "Divergent Destinies: Children of Immigrants Growing Up in the United States." *Annual Review of Sociology* 45 (1): 383–99. https://doi.org/10.1146/annurev-soc-073018-022424.

Zhou, Min, and Jennifer Lee. 2017. "Hyper-Selectivity and the Remaking of Culture: Understanding the Asian American Achievement Paradox." *Asian American Journal of Psychology* 8 (1): 7–15. https://doi.org/10.1037 /aap0000069.

Index

The italicized abbreviations *fig* or *tab* following a page number indicates that an illustration or table appears on that page.

Founded in 1893,
UNIVERSITY OF CALIFORNIA PRESS
publishes bold, progressive books and journals
on topics in the arts, humanities, social sciences,
and natural sciences—with a focus on social
justice issues—that inspire thought and action
among readers worldwide.

The UC PRESS FOUNDATION
raises funds to uphold the press's vital role
as an independent, nonprofit publisher, and
receives philanthropic support from a wide
range of individuals and institutions—and from
committed readers like you. To learn more, visit
ucpress.edu/supportus.

www.ingramcontent.com/pod-product-compliance
Lightning Source LLC
Chambersburg PA
CBHW071736270326
41928CB00013B/2704